D1301104

The Proletarian Episode in Russian Literature, 1928-1932

STUDIES OF THE
RUSSIAN INSTITUTE
COLUMBIA UNIVERSITY

Edward J. Brown

The Proletarian Episode in Russian Literature 1928-1932

1971
OCTAGON BOOKS
New York

The transliteration system in this series is based on
The Library of Congress system with some modifications

Reprinted 1971
by special arrangement with Columbia University Press

OCTAGON BOOKS
A DIVISION OF FARRAR, STRAUS & GIROUX, INC.
19 Union Square West
New York, N. Y. 10003

LIBRARY OF CONGRESS CATALOG CARD NUMBER: 77-120236

Manufactured by Braun-Brumfield, Inc.
Ann Arbor, Michigan

Printed in the United States of America

THE RUSSIAN INSTITUTE

OF COLUMBIA UNIVERSITY

THE RUSSIAN INSTITUTE was established by Columbia University in 1946 to serve two major objectives: the training of a limited number of well-qualified Americans for scholarly and professional careers in the field of Russian studies and the development of research in the social sciences and the humanities as they relate to Russia and the Soviet Union. The research program of the Russian Institute is conducted through the efforts of its faculty members, of scholars invited to participate as Senior Fellows in its program, and of candidates for the Certificate of the Institute and for the degree of Doctor of Philosophy. Some of the results of the research program are presented in the Studies of the Russian Institute of Columbia University. The faculty of the Institute, without necessarily agreeing with the conclusions reached in the Studies, believe that their publication advances the difficult task of promoting systematic research on Russia and the Soviet Union and public understanding of the problems involved.

The faculty of the Russian Institute are grateful to the Rockefeller Foundation for the financial assistance which it has given to the program of research and publication.

Foreword

THE RESEARCH for this book was begun in 1947 during a year of graduate work in the Department of Slavic Languages and the Russian Institute at Columbia University, made possible by a grant from the American Council of Learned Societies. It was accepted as a doctoral dissertation at Columbia University in May, 1950. In the present revised and abridged form it was submitted for publication by the Russian Institute.

There are many people to whom the author is indebted for criticism and suggestions. Among these should be mentioned Professor Clarence A. Manning and Professor Manfred Kridl of the Columbia Department of Slavic Languages, Professor André von Gronicka of the Columbia German Department, Professor Geroid T. Robinson and other officers of the Russian Institute, and particularly Professor Ernest J. Simmons, whose interest in the project, encouragement, and criticism were extremely helpful in bringing it to completion.

Contents

The Proletarian Episode in Russian Literature, 1928-1932

Introduction

THIS STUDY is devoted almost entirely to one organization which rode a wave of dubious power and glory for about four years in the Soviet Union. It was the Party's own literary organization, called the Russian Association of Proletarian Writers and usually referred to by its initials as RAPP. Its peak membership during the best days has been variously estimated at from two to three thousand self-styled proletarian writers. A few of these were very good writers who added something to Russian literature. With the support and encouragement of the Communist Party their organization became a potent force in Soviet literature. Yet it was liquidated by the Politburo in 1932, and many of its leaders accused of "errors" and "deviations from the Leninist line." Some years later those same leaders were officially discovered to have been "Trotskyites," and "enemies of the people" who had used the influence bestowed upon them by the Party to disorientate literature and impede its development. Such is the official Soviet evaluation of RAPP.

It is no easy matter to investigate the various phenomena of what is sometimes called "Soviet reality." The Soviet sources—to which one would naturally turn for a first-hand account of historical events—prove to be a poor fabric of palpable half-truths and obvious obscurantism, especially those written since the trials of the mid-thirties, and especially where they touch upon the period of the twenties in Soviet literature. The leaders of the Communist Party in the intellectual life of the twenties have almost all disappeared from the scene, and the Soviet sources tell us simply that many of them were "enemies" exposed and defeated through the vigilance of the Party. The list of such enemies includes the most active Communist literary figures of the decade of the twenties: Trotsky, Voronskii, Bukharin, Radek, Averbakh, Kirshon, Rodov, Lelevich, and a number of others. Thus it is impossible for the Soviet literary historian to tell us that Bukharin was one of the chief authors of the 1925 resolution of the Communist Party on belles-lettres—an extremely interesting fact—or that Voronskii as editor of the magazine *Red Virgin Soil* made a substantial contribution to the revival of Russian literature after the end of the civil war. For these men were "enemies" and their services—even their names—must be erased from the chronicle of events.

In place of clear, objective information on the history of RAPP we have been given a highly prejudiced stereotype in which the leaders of RAPP appear as pseudo-Marxist vulgarizers and drillmasters of the literary world. They are supposed to have been indifferent to the culture and literature of the past and to have ignored literary factors in their criticism of the current product. They were a force, we are told, which made for the vulgarization of Soviet literature to the level of propagandist and journalistic activity in support of the first Five-Year Plan. The liquidation of RAPP in 1932 has been presented as a liberalizing act prompted by dissatisfaction with the RAPP regime.

The history of RAPP is indeed confused. At some points it has been almost hopelessly obscured. The written records from which it must be reconstructed are often ambiguous, sometimes deliberately equivocal, and not infrequently self-contradictory. The preponderance of evidence, however, is not in agreement with the version of RAPP which has just been outlined.

On the basis of this evidence the present writer has rejected the interpretation of RAPP as a source of the utilitarian and vulgarizing emphasis so conspicuous in Soviet literature during the period of the first Five-Year Plan. The source of the demands made upon literary men in those years was not RAPP at all but the Central Committee of the Communist Party. That is written large in the evidence. RAPP, along with all other literary organizations, had to carry out or seem to be carrying out these demands. However, the RAPP leaders were themselves writers and critics who had ideas of their own about Marxism in literature. In fact they had a full-blown theory. Evidence from various sources does make sense as soon as one becomes aware that the RAPP leaders were resisting the Party demand and stubbornly propagating their own ideas and their own "literary method." RAPP was therefore one of the eventual victims rather than the source of a determined Party program to control and utilize literature.

This study is not an apologia for the RAPP leaders. We shall see that they were limited, sectarian, and dogmatic in their treatment of literary problems. But during the hectic years of the first Five-Year Plan they did attempt to maintain a minimum of literary quality in their proletarian product. For this they no doubt deserve at least a footnote in a universal history of literature.

It has been the purpose of this study to remove the successive deposits of partisan Soviet criticism and official vilification and to discover what RAPP really was. We shall read the literary criticism and theory of its leaders and sample a good cross section of the literature they produced. We shall try to estimate as objectively as possible the effect of their activity on the development of literature. Finally we shall seek to learn what was the source of their conflict with the leaders of the Party, and why they were first disgraced as heretics, and later exorcised as devils. It is hoped that this study will throw light on the history of Soviet literature and of Soviet institutions generally.

Chapter I

Proletarian Literature

1. The Proletcult

THE GROWTH of the working-class movement in Russia under the influence of Marxist ideas led to the formation shortly before the October revolution of an organization whose aim was the creation of a "culture" proper to the new and rising class, the proletariat. Certain passages in the works of Marx had stressed that the religion, art, and literature of a given epoch are built upon the basis of productive relations, and in a society divided into classes reflect the ideas of the dominant class.[1] The partisans of "Proletarian Culture" concluded that since the *bourgeoisie* would soon disappear from the world arena, their culture would disappear with them, to be replaced by an entirely new phenomenon, the culture of a new ruling class. They maintained, further, that the development of a proletarian culture was a necessary prerequisite for the establishment of proletarian power in politics or in the economic sphere.[2] The proletariat, however, was admittedly without its own art and literature. It must, therefore, undertake to create them.

Under the leadership of the Marxist theoretician A. A. Bogdanov[3] and with the active cooperation of the future Commissar of Education A. V. Lunacharskii[4] an organization arose in 1917 which took upon itself the project of developing a proletarian art and literature. It was called the Proletarian Cultural and Educational Organization, soon abbreviated to "Proletcult."[5]

It was a basic tenet of Bogdanov and the Proletcult that art is a social product the nature of which is conditioned by the social environment in which it arises. In enunciating such views he contributed nothing original, for these ideas were developed by the Marxist writer and critic G. V. Plekhanov, who first attempted systematically to apply the Marxian dialectic to literature and art. Wrote Plekhanov:

I hold to the view that social consciousness is determined by social existence. For a man who maintains such a view it follows that art, and so-called belles-lettres, expresses the strivings and the mood of a given society, or, if we have to do with a society divided into classes, of a given social class.[6]

However, Bogdanov did add something of his own to this traditional Marxist analysis of art, and the ideas he contributed were connected with his general philosophical views. Art and literature he regarded not merely as a reflection of life from the viewpoint of a given class nor merely as an expression of its ideas, but as a means of organizing its collective labor.[7] Art has as its chief reason for existence this task of organization. A resolution adopted by the First All-Russian Conference of the Proletcult set forth that the proletariat must have its own "class" art to organize its forces in the struggle for socialism:

Art organizes social experience by means of living images, not only in the sphere of cognition, but also in that of feeling and desires. As a consequence it is a most powerful weapon for the organization of collective forces, and in a class society, of class forces.

The proletariat must have its own class art to organize its own forces in social labor, struggle, and construction. The spirit of this art is that of labor collectivism: it perceives and reflects the world from the point of view of the labor collective. . . .[8]

Bogdanov was insistent on this organizing role of art. In discussing the beauty possessed by such a creation as the Venus de Milo, he wrote:

The temple was the center of the community, and the goddess was the center of the temple. Therefore she was the center of organization of the collective.[9]

It did not at all follow from these propositions that the art and culture of past ages would be of no use to the proletariat. On the contrary, even the goddess of Melos was capable of adaptation to the needs of the modern proletariat. In an article on the "cultural heritage". Bogdanov maintained that the art of past ages could and should become the possession of the working masses: "through critically reworking it from the collective-labor point of view."[10] He not infrequently uses the term "the beautiful" to describe that quality which gives to great masterpieces their eternal value. Still speaking of the Venus de Milo, he says:

> The gods have died. The goddess has ceased to organize her former collective; however, people have felt the great organizing force of this statue, they have beheld the beautiful. And from the moment they behold it they are forever bound to one another by something in common.[11]

The organizers and theorists of the Proletcult were not themselves members of the working class, but were distinctly non-proletarian intellectuals. Logically enough they concluded that the new art and literature would be created not only by people of pure proletarian origin but also by people of proletarian "orientation," like themselves.[12]

It is nevertheless true that the primary aim of the organization was to impart education to the working class and to develop new proletarian artists. For this purpose special literary studios were set up to give working-class readers and writers an elementary literary education. On this subject the resolutions of the Proletcult said:

> For the accomplishment of our aim it is necessary to create a wide network of literary studios in which work should be carried forward in two main directions:
>
> a. In order to acquaint the members with the literary heritage of past epochs, courses should be given in ancient and modern literature, both Russian and foreign . . . and in the history of culture. . . . All of these courses should be given from the viewpoint of the working class.
>
> b. . . . The writer and working-class reader should become acquainted with the technique . . . of literary creation, and for this purpose theoretical courses and practical exercises should be given in metrics, rhythm, and the general theory of versification, in the theory of dramaturgy, artistic prose and criticism.[13]

Among the working-class writers active in the affairs of the Proletcult were some who had published verse even before the revolution. Many of the early proletarian poets were associated with Bogdanov in the work of the Proletcult.[14] The extent of its literary and educational activity during the revolution and civil war (1917–21) indicates that it received considerable support from the state. It was claimed that there were over one hundred provincial branches of the Proletcult and eighty thousand workers enrolled in its studios in 1920.[15] The list of periodicals which it was able to publish in those dreadful years is an impressive one. There were about twenty of these, bearing such titles as *Proletarian Culture*, *The Future*, *The Furnace*, *The Siren*, and many others.[16]

Yet the work of the Proletcult under the leadership of Bogdanov soon met with determined opposition from the Communist Party itself. The chief reason for this opposition was the thesis of Bogdanov and his associates that the cultural organization of the proletariat must be an autonomous body entirely independent of the Party and the government apparatus. Bogdanov maintained that there were three "independent roads" to socialism: the political, the economic, and the cultural. The cultural work of the proletariat—"the organization of its experience as a class"—must develop, he believed, free of interference from bodies concerned with the political and economic struggle.[17] Such bodies (the state apparatus of control, for instance), moreover, were not purely proletarian, he said, but were mixed with "bourgeois" elements.[18] Toward the end of the civil war the leaders of the Party betrayed a distinct distrust of the proletarian cultural movement as fostered by the Proletcult. Trotsky argued with great cogency that a specifically proletarian culture was simply not possible.[19] Bukharin expressed doubt as to whether such a phenomenon could be artificially induced, and he also took exception to the idea that it could develop independently of the Party and the state.[20] Lenin revealed a vigorous contempt for the theoreticians of the movement,[21] and in 1920 forced its congress to pass a resolution which affirmed that: (1) a proletarian culture could arise only on the basis of the "bourgeois" thought and culture which already existed; and (2) the Proletcult must function as a subordinate body within the People's Commissariat of Education.[22]

This very brief sketch of the ideas and activity of the Proletcult is important background for an understanding of the proletarian literary movement of the twenties, and even for subsequent developments in Soviet literature. For the idea of a separate proletarian literature with special revolutionary tasks is one which persisted in Russia until the thirties. We shall see that the leaders of proletarian literature insisted on the function of literature as an instrument for the organization of labor. Now this idea, expressed in different terms, has become the cornerstone of contemporary Soviet literary theory. It is perhaps important to realize that Marx, Engels, and Plekhanov did not express themselves in such terms when discussing the nature of literature and art. The idea that literature must serve as an instrument for mobilizing and educating the masses and that writers should be, as Stalin is supposed to have said, "engineers of the human soul" did not, apparently, derive from the classics of Marxism. It is rather the contribution to Soviet literary thought of Bogdanov and the Proletcult.[23]

2. The Smithy

A few of the proletarian poets active in the Proletcult seceded from that organization late in 1919 and organized under the auspices of the Literary Section of the People's Commissariat of Education a new literary group which they called Kuznitsa (The Smithy).[24] Among them were such proletarian poets as Gerasimov, Liashko, and Kirillov, who had achieved some literary recognition even before the revolution. The statement announcing their withdrawal from the Proletcult gives as the reason for this step that "the work of the Proletcult is holding back the development of the creative possibilities of proletarian writers."[25] The Smiths preferred to work within a small organization of active writers, and it would seem that they withdrew from the Proletcult in order to avoid involvement in mass activity and mass education.[26]

There was no essential disagreement between the Smiths and the Proletcult regarding the nature of literature. They too believed that all art is a social product serving as an instrument in the hands of a particular class. The declarations of the Smithy are perfectly clear on this point:

Art is just as necessary for the proletariat as are its army, its transportation system and its factories. The far horizons of a new epoch, unlimited perspectives of activity, an unheard-of panorama of revolutionary life, all await the new art. . . . It is becoming an exceptionally keen instrument for the organization of the future communist society.[27]

The main product of the Smithy in this early period was lyric poetry, for the most part conventional in form, devoted to such themes as the factory, the "iron proletarian," and the coming world revolution. The Smith N. Liashko attempted on the basis of the literary product of this early period to point out the specific qualities which characterized proletarian poetry. One of the outstanding features of this poetry he found to be "the consciousness of the power of labor . . . and . . . only by and through labor will proletarian ideals be achieved."[28] The feeling for labor permeates much of the work of the Smithy poets, and is often expressed in the images they devise: "The moon, the trilling of the nightingale, the stars, the sun, the cuckoo,—all of these suggest to the proletarian writer images of work." Thus the stonemason-poet V. Kazin beholds "how the morn lifts up its brick, the sun," and sees the evening sky with its stars as "a hive full of bees." Gerasimov calls upon the sun to "plane off the grief from sad faces."[29]

Another *motiv* frequently heard in Smithy poetry is the metallic world of machines. The proletarian looked forward to the day when "labor would be joy and the machine a friend and deliverer."[30] The factory was for the proletarian poet Samobytnik the pledge of future happiness and freedom, and he overheard in his factory "the confusion of the fiercely groaning machines, and under the darkling vault the birth of a throng of servitors."[31] Not the individual proletarian but the "mass" is the hero of the Smithy lyric. Liashko maintained that the collective "We" had driven out the personal "I."[32]

This early period of proletarian poetry witnessed the curious development known as "cosmism," or "planetarity." It is characteristic of many of the Smithy poets and particularly of Gastev and Kazin that their revolutionary emotion not only arises from the contemplation of the coming victory of the world proletariat, but attempts to go beyond the bounds of earthly life and include the universe itself in the revolutionary movement of which they felt themselves a part. Some observers saw in this a kind of "escapism," a search for a better and purer world.[33] Yet the early Marxist critic Kogan felt that "cosmism is the result of the poet's faith in the unlimited might of labor and science. . . . Our social struggle is for him only part of a world-wide drama, and the factory with its machines becomes part of a universal workshop."[34] A better interpretation is, perhaps, that this cosmism is the obverse of their militant atheism: the poet sought in the revolution an answer to the ultimate questions of life and death, and finds it in a continuing, cosmic development of which he himself is a part.[35]

It would appear that reality dealt a rude shock to the revolutionary lyricism of the Smiths. Not only did the world proletariat fail to rise in its strength, but with the introduction of the New Economic Policy (NEP)[36] in 1921 the advance of communism in Russia itself was indefinitely postponed. Many of the Smiths could not accept the new course, which they regarded as a betrayal of communism.[37] Some of these left the Party in melancholy disillusionment.[38] A note of defeat was heard in the work of those who continued to produce.[39]

The ending of the period of revolution and strife soon brought about an important regrouping in the ranks of proletarian literature.

3. October and VAPP

The writers of the Smithy had organized in May of 1920 an All-Russian Conference of Proletarian Writers.[40] In October of the same year the Smithy called an All-Russian Congress of Proletarian Writers, in which many provincial groups were included in order to organize proletarian literature on a national scale.[41] At this Congress the All-Russian Association of Proletarian Writers was founded. The Association (Vserossiiskaia Assosiatsiia Proletarskikh Pisatelei) became known by its initials as VAPP. This All-Russian Association continued to be called VAPP until its reorganization in 1928, when Vserossiiskaia was dropped in favor of Rossiiskaia. Thereafter the abbreviated title became RAPP. Thus we see that RAPP, the Russian Association of Proletarian Writers, traced its lineage ultimately to the Smithy, and was the final flowering of a proletarian literary movement which had begun in the early days of the revolution.

A serious schism developed in the ranks of the Smithy and of VAPP during the early days of NEP. According to the poet Semën Rodov, one of the founders of the Smithy, the split within that organization began in the spring of 1922, when many of its members, disillusioned as they were with the developments of the NEP period, abandoned the Party and suggested that VAPP be disbanded, leaving only small organizations of established writers in Moscow and Leningrad.[42] The main body of the Smithy thus tended to dissociate itself from the Party and also from the new effort to organize proletarian literature on a national scale. They insisted that only developed and mature writers should enter into the Smithy, an attitude which Rodov ascribes to their desire to "isolate themselves in their own little world," and also to their "contempt for the younger writers."[43] As indicated above, it seems more likely that they felt a small organization of developed writers could best serve the interests of a proletarian literature.

As a result of a series of disagreements on current problems, both political and literary, several members of the Smithy abandoned that group and joined with other proletarian littérateurs to found a new group which they called "October." The new group came into existence one December day in Moscow in 1922,[44] when a number of youthful and enthusiastic writers gathered in the editorial offices of the Youth League magazine *Molodaia Gvardiia* (Young Guard) and after a prolonged discussion of the point at issue composed a "manifesto" announcing the formation of the October group:

The group of proletarian writers calling itself the Smithy, formed in the beginning of 1920, has lately, in our opinion, turned into a small, insignificant and isolated circle of comrades with interests which are far from answering to the tasks of the developing struggle of the proletariat on the ideological front. In view of the fact that in such a situation the Smithy is an organization which retards the development of the younger forces of proletarian literature . . . the undersigned have formed a group of proletarian writers under the name October, which will have as its chief aim the strengthening of the Communist line in proletarian literature and the organizational strengthening of the All-Russian and Moscow Associations of Proletarian Writers.[45]

It would appear, then, that the chief reasons for the formation of this new group were the demand of the younger writers for recognition, their fierce loyalty to the Party, and their belief in the need for a "mass" organization of literature.

The manifesto was signed by several dissidents from the Smithy, and by a number of aspiring proletarian writers from the Communist Youth League. The leaders of the group were Semën Rodov, one of the founders of the Smithy and a Communist critic and poet who produced rhymed inspirational verse on the heroism and self-sacrifice of the Party;[46] Alexander Bezymenskii, a poet-agitator among the Communist Youth; the very able young novelist Iurii Libedinskii;[47] a literary theorist and critic G. Lelevich;[48] and the teen-age editor of the magazine *Young Guard*, Leopol'd Averbakh.[49] All of them were members of the Communist Party. Though they took considerable pride in calling themselves "proletarian writers," they were without exception "bourgeois" in origin, all of them being products of a middle-class and intellectual milieu.[50]

The new group continued to support without question the basic ideas of the Proletcult and the Smithy on the nature and function of literature. The October platform declared:

Before the proletariat there now arises the task . . . of creating its own class culture, and consequently its own literature as a mighty instrument for influencing the sense perceptions [*sic*] of the masses. . . .

In a class society literature, as well as other things, serves the interests of a particular class and only through that class does it serve all humanity; therefore proletarian literature is such a literature as organizes the psyche and the consciousness of the working class in the direction of the final tasks of the proletariat as the creator of a communist society.[51]

The October movement did, however, represent a new orientation in the literature of the revolution. The members of the new group were realists in the sense that their literary efforts were given to reflecting and inspiring both in prose and in verse the day-to-day tasks of the proletariat. They repudiated with obstreperous scorn the lyrical and romantic note which the Smiths had been sounding on the cosmic proportions of the world revolution. Indeed the rise of this new group is an important symptom of the temporary retreat from world revolution in order to restore the economic life of the USSR. Poetic expression was given to this idea by Bezymenskii:

TO THE POETS OF THE SMITHY

It's fine to toss the planets about as though they were little lumps of something, and in galvanic verse to celebrate the cosmos. But can you show us the dawn of the future in some chairman of a lumber commissariat. . . . Give up the heavens, forget about *things*, and give us instead the earth and living people.[52]

The critic G. Lelevich, in the first issue of the literary magazine published by the group and called *October*, pointed out:

The civil war is over and done with, the period of "storm and stress" is past. . . . A period of gray "workdays" is approaching . . . though new "storm and stress" is in preparation. . . . The emotionalism of the Smithy lyric no longer has any effect on the reader. . . .

New methods and a new approach are needed. The Smithy group has not sensed this in time. It continues to sing out its sonorous but no longer convincing "iron psalms"; it continues to speak its resounding words about the "cosmic" sweep of the revolution. . . . In contrast to this tendency *October* intends to cultivate a literature which will help the reader see the close connection between the most trifling workaday fact . . . and our mighty tasks. . . . The magazine *October* will attempt not only to show forth "living people" but to show them in their proper perspective.[53]

In both of these selections we find the term "living people," which later became so important in the critical literature of RAPP, used to give emphasis to the new approach of the October group. As it was first used the term "living man" meant primarily realism in the portrayal of character and in the treatment of themes drawn from contemporary life. This new emphasis on realism led to a relative decline in the production of lyric poetry. The contribution of the October group in this early period consisted almost entirely of agitational poetry and prose works concerned with problems of the day. The novels of Iurii Libedinskii and the topical poetry of Demian Bednyi were held up as models for imitation and an earnest of what proletarian literature might be expected to accomplish in the near future.[54]

Libedinskii himself devoted one enthusiastic article to an outline of the kind of material which proletarian literature might be expected to treat. His "Themes Which Await Their Authors" concerned such things as the activity of Communists, new moral and ethical values, the new family life, the struggle for socialism, etc.[55] Averbakh in 1923 wrote that the proletarian writer should "show the Red Army man in his barracks learning to read and write; the Young Communist fighting against the evil of drink in the name of the world unity of the proletariat; he should be able to find the pathos of the revolution in the awkward dispatch of a worker-correspondent on the poor organization of his factory."[56] The immediate and practical aim of the themes recommended in this early period was service to the proletariat in its struggle for a new culture. Libedinskii maintained that such themes as these could be handled only by the proletarian youth. Their literary production, he conceded, was as yet a meager and poor thing. Yet the early writings of the October leaders express a faith, perhaps naive, in the proposition that the true inheritors of the Russian literary tradition are not the descendants of the *bourgeoisie* or the intelligentsia, but the young and as yet unformed proletarian writers.[57]

4. VAPP and the Organization of Literature

The October leaders believed in the need for a broad and firm organization of proletarian writers. Since the Smiths preferred to withdraw from "mass" literary work, the new group was soon able to gain control of the All-Russian Association which the Smithy had founded: VAPP. The program of the October group became the policy of VAPP.

Perhaps the most striking characteristic of proletarian literature under the leadership of the October group was this effort to organize the work of literary men. The new literature was to be built by many hands cooperating in the work. A contemporary observer remarked: "History knows of no example of a similar effort to build a literature, and in no other epoch was the demand so loudly sounded that creative inspiration be included in the general plan, and the enthusiasm of the poet subjected to a common task."[58]

The October group believed that proletarian writers should break decisively with the traditions of individualism in literature. The proletarian writer must feel himself to be a member of a group working under firm discipline. Semën Rodov thus expressed the need for organization and discipline:

> If proletarian literature was to be victorious it must be organized, and firmly organized. For proletarian literature this was just as necessary as it was for any other branch of the working-class movement. . . . And in any organization at least two things are necessary: unity of views and unity of action. The particular advantage of this is that it makes a particular systematic outlook obligatory upon every proletarian writer.[59]

That the discipline imposed was indeed strict, and that the model for the literary organization was the Party itself is revealed in the following paragraph from an Agreement between MAPP and LAPP:[60]

> Both Associations oblige their members to carry out the policy agreed upon. . . . Executive boards will take the sternest measures, including expulsion, against those members who fail to carry out the orders of their respective executive boards.[61]

Rodov at one point explained that a great deal of time and effort had to be taken up in the writing of manifestoes, programs, platforms, directives, and the like because of the need to define clearly the ideas and aims of proletarian literature and the thematic framework within which the proletarian might create.[62] The need for clear and explicit directives was felt especially in the work with the newcomers to literature, the factory workers and Communist youth who were organized in VAPP's literary circles. Much of the energy of professional writers was given to the organization of these groups, to the conduct of "study sessions," and to consultations with aspiring authors.[63]

The "organizational" work of the October group and VAPP thus included an activity quite comparable to the literary studios of the Proletcult. The literary circles of VAPP appear to have been numerous and widespread, though there is great difference of opinion concerning their size and importance.[64] We learn that MAPP in 1923 organized a network of such circles in co-operation with district committees of the Party.[65] Typical of such enterprises was the literary circle called Zakal (Tempering), the members of which were adult worker-correspondents who read their sketches, poems, and stories at the meetings of the group and "had the advantage of comradely criticism."[66] Here they learned that "literary creation is a difficult task, requiring long study and serious work."[67] It was admitted that after three years of such work the members of the group had not published much, though one, Filippov, had had his sketches published in *October*.[68]

Another such group was called Rabochaia Vesna (Workers' Spring). The members chose this name for their circle because it suggested to them the burgeoning of the workers' strength.[69] At the "literary evenings" of this group a number of professional writers read their works aloud and submitted them to "proletarian criticism." Serafimovich is said to have read parts of his *Zheleznyi potok* (Iron Flood), a novel that achieved widespread popularity, at such meetings before giving it to the publishers. And he "listened closely to the workers' criticism."[70]

Usually an established authority, a critic or a writer, was directly responsible for the work of one or more of these circles. A circle called "Antenna" was founded and supervised by the October critic Lelevich. Bezymenskii, Libedinskii, and Lelevich were deeply involved in the preparation of study programs for these literary circles.[71]

The novelist Dmitrii Furmanov, whose *Chapaev* (1925) became an international literary and cinema success, was a staunch partisan of proletarian literature and its emphasis on organization. At a conference of VAPP in 1925 he defended the idea of organization against the objection of the Smithy writer Makarov that it was crushing the creative initiative of proletarian writers.[72] Furmanov argued that because the "class enemy" still roamed abroad in the country proletarian writers had to organize themselves. Without organization the relatively uneducated proletarians would be at a disadvantage in competition with their bourgeois enemies who possessed a long literary and cultural tradition. He believed that organization actually aided creative work, since proletarian writers were enabled through it to help one another with the problems and difficulties involved in creation. In addition, the member of an organization was in a far better position than the lone individual in his dealings with the publishing houses and editorial boards.[73]

The program of the October group as we have outlined it up to this point presents a new and interesting approach to the problems of literature. It is an approach which might even have borne fruit over a long period in the education of ambitious but underprivileged writers. Yet it seems that the whole program was vitiated by the dogmatism and uncompromising orthodoxy of the leaders, and especially by their demand that the Party regard VAPP as the only bearer of a true literary faith. The Octobrists were a completely exclusive group. Other left-wing groups such as LEF[74] and the Smithy were anathema to them. Indeed they were particularly violent in their attacks on groups close to them in ideology.[75] The diaries of Furmanov, published many years later, reveal that questions of politics and organization eventuallly took precedence over literary creation, and that the policy of the leadership had turned VAPP into a kind of sect with new "enemies" arising every day.[76]

Yet the proletarian literary movement under this leadership continued to grow in numbers and influence, though it still had little to offer in the way of literary production. A number of leaders of the Party and the government lent their support to the movement. Among these were Leon Kamenev, Karl Radek, and Emelian Iaroslavskii.[77] In August, 1923, the group had been granted authority to publish its own critical and theoretical journal, which it called *Na postu* (On Guard). In this publication the editors attacked their "enemies" with fanatical violence.

It soon appeared that the chief cause of worry to the editors of *On Guard* was those writers who, though sympathetic to the revolution, were developing outside the Communist and proletarian milieu. Indeed the revival of literature which was even then taking place under the NEP regime of the twenties was largely the product of nonproletarian writers whose ideology was seldom strict and often suspect. It was against this "alien" element that the October group stood "On Guard":

> We shall stand firmly *on guard over a strong and clear Communist ideology in proletarian literature.* In view of the revival, ever since the beginning of NEP, of the activity of bourgeois literary groups, all *ideological* doubts are absolutely *inadmissible,* and we shall make a point of bringing them to light.
>
> We shall fight those Manilovs[78] who distort and slander our revolution by the attention they pay to the rotten fabric of the Fellow-Travellers' literary creation, in their attempt to *build* an aesthetic *bridge between the past and the present.*[79]

Chapter II

The Fellow-travelers and the Orthodox

1. The Serapions

The adoption of the New Economic Policy in 1921 was an event of prime importance in the history of Russian literature. For the new departure meant the end of the virtual monopoly over literature and the arts which had been exercised up to that time by groups claiming to speak and create in the name of the proletariat. Private and cooperative publishing companies were now established, literary and bookselling activities were once again revived, literary journals began to flourish, and literature developed in relative freedom from organized control and official directive. The result was a rich growth both in belles-lettres and in criticism.[1]

The liberalism of the authorities in permitting this literary growth is attested to by a number of facts. Meshcheriakov, the head of the State Publishing House, revealed in 1923 that a large part of the product of private publishers was devoted to what he called "mystical" themes,[2] and the October leader, Rodov, complained that the product of the State Publishing House was itself "heterodox," and out of tune with the revolution.[3] With the beginning of 1921 Soviet literary men began to manifest a tendency to free themselves formally from the domination of official theory and from the constraint of official or semiofficial literary organizations.

Of course the liberalism of the NEP period in Russia had its strict limits. It was at all times understood that nothing "counterrevolutionary" could be written or published. There is evidence that censorship bodies sometimes allowed this term to cover a rather wide range of literary phenomena. Voronskii, writing in 1924, complained that "every attempt to represent the grotesque, Shchedrinian, Chekhovian aspects of our life" is considered by our censorship "a mortal attack on the revolution." Even then such themes were often suspect. Voronskii cites cases of literary works being forbidden on grounds of "decadence," "pessimism," "formalism," and other qualities having no clear connection with counterrevolutionary activities. Indeed the liberalism of the NEP period was only relative at best, and those days seem to us so amazingly free only because of the dismal contrast with the present state of Russian literature.[4] Yet the Soviet writers eagerly embraced the "new freedom," such as it was.

One of the boldest announcements of this tendency was a manifesto published in 1921 by a group of writers who signed themselves as "The Serapion Brothers." They had taken as their spiritual model the hermit Serapion, a character in one of E. T. A. Hoffman's stories, who "believed completely in the reality of his poetic visions." Their manifesto proclaimed the inviolability of artistic creation as a process independent of ideologies, parties, and groups. This "statement of principles" provides a surprising and refreshing contrast to the proletarian documents which have so far been examined:

> We have gathered together in days of powerful and revolutionary political tension. "Whoever is not with us is against us," we have been told from the right and from the left—"Whom are you with, Serapion Brothers? With the Communists or against the Communists? For the revolution or against the revolution?"
>
> Whom are we with, Serapion Brothers?
>
> We are with the Hermit Serapion.
>
> That means—with nobody? . . . Without ideology, without convictions? Standing aside? No.
>
> Each of us has his ideology, his political convictions, each paints his hut to suit himself. Thus in life and thus in our stories, tales and dramas. We all together, we—the Brotherhood—demand only one thing: that the tone not be false. That we may believe in the work, whatever color it may have. . . .
>
> Too long and painfully has the public welfare directed Russian literature. It is time to say that a non-Communist story may lack

talent, but also it may show genius. And we do not care whom Blok the poet, author of "The Twelve" was for; nor Bunin the writer, author of the *Gentleman from San Francisco.*

These are elementary truths, but every day convinces us that they must be said over and over again.

Whom are we with, Serapion Brothers?

We are with the Hermit Serapion. We believe that literary chimeras are a special reality, and we will have none of utilitarianism. We do not write for propaganda. Art is real, like life itself. And, like life itself it has neither goal nor meaning; it exists because it cannot help existing.[5]

The Serapions, who thus flouted the literary demands of the orthodox, were not by any means a small or isolated group, but included many young men of rare talent, most of whom have since established their reputations in Soviet literature. According to a recent study, "every one of the surviving Serapion Brothers has achieved literary distinction."[6] They contributed generously to the revival of literature in the twenties. Trotsky, in a series of *Pravda* articles on literature later published in book form,[7] applied the term "fellow-traveler" to the Serapions and other writers who, though generally sympathetic to the revolution, were neither Communists nor proletarians.[8] The group to which the term "fellow-traveler" was applied included such outstanding literary figures as Veniamin Kaverin, Valentin Kataev, Boris Pil'niak, Vsevolod Ivanov, and Konstantin Fedin. Such names as these are the meat and substance of Soviet literature.

The apolitical stand of this group immediately provoked a lively controversy which continued for many years in the Soviet press. The critic and historian of literature P. S. Kogan, whose Marx was mixed with Bogdanov, wrote that "a truly artistic work always serves special purposes, it always organizes the thoughts and feelings of one collective or another, and guides its will in a specific direction."[9] Lebedev-Polianskii, a close associate of Bogdanov at one time, maintained that the masses should see in the writer, "not a rogue or a playboy, but their teacher, their elder brother, with whom they are united in thought and action."[10] We have seen that the leaders of VAPP sounded an alarm against the "alien" element, calling upon the defenders of the true faith to stand "On Guard" against the ideologically impure.

In this as in other literary controversies of the period the Communist Party itself did not take sides. Party members and Marxist theoreticians expressed their views quite forcefully, though without claiming ex-cathedra sanction for their pronouncements. A number of important and official Communists defended and supported the fellow-travelers. Alexander Voronskii, whose position as editor of the important literary journal *Krasnaia nov'* (Red Virgin Soil) lent considerable weight to his judgment in these matters, defended the Serapions and other fellow-travelers as artists whose products had real value quite apart from the conscious ideology of their producers. In the course of a prolonged and ever more embittered controversy with the Communist "left" Voronskii presented his own analysis of the nature and function of literature.

2. Voronskii and the Cognition of Life

Voronskii, perhaps more than any other single person, was responsible for the revival of literature which took place in Russia in the middle twenties. In 1921 the Party, having relieved him of all other duties, commissioned him to edit a Soviet version of the literary "fat" journals which had reflected intellectual life in prerevolutionary Russia. He helped to found the journal *Red Virgin Soil* in 1921 and was its editor until 1927. In its pages appeared the work of "Serapions," fellow-travelers, Communists, and even some writers who could be labeled "bourgeois"; for Voronskii's chief concern as an editor was that the quality of Russian literature be restored and maintained. He was less interested in the class origin or ideology of his authors than he was in the literary value of what they submitted to him. The non-Communist intellectuals whose work was appearing in *Red Virgin Soil* he regarded as "literary specialists" who should be used in the interest of the proletariat just as specialists in other fields were being used.[11]

The attacks upon his policy from the "left," which became particularly violent after the appearance of the journal *On Guard* in 1923, evoked a series in which Voronskii developed his own ideas on the nature of literature in a "class" society. For these ideas he laid no claim to any special originality, asserting, on the contrary, that his position was more "Marxist" and more orthodox than that of his opponents. He relied largely on the aesthetic ideas of the Russian philosopher Belinskii,[12] as reworked and developed by the Marxist theoretician G. V. Plekhanov.[13] Marx and Engels had expressed themselves on literary matters only in random and incomplete statements, and the works of Lenin are, surprisingly, almost devoid of specifically literary studies.[14] Thus Voronskii invoked the only available authority in drawing up his counter-theses.[15]

Voronskii defines art as one of the *means* by which men obtain knowledge of the external world. Art, he believed, is like science in that it deals with objective reality and that its primary function is to provide knowledge of this reality:

> Primarily art is cognition of life. Art is not an arbitrary play of fantasy, feelings, or moods; art is not the expression of the purely subjective sensations and experiences of the writer, nor does it have as its primary aim to awaken "good feelings" in the reader. Art, like science, supplies us with knowledge of life. Both art and science have the same object: reality. But science analyzes, art synthesizes. Science is abstract; art is concrete. Science is aimed at man's mind; art at his sensuous nature. Science perceives life by means of concepts; art by means of images. . . . [16]

Though art and science are alike in that both deal with reality, the distinction between them is of the first importance for Voronskii's system of ideas. Art differs from science in that it perceives life by means of sensible images, rather than by means of concepts. The language of science is logic, that of art is the image. Science proves and demonstrates from observation of reality; art portrays that reality. When the language of science—proof and demonstration—appears in a work of art in the form of ideological preachment or propaganda it vitiates the artistic image.

Voronskii maintained, moreover, that the artist in revealing life uses a faculty which is quite different from the rational process of the scientist. Voronskii called this faculty "intuition," and he regarded it as an activity of the subconscious part of man and quite independent of the artist's rational equipment:

Intuition is our subconscious in its active operation. Intuitive truths are stored in the subconscious realm of life and reveal themselves in the consciousness suddenly, quickly, unexpectedly, as it were independently of the ego.[17]

Voronskii characterized this essentially subconscious and intuitive activity of the artist as "removing the coverings" from the real world in order to see it as it really is. The chief criterion of the beautiful in a work of art is its faithfulness to reality: "Art has always sought and must seek to recover, restore, and reveal the world, which is beautiful in itself, to represent it in the purest and most direct impressions."[18]

For Voronskii, a practicing Marxist who had spent a large part of his life in the underground revolutionary movement, this view of the nature of art was not at all inconsistent with the Marxist doctrine that art is the product of a particular milieu, and thus reflects the class viewpoint and class psychology of its producers. He did not at all reject the statement of Marx, so often quoted by the On Guardists, that the "dominant ideas of any epoch are those of its dominant class," nor their conclusion from this that literature reflects a particular "class" psychology.[19] However he did insist that the analysis of literary phenomena must not be limited to the discovery of such things:

For the definition of art the class concept is inadequate. Yet the magazine *On Guard* limits itself to such general pronouncements [on the class nature of literature]. Nowhere in this magazine is the idea clearly and firmly expressed that art is a special means for the cognition of life, and that in genuine art there is just such an exact, objective element as in philosophy or science. Not to point this out while operating exclusively with the "class" concept means to throw overboard one of the most important elements which make up the "soul" of art. . . . [20]

In resolving the apparent contradiction arising from the view of art as truth in "images," and at the same time as a reflection of "class" psychology, Voronskii used his own version of the critical method of G. V. Plekhanov, who had explained that every work of art possessed an aesthetic as well as a "sociological" aspect. The task of the critic is to separate these two aspects. He must determine first the "sociological equivalent" in a work of art, that is, what social factors entered into its production.[21] Those elements in a work of art which are the product of the social psychology of the artist Voronskii calls *subjective*. But the critic who only reveals this much has not completed his work. He must perform a "second act": he must evaluate it aesthetically. And for Voronskii this meant an appreciation of its *objective* value as cognition of reality:

No matter how far our analysis might go in this sociological direction, we would still be unable to establish the relationship of a scientific or artistic discovery to objective truth. Therefore the great theoretician of Marxism (Plekhanov) supplemented his first requirement with another: the necessity of an aesthetic evaluation of an artistic production. . . . In evaluating a work of art aesthetically we determine to what extent its content . . . is faithful to objective artistic truth; for the artist thinks in images, and his image must be artistically truthful, that is, it must be faithful to the nature of that which is portrayed. Herein is the perfection and the beauty of a work of art.

Therefore the great literature of the past as well as the work of contemporary bourgeois and fellow-traveler artists is a permanent possession not only of the Russian proletariat but of all mankind, for such a literature is a revelation of the world. Because he believed that the work of Serapions and even of bourgeois writers often possessed an *objective* value he defended them with great courage against the ideologists of the left.

Voronskii did not agree with the theorists of proletarian literature who, up to this time, had insisted on the definition of art as an *instrument* in the hands of the dominant class. In plain words, he did not believe that belles-lettres could be devoted to agitation and propaganda, the service of the proletarian state, or the conscious promotion of any set of ideas and values. The production of literature by directive under the leadership of proletarian groups he held to be quite impossible, for literary creation, as he constantly emphasized, involves a subconscious element which cannot be regulated by rational factors.[22]

He believed that no "proletarian culture" existed in Russia, and that it could never arise as long as the Russians had before them the task of assimilating the already existing bourgeois thought, science, and art.[23] He was deeply concerned over the tendency of his younger comrades to arrogant neglect of this essential cultural work:

In their writings there is much of simple Russian "Asianism," the inability and unwillingness to pay careful attention to every useful cultural force. But isn't it clear that we are dreadfully poor, beggarly, and illiterate. Our economy is ruined, there is darkness and savagery in our forests and villages. . . . Ours is a sad and often nightmarish way of life. Our culture is only a thin layer—as thin as it could possibly be. We would have to be self-enamored Narcissuses or else blind and deaf to reality . . . to declare the Ivanovs useless to the Party and the working class, push them into the "NEP," and have the hardihood to remain with "October."[24]

Considering the recent state of art and letters in the Soviet Union, when a brutally ignorant Zhdanov[25] stood forth as the chief Soviet critic and Stalin's remark that writers should be "engineers of the human soul" was received as an inspiration, it will no doubt surprise many readers to learn that Voronskii was the most important literary figure of his day, and that he had the active support of the most influential Party and government leaders. Trotsky's ideas on the place of literature in the Soviet state agreed almost completely with his. The Commissar of Education, Lunacharskii, supported him against his critics. Riazanov, the founder of the Communist Academy, and Meshcheriakov, head of the State Publishing House, were both on his side. It should be borne in mind that the ritual of subservience to authority was not imposed on Soviet literature until some years later, when Voronskii and most of his friends had disappeared from the scene.

3. The On Guard Campaign

The magazine *On Guard*, published by the October group, was not only opposed to Voronskii's activity in the literary field, but it also attacked with incredible violence the total production of the fellow-travelers. Voronskii defended them on the ground that they were describing and illuminating the Russian revolution and the civil war, and thus helping Russians and even Russian Communists to know themselves and their country better. *On Guard* accused the fellow-travelers of distorting the picture and slandering the proletariat.[26] The fellow-travelers were "a reserve from which the bourgeoisie could recruit aid for its failing strength."[27] Voronskii himself was guilty, they said, of betraying the best interests of the working class in providing these elements with a forum for the dissemination of their "poison." "Voronskii's policy is making it possible for bourgeois elements to use our own literature against us," said Vardin, the editor of *On Guard*, "and thus it happens that under the seal of the Communist Party a great deal of filth is being turned out" and no one criticizes it from the Marxist point of view.[28]

The Marxist point of view taken by the On Guard group[29] is perhaps expressed most concisely in the following resolution, passed by the First All-Union Conference of Proletarian Writers in January, 1925:

1. The rule of the proletariat is incompatible with the dominance of nonproletarian literature.

2. Literature in a class society cannot be neutral; it must serve one or another class.

3. Competition of various groups in this field is an impossible utopia. Such a utopia is unbolshevik, as are all utopias.

4. Belles-lettres is one of the last arenas in which an implacable class war is taking place between the proletariat and the *bourgeoisie* for hegemony over intermediate groups.

. . . .

7. The path by which the proletariat has proceeded in the fields of general politics and economics must be the same path that it follows in literature, that is, the path of hegemony, of the seizure of power by the proletariat in the field of art.

. . . .

9. The old literary heritage must of course be mastered, but we should go beyond it.

10. The predominant type of fellow-traveler is one who slanders the revolution. War upon this type must be waged.

11. The genuine fellow-traveler is to be made use of. This can happen only if he is influenced by the proletariat, and such influence can be exerted only if the fellow-travelers are grouped around a proletarian nucleus in literature.

12. VAPP should become and is becoming just such a nucleus.[30]

The On Guardists shared the basic idea of Bogdanov and the Proletcult that the proletariat must have its own "class" literature to be used as an instrument in its struggle. Unlike the Proletcult, however, they did not believe that the cultural organization of the proletariat should be independent of the Party and the state. Rodov declared that "what we demand is a workers' and peasants' government in belles-lettres."[31] It was through the power of the Party over all Soviet life and its direct intervention in literature that they hoped to carry out a seizure of power in favor of VAPP:

Considering that proletarian literature will be the only serious factor in literary production, it must be acknowledged that even now the interests of the ideological front demand that proletarian literature obtain the leading influence in the basic literary organs of the Party and the Soviet press.[32]

The outstanding characteristics of the On Guard group are its vociferous orthodoxy, and its insistence on the realization of its program for literature through decisions on the part of the Central Committee of the Communist Party. It is difficult to characterize the group in a literary sense, for up to 1925 its members had produced only a trickle of belles-lettres.[33] Perhaps the On Guard group should be remembered in the field of cultural history as the group which first called upon the Communist Party to render decisions in the field of belles-lettres, a province which it had hitherto allowed to develop more or less freely, with only general ideological supervision.[34]

4. The Personality of the On Guardists

Let us pause at this point to consider briefly the human material of which the On Guard leadership was composed, the personality of the leaders and their motivation in the struggle for "proletarian hegemony." Perhaps the most outstanding characteristic of the group is their extreme youth: most of them were in their early twenties or even younger at the time they made their demand for the leading voice in the development of Russian literature.[35] They were of course all members of the Communist Party, and most of them had participated in the revolution and the civil war, though the majority of them were by no means proletarian in origin. With the exception of Libedinskii and Demian Bednyi, none of the leading members of the group was distinguished as yet by outstanding literary production.[36]

Their critical writing during this period was a display of youthful arrogance coupled with ignorance and lack of the most elementary education in matters literary. Even an observer who was generally friendly to the group, Ivan Maiskii, the future ambassador to England, found that one of their chief "sicknesses" was lack of education: "education of every kind, general, political, and literary-artistic."[37] Their youth, their ignorance, and their enthusiasm for the Communist cause led them into gross oversimplification of all problems, and crude verbal excesses in their criticism of those who disagreed with them. They had no patience with people who expected cool detachment and fair-minded objectivity in the discussion of literary problems. Rodov thus answers Voronskii's complaints against their blunderbuss methods in dispute:

> Real life, which is rolling past Voronskii, disturbs him and upsets him. The laughter of youth irritates him. A straightforward and bold word, especially if it is loudly spoken, sounds to him like blasphemy. And how could it be otherwise? In graveyards and museums there is always quiet and the stillness of death. . . .
>
> He abjures the "insulting manners" which characterize our magazine *On Guard*. For, you see, he is a fine gentleman. The sensitive and delicate manners which he has cultivated in his literary association with *émigrés*, inner and outer, past and present, cannot bear with our direct, decisive, and honest behavior.[38]

Attacks on the fellow-travelers in the magazine *On Guard* were full of gross accusation and unprincipled innuendo. Even mild approval of a Soviet writer (for instance, the critic Voronskii) by an *émigré* journal would be used as evidence that that writer was in some kind of league with "hostile forces."[39]

Their motives in this struggle for "proletarian hegemony," that is, for a preferred position for their own group, were mixed. Many of them may have been genuinely concerned about the wide circulation and popular favor enjoyed by writers they believed to be out of sympathy with the Soviet regime. The right-wing critic Polonskii, who cannot be suspected of sympathy for the group, thus describes the reasons for its growth:

The revolutionary youth, which had just returned from the front, where with rifle in hand it had destroyed the bourgeois counter-revolution, discovered that in literature a tendency was dominant which was far from proletarian. This seemed to them strange and suspicious. The youth supposed that it was possible to create immediately a new art, an art of the proletariat.[40]

No doubt some of them were influenced by the idea that only a proletarian literature could aid the proletarian struggle, and that the art of any other class, if allowed free development, would harm their cause. Many were genuinely alarmed at the prominence of writers such as Zamiatin and Pil'niak[41] whose work, they believed, did not promote that cause but hindered it. Hostility to Communist ideas, or at best indifference to them, was what they found in much of fellow-traveler literature. Rodov complained that most of the writers supported by Voronskii were not fellow-travelers at all, but actually enemies.[42] He was no doubt genuinely afraid of them as a reflection of the growth of kulak and bourgeois strength under the regime of NEP.[43]

There were other forces and motives at work within the group. Some of these are only hinted at in the literature of the time, and others are obvious at every move. First, there was the proletarian writer's personal economic problem, his need for money. A large part of the funds distributed by the workers' and peasants' government in the form of royalties to writers was going, not to Party members or even to sympathizers, but to writers remote from the Party organization and to those suspected of hostility. The angry cries which greeted the mention of names such as Ehrenburg, Alexei Tolstoy, Anna Akhmatova, Boris Pil'niak, Vsevolod Ivanov, and many others, can be explained in part by a perfectly natural envy of their favored position in the journals and publishing houses of the country. "Is it for this we've shed our blood?" asked the proletarians of VAPP.

This is of course seldom stated specifically, though it is implicit in the frequent demands for "support," and "ideological *and material*" assistance for the young writers. However, the proletarian G. Seryi is quite honest about the meaning of this dispute. In a style both frank and fresh he wrote:

It costs from 70 to 100 rubles to print one short story written by a fellow-traveler. (This is his honorarium.) On this money a literary circle could be supported for two or three months. Not every factory can permit itself the luxury of supporting a literary circle. But that's where the money ought to be rolling. Why conceal facts. . . .

I remember once that a very important Party comrade, having in mind the On Guardists, made the following offer: "Write like Seifullina—we'll put out millions for you." No one answered: "Put out the millions and in a year we'll give you a hundred Seifullinas." But isn't it the truth? . . .

That's just what all the talking is about. The root of all the contemporary discussions about the fellow-travelers is right here. *Da ist der Hund begraben.*[44]

The manifestoes and agreements of the period frequently contain references to this need for material help. An agreement between MAPP and LEF, for instance, contains a paragraph which provides that measures will be worked out to improve the material condition and protect the rights of proletarian authors.[45] The Party Resolution on Belles-Lettres of 1925 contains one section which guarantees "material help to these writers."

In addition there was the perfectly natural desire of young and ambitious writers to supplant the old and established ones and to gain for themselves position and prestige as literary men. This is a commonplace phenomenon and not at all peculiar to the Soviet state. The difference here is that the young and ambitious writers were closely associated with the ruling Party, whereas the old and established ones were not, for the most part. The newcomers felt that the ruling Party, which was their own, should intervene directly to guarantee their hegemony over the old writers and their champion, Voronskii.

At one point Lelevich appears to have spoken a little more frankly than he intended regarding the aims of the On Guardists. He complained that the question was not so much the "quality" of the fellow-travelers' writing, but rather the "quantity" of this material being carried in the Soviet press. He can only have meant that the quantity of fellow-traveler literature should be reduced—of course to the advantage of the proletarians. In their struggle against established reputation and talent the leaders of VAPP attempted to achieve by administrative pressure what they could not achieve in open competition.[46]

Voronskii has left the following account of the impression made on him by the On Guard writers:

At the time of October and afterwards during the period of the civil war a great many youths joined our Party. There were many workmen, but the offspring of peasants, *petit-bourgeois,* and the democratic class of the intelligentsia (clerical workers, etc.) prevailed. They had passed through the cruel training of the civil war and had acquired wide knowledge from the rank and file of the Communist Party, but they had no solid bond with the life of the workmen. . . . While the war was being waged they had no time to study Marxism seriously, but they are doing it now. This generation . . . had borne arms, and from its midst came the *politruks* and regimental commanders; it fought the battles of Petersburg, Orël, and Rostov . . . it led a camp and nomadic life. . . . Now, however, instead of carrying a heavy rifle these youths handle pen and paper. They are strong, hardy . . . eager, mirthful, conceited, and resolutely self-reliant. They are accustomed to taking everything by storm: so give them Europe, give them schools, science, and art. They abound in youthful enthusiasm, and they are reluctant either to estimate their own strength soberly or to set themselves any limits. . . . Rather unmannerly, they step on your feet, they spit, and they talk arrogant nonsense.[47]

Chapter III

The Compromise

1. The Party Discussion

THE CAMPAIGN initiated by the October leaders of VAPP against the prevailing literary policy of the day could only be answered by a decision of the Communist Party. The Party itself, however, though it allowed both sides access to the public press and permitted the embittered literary controversy to go on, did not at first attempt to intervene on either side.

But the leaders of VAPP were both loud and insistent and as representatives of the Party youth they were able to make their arguments heard. The Party leaders most competent and most influential in the intellectual fields, Bukharin and Trotsky, for instance, tended to discourage their campaign. The latter were well aware that literary growth was possible only in an atmosphere of relative freedom. Yet the "Party's own" literary group continued to demand that the dispute which they had initiated be resolved by a clear and firm decision of their Party. Thus it came about that problems of literary history, theory, and criticism were threshed out on the highest level of the Party and government hierarchy. It would seem that the precedent set here was a fatal one. For the relatively sophisticated policy of a Bukharin or a Trotsky was soon replaced by the policy of Kaganovich in 1931, and of Zhdanov in 1934.

The Party leaders most prominent in this controversy included Trotsky, Bukharin, Ivan Maiskii, Lunacharskii, Karl Radek, and the Red Army leader Frunze.[1] There is no record that Stalin had anything to say about literature at this time.

Lenin, whose health was permanently impaired by a series of paralytic strokes and who died early in 1924, did not take an active part in the dispute. His authority, however, was enlisted by both sides. Statements could be found in his works both for and against the idea of a proletarian literature, and he was quoted at length by both the On Guardists and their opponents.[2] It is clear that his writings offered no clear scriptural authority for the solution of the specific problems raised by the On Guard group.[3]

The most prominent and the most persuasive opponent of the On Guardists was Leon Trotsky, whose ideas were for the most part in complete harmony with those of Voronskii. He was far more dogmatic than Voronskii, however, regarding the impossibility of a proletarian art and literature. Trotsky's viewpoint was that the proletarian state in Russia was a temporary, transitional phenomenon, which would disappear with the final victory of the world revolution. He argued that therefore a proletarian culture would simply not have time to develop.

He pointed out that no analogy was possible between bourgeois and proletarian culture, citing the example of the *bourgeoisie* in France. When they seized power they had behind them five centuries in which they had been developing their own culture; thus by the time of the French revolution theirs was already a rich culture. The Russian proletariat, on the other hand, had been the "stepchild" of culture, and had come into power without any tradition, literature, or culture that was peculiarly its own. Would it be able to develop its own literature? Trotsky's answer was a very definite "no." Said he:

> Our basic perspective is for a period of prolonged civil war, in the course of which the bourgeois world will be transformed. Such a period does not help the development of literature—for literary men are silent at such times.[4]

And again:

> It is impossible to think of a proletarian culture as analogous to bourgeois culture. The *bourgeoisie* were rich and already cultivated when they seized power, and they seized it in order to perpetuate

their own power. The object of the proletariat in seizing power is to destroy those conditions which have made them proletarian.[5]

Trotsky did not deny the propaganda and even educational value of such proletarian poems and novels as had appeared, but he did deny that they constituted a proletarian literature, or that they might be characterized as literature at all:

One cannot deny that even weak, colorless and illiterate verses can show the political growth of the poet and his class and may have considerable importance as cultural symptoms. But weak, and moreover illiterate, verses do not constitute a proletarian poetry, for they are not poetry at all.[6]

While Trotsky thus contrived to answer the theoretical questions raised by the proletarians, within the framework of his own political ideas regarding the continuing and "permanent" nature of the revolution, yet it is evident that he was also concerned about the immediate and practical results of a surrender to the On Guardists' demands. He seems to have been somewhat concerned at their neglect of the Russian literary tradition. He was at some pains to point out that even the worth-while examples of proletarian literature which had so far appeared were part of that tradition, and had taken form under the influence of particular "bourgeois" authors. He felt, I believe, that the normal development of Russian literature was threatened by the demands and the tactics of the On Guardists.

Like Voronskii, he rejected the prevalent tendency among the proletarians to understand all art as a purely "class" phenomenon:

When Raskolnikov[7] says that the *Divine Comedy* is valuable to us only because it portrays for us the ideology of a particular class at a particular time he is treating it simply as ideology and not as literature. He is ignoring that which makes it literature. . . .

The notion of a simple class analysis is insufficient. The works of Pushkin, Shakespeare, and Dante have value for us because through their artistic power these writers raised the experiences of a particular time and place to a high level.[8]

Trotsky offers as his fundamental argument against the proposals of the On Guardists the thesis that artistic creation has specific laws of its own which cannot be violated with impunity:

> We must not approach the problems of art as we approach those of politics; not because artistic creation is a holy or mystical activity . . . but because it possesses its own devices and methods and its own laws of development, and most of all because in artistic creation so large a part is played by subconscious processes. Such processes are slower and more gradual in their development, less subject to administration and direction, just because they are subconscious.[9]

In support of this idea he pointed out that those works of Pil'niak and Maiakovskii in which they attempt consciously to work out Communist ideas had been artistic failures.

Trotsky was merciless in exposing the flatulent ignorance of the On Guardists in the discussion of literary and political questions, their unprincipled attacks on Voronskii and the fellow-travelers, and, above all, the literary poverty of this small group which laid claim to the central place in the development of Russian literature. Rejecting the demand of the proletarians for "hegemony," he maintained that all writers not opposed to the revolution should be given a large measure of autonomy in the sphere of artistic creation.[10]

The Commissar of Public Education, Lunacharskii, was in complete accord with the supporters of Voronskii in their belief that administrative methods of control and direction were unfeasible in the area of literary creation, but he attempted at the same time to refute (utilizing appropriate excerpts from the works of Lenin) Trotsky's idea that there was not and could not be a proletarian literature and art. He announced it as his belief that the state must "work for the creation of a proletarian art and culture."[11] Yet he was no less emphatic than the others in rejecting the demand that such a literature be created through the support of an exclusive Party "cell" in the literary field:

> Vardin demands that the Party approach literary phenomena from a purely political point of view. But the sphere of pure politics is a narrow one. How is it possible, for instance, to approach questions of military policy, transport policy, or trade policy from a purely political point of view, without taking into account the special peculiarities of war, transport, and trade? In the same way the peculiarities of literary creation should be taken into account. . . .

A work of art with political content which does not have artistic quality is an absurdity. . . . Why not set forth political ideas in the form of propaganda?

If a good novel has no counterrevolutionary intent, but suffers, let us say, from a rather unpleasant deviation, or is completely apolitical, we must, of course allow such a novel to live. . . . Any really talented work of art is useful to us because it organizes experience, and a flourishing art will be a magnificent source to us of *knowledge* of the land.[12]

Yet Lunacharskii finally arrived at a compromise position which was not at all unfavorable to the proletarian literary movement:

I consider the only correct conclusion from our whole discussion to be that proletarian literature must be supported in every way as our chief hope, but that the fellow-travelers should by no means be alienated from us.[13]

Nikolai Bukharin[14] was at this time one of the most important members of the powerful Party Politburo. He was the person chiefly responsible for the Party policy in literature which was evolved in the course of this discussion and embodied in a Politburo resolution dated July 1, 1925.[15] Bukharin was a leader of the right wing of the Party. He held that the transition from a capitalist to a socialist society would be slow and gradual, and that the new socialist institutions would develop "at a snail's pace." His ideas were at the opposite extreme from those of Trotsky, who believed that the transition period would be "short and bloody." Bukharin therefore maintained that a proletarian culture would have time to develop during this lengthy transition period.[16] At the same time he insisted that while moving in the direction of a classless society the proletariat must permit the existence of the *bourgeoisie* and the peasantry, and even allow a certain amount of collaboration with them. He believed that the tasks of the Party in this period would in the main be peaceful ones, and that its policy in the domestic sphere should be to "soften and abate the class struggle." It followed from this that nonproletarian literature should be allowed to thrive alongside the proletarian product.[17]

Bukharin believed that the Party should scrupulously abstain from issuing directives in the literary sphere.[18] The methods applicable to the military and political struggle could not, he insisted, be employed in the cultural sphere. Direct coercion might be used successfully in a political seizure of power, but literary problems were not susceptible of solution by such means.[19] He therefore advised the proletarians to give up the composition of theses, directives, and manifestoes in favor of novels, plays, and poems, their proper sphere.[20] He insisted that only free competition of writers and groups would guarantee the emergence of a valuable literary product:

It seems to me that the best way to destroy proletarian literature is to reject the principle of free and anarchic competition. . . . Proletarian literature should attempt to develop the fellow-travelers, to educate and attract them to our side, not beat them over the head with a club, nor hold them in a vise.[21]

And in the development of such free competition Bukharin believed there should be no limit set on the number and variety of the competing literary schools and groups. "There should be many different groups," he said; "the more there are the better it will be." Of course groups and individuals that revealed counterrevolutionary tendencies should be forbidden, but a proletarian literature would be created in the end "only if the Party does not squeeze everyone into a single fist, but rather . . . allows competition."[22]

When we examine in detail the Party resolution on belles-lettres which resulted from this discussion we shall see that it includes Bukharin's main ideas and that even the phrasing and emphasis of his speeches and articles reappear in many sections of the official statement. The relatively liberal policy which characterized the decade of the twenties, was, we must conclude, largely the result of Bukharin's influence as a leading political figure.

2. The Difficult Decision

We have now examined the statements of the most important political figures who took part in the debate on proletarian literature. Voluminous articles and long speeches were contributed by lesser figures, but these seem to have had little effect on the outcome of the debate.[23] This discussion held a prominent place in the press of the country from 1923 to 1925.

In May, 1924, a special meeting of the Press Section of the Central Committee was called to discuss the issues raised by the On Guardists. The Thirteenth Congress of the Communist Party at the same time touched upon literary problems in its resolutions on the press. A special commission of the Central Committee met in February, 1925, to work out a policy with regard to competing literary groups, and its conclusions were embodied in the famous Politburo resolution published on July 1, 1925.[24] This resolution is often referred to in non-Soviet histories of the period as though it were a kind of "Charter of Liberties." The manner of its adoption is interesting for the light it throws on the operation of the Russian Communist Party in the mid-twenties.

At the Press Section Meeting of May, 1924, both sides were heard in full, and a number of important Party functionaries participated in the debate. There were representatives from the State Publishing House, and the Communist Academy, spokesmen of various literary groups, and individual literary figures. The discussion lasted for two days: May 8 and 9.

The order observed in the debate was similar to that adopted on many other occasions when thorny questions had to be threshed out prior to a decision by the Central Committee.[25] Each side selected a main speaker to present its basic arguments in a speech lasting about twenty minutes. The main speaker for the "right" was Voronskii, and for the "left" (the On Guardists), Vardin. After their speeches individuals were allowed the rostrum for a five- to ten-minute statement. No rebuttal was allowed to the individual speakers, but speeches were frequently interrupted by remarks from the floor. Curiously enough, a speaker usually felt himself obliged to interrupt the flow of his argument in order to answer each "irregular" remark. Finally the two main speakers were allowed a final word to sum up the opposing arguments, and at the end a resolution was presented by the chairman of the meeting. This was voted upon and accepted.[26]

Except for the October leaders themselves no one appeared at this meeting to support the program of VAPP in its entirety. The demand that VAPP become the administrative center of literary life was supported only by the spokesmen of that organization. The resolution approved by the meeting rejected this demand. It also censured VAPP and its publication *On Guard* for alienating many fellow-travelers from the Party and the Soviet power. Yet it is surprising to find that the wording of the resolution is not at all a complete rebuff to VAPP, but rather seeks to discover a means of compromising the dispute. Thus it is emphasized that: "The basic work of the Party should be oriented on the creation of those workers and peasants who are becoming worker and peasant writers in the process of the cultural rise of the broad masses of the Soviet Union."[27] And again that "material help be given to the writers of the Youth League."[28] Such statements betray an affection for the young proletarians and an interest in their organization, and they suggest that though competition might continue it would not be completely "free" and "anarchic." On the contrary, one particular group is to be the object of special concern. Yet the main tenor of the resolution was support of Voronskii's policy in utilizing and encouraging the fellow-travelers.

The resolution of the Thirteenth Party Congress on the press (June, 1924) included a statement on belles-lettres which was substantially the same as this Press Section resolution. It was somewhat more definite, however, in rebuffing the VAPP claim to speak for the Party in literary matters:

While it considers that no single literary program, school, or group can or should speak in the name of the Party, the Congress nevertheless emphasizes the necessity of regulating questions of literary criticism, and of the fullest possible interpretation from the Party viewpoint of those literary works which appear on the pages of the Party and Soviet press.[29]

Such a statement gives a negative answer to the demand of the On Guard leaders for the immediate hegemony of their group, but it also recognizes the necessity for closer attention to belles-lettres on the part of official organs, which was one of the chief demands of the On Guardists. Another paragraph of the resolution betrays the influence of that group's supporters:

Material support to the proletarian and peasant writers, who have entered our literature, in part from the plow and the work-bench, in part from that intellectual element which in the days of October and in the epoch of War Communism entered the ranks of Russian Communism and the Young Communist League, should be in every way strengthened.[30]

It is no wonder that both sides in the dispute over proletarian literature received this statement as a vindication and a victory. The spokesmen of the On Guard group and the partisans of Voronskii both published statements indicating they felt the Party policy to be in the best interests of literature generally; Bezymenskii and Lelevich added that the statement of the Congress had granted the proletarians "all that they had asked for."[31] That of course was simply not so; and yet the statement is remarkable as an attempt to settle an intra-Party dispute without alienating either side. For the Party was not yet ready to declare itself in favor of any one literary group, nor yet against the policy of supporting its own group; but it gave the Young Communist writers of VAPP good reason to hope that the future might be theirs. They would be given both material and moral support.

Let us now turn to the most important document we have, the resolution "On the Policy of the Party in the Field of Belles-Lettres" of July 1, 1925. A close reading of this resolution and an awareness of the fact that it was used by diametrically opposed groups to justify their behavior from 1925 to 1932, leaves no doubt that this document, too, instead of being a clear statement of policy, is an evasion and a postponement of the issues raised by the On Guardists. It betrays an ambivalence which probably arose from the fact that the Central Committee itself was not at this time a single-minded body, but contained bitterly opposed factions in a fierce struggle for power,[32] and neither side cared to alienate finally any large group of possible supporters, even in the intellectual field.

The most important ideas in the official statement of literary policy were contributed by Bukharin. One is that in the rather lengthy "transition period" the Party has before it the peaceful task of "living with," utilizing, and gradually winning over to its own program the nonproletarian intelligentsia.[33] Therefore the fellow-traveler writers, as "specialists of literary technique,"[34] should be highly valued and carefully cultivated in order to insure their loyalty to the Soviet regime and their eventual acceptance of its ideology.[35] The Communist critic is therefore cautioned to exhibit great tact in dealing with any literary group which is not clearly counterrevolutionary.[36] For literary specialists must be cherished and guided "onto the rails" of the proletarian revolution.

The Party in this statement rebuffs as premature the demand that it support any one group or faction in the literary sphere, and it eschews as "quasi-bureaucratic" any attempt at controlled literary development. Free competition of various groups and tendencies is called for.[37] Communist literary men and critics should, therefore, overcome their semiliterate "arrogance," and drop their pretentious "tone of command."[38] The Party itself, moreover, attempts to set limits to its own activity in literature, though it is explicitly stated that the Party is the leader of "literature as a whole."[39]

Taking the sections of the resolution so far quoted in isolation from their context, we might conclude that the policy of the Central Committee at this time was indeed one of encouraging competition among literary groups, of eschewing authoritative statements on aesthetic and literary matters, and of denying support to the demand of the proletarian writers for hegemony. This was, as a matter of fact, the policy of Bukharin, and those sections of the resolution so far quoted were largely his contribution, as a comparison of them with his speech at the May, 1924, meeting makes quite clear. But the On Guard group was not without support on the Central Committee, nor did the latter wish to alienate the writers of the Young Communist League and their allies. Its supporters were able to incorporate some of their views, too, in the resolution.

Certain sections of the resolution gave the proletarian writers reason to hope that their defeat was only temporary, and that the future would be theirs. For the resolution accepts without cavil the On Guard tenet that a "class war" is in progress in the literary world, and that art cannot be neutral as between the warring classes.[40] It is conceded, however, that in literature such a phenomenon is infinitely more complex than, say, in politics.[41] All discussion of the possibility of a proletarian literature is ended with the appearance of the Party statement, which affirms that a proletarian literature already exists,[42] and that while it does not yet enjoy "hegemony," yet it will surely win the right to such a position in the future.[43] In fact all concerned are warned against underestimating the importance of the struggle for "proletarian hegemony."[44] Moreover, the future hegemony of the proletarians is not to be achieved by the superiority of proletarian literature alone and unaided. Quite the contrary: the Party solemnly promises that the proletarians are to be given "material and moral" assistance.[45] It is true that a measure of recognition is given to the rights of the fellow-travelers, but at the same time the On Guardists are encouraged in their struggle against "neo-bourgeois" literature. We shall see later that good use was made of this statement in the ensuing period in attacking a large group of fellow-travelers.

We have examined this curious document in some detail because of its importance in Soviet literature, and also because it is a phenomenon almost unique in literary history. Seldom has there been such a close connection of literary development and party politics. Seldom has a government body been called upon to render such sweeping decisions in the field of belles-lettres. The manner in which questions were raised by the On Guardists made such intervention by the Party inevitable. Yet several sections of the resolution, as we have seen, show the influence of those who would exercise restraint in asserting Party authority in this field and would discourage the intransigents among the youth.

However, the idea that the Party as such has authority in the literary sphere is implicit in the resolution; regarding the field of aesthetics generally, the Party avers that Marxism has not "penetrated" it, but will surely do so in the near future.

The Party Resolution on Literature of July, 1925, is a rambling, repetitious, verbose, and pompous document. It is possible to interpret it in a number of ways. Its chief importance for us is that it did represent a rebuff to the leaders of the proletarian literary movement, and seemed to call for a change in their policy and tactics.

Chapter IV

On Literary Guard, 1925–1928

1. The New Leadership of VAPP

The resolution of July 1, 1925, was understood by the fellow-travelers and by Party spokesmen as a serious defeat for the leaders of the proletarian literary movement. A new approach to the problems of proletarian literature and of Soviet literature generally was clearly called for.[1] This situation presented an opportunity for advancement to a group of critics and writers within VAPP who had frequently disagreed with the leadership and opposed its sectarian policies.[2] The most important of these figures were the young critic Averbakh, the novelists Libedinskii and Furmanov, and the playwright Kirshon.[3] They led the opposition within VAPP to the policies of Vardin and Rodov, the leaders whose immediate demands had been rebuffed by the Party resolution.

The group of which Averbakh was the leader accepted without cavil the Party resolution and the criticism of VAPP contained in it. They attempted to understand and explain it as a victory for proletarian literature. "The resolution of the Central Committee gives us all that we have asked for," said Averbakh. "We must work on the basis of this resolution, for all the conditions which the On Guardists called for have been granted."[4] Vardin, Rodov, and their followers did not accept the Party decision with complete good grace. They were reluctant to admit that the criticism directed at them by the leaders of the Party was entirely "correct," and they continued to maintain that proletarian literature could thrive only if its organization were given the leadership of all contemporary literature and a preferred position over the "bourgeois" writers.[5]

The propagation of such views, though "condemned by the Party," was still possible in the years 1925 and 1926, for an opposition to the Party leadership still existed at that time. It should be emphasized that this "literary discussion" was taking place within the Communist Party at a time when it was divided by a bitter factional dispute. The violent arguments among Communist literary men were a part of this internal strife, and literary problems were discussed in terms which can hardly be understood without reference to political events. The future program and leadership of VAPP were in the balance at the time when the opposition led by the Old Bolsheviks Zinoviev and Kamenev was developing within the Party.[6] This opposition had a not inconsiderable following, especially in the city of Leningrad.[7] The factional fight within the proletarian literary organization was a reflection of the Party struggle itself. Vardin, Rodov, Lelevich, and many of their followers in VAPP were in opposition not only to the literary policy of the Party; they were in opposition to the leadership on other questions as well, and had joined their forces to Zinoviev's movement.[8]

Averbakh's group, which was distinguished at this time for its devotion to the Party line in all matters, received the support of the Central Committee and was able to remove the oppositionists from the executive bodies of VAPP. We learn that at a meeting of the VAPP executive in February, 1926, the members of the left-wing group within VAPP, "because they objected . . . to the Resolution of the Central Committee on Literary Policy," were relieved of administrative work.[9]

The evidence is conclusive as to the connection of the literary dispute with the bitter struggle within the Communist Party. It must be admitted, however, that the history of these events is not easy to reconstruct from the documents which purport to describe them, and that developments within the Soviet Union have made it largely impossible to get a clear account of them from the surviving participants. Nearly all of the men involved in this dispute had disappeared from the scene by the end of 1937, and later Soviet accounts only say that both factions were made up of "enemies" and "fascist agents."[10]

Shortly after the change in leadership was effected, VAPP was given authority to publish again its own critical and theoretical journal. The former organ of VAPP had borne the title *Na postu* (On Guard). The new magazine appeared in March, 1926, and was called *Na literaturnom postu* (On Literary Guard). Its editorial board consisted of Averbakh, Volin, Libedinskii, Olminskii, and Raskolnikov. The appearance of the word "literary" in the title was not without significance. A lead editorial in the first issue of the publication announced that "henceforth the center of our attention will be transferred to the field of literary creation."[11]

2. The New Approach to "Proletarian Hegemony"

The most important question which faced the new leadership in 1926 was the relationship of the proletarian and Communist writers to the numerous and successful group of writers who were nonproletarian and non-Communist: the fellow-travelers. "Hegemony" in the literary field had been denied to the proletarians for the present by the Resolution of the Central Committee. Therefore they were faced with the necessity of living with, and gradually, as they put it, "winning over," this group of writers while earning the right themselves to leadership. Since this could hardly be accomplished if the proletarians isolated themselves completely from the "bourgeois" writers, the new leadership of VAPP, early in 1926, applied to the Press Section of the Central Committee for permission to organize a Federation of Organizations of Soviet Writers (FOSP) which would include both proletarian and fellow-traveler writers' groups. The most important organization which was to enter this Federation along with VAPP was the Union of Writers (VSP), the membership of which was for the most part composed of fellow-travelers.[12]

This project met with the bitter opposition of VAPP's former leaders, who were still unwilling to adopt a conciliatory attitude toward non-Communist writers. The "left opposition"—Vardin, Lelevich, Rodov, Bezymenskii, and others—felt that in the circumstances proletarian literature could lose more than it stood to gain from close association with the "bourgeois" writers' group: for the fellow-travelers were, in their education, general culture, and artistic accomplishment so far superior to the struggling proletarians (the "stepchildren of culture") that association with them might vitiate the ideological purity of the latter. We have had occasion to observe the intransigence under the leadership of Vardin of VAPP's attitude toward "bourgeois" literature. And even after its repudiation by the Party the old leadership in its role of "left opposition" maintained an uncompromising attitude toward the non-Communists and opposed the adoption of a somewhat more conciliatory policy. For Vardin regarded the Union of Writers as "the banner of the Nepmen, the organization in literature of the *bourgeoisie.*"[13]

In spite of opposition from the left the proposed Federation was formed on December 27, 1926, at a meeting which included representatives of VAPP, the Union of Writers, and the All-Union Society of Peasant Writers. VAPP and the VSP were numerically the most important organizations. Shortly thereafter other less important groups joined: the Left Front of Art, Pereval, and the Smithy.[14]

It is important for an evaluation of the influence of VAPP upon Russian literature to understand that the leadership of that organization after 1926 did not anathematize fellow-traveler literature as a whole. We shall see in a later chapter that their criticism was more moderate than has been generally supposed. However, the "left opposition," though defeated and removed from participation in the work of the executive, did remain within VAPP (and later, RAPP) and was not without influence in literary affairs. Critics and writers of that persuasion continued to write and to publish books. The *Literary Gazette*, a weekly newspaper published by the Federation, was during a part of this period the avowed organ of the "lefts."[15] Much of what appeared in it has been quite unjustly ascribed to RAPP as a whole and has given rise to a mistaken interpretation of its activity.[16]

The new leadership of VAPP, equipped with new Party directives regarding proletarian hegemony, no longer spoke of the need for a "Party cell" to which all literary work must be subordinated. They believed that hegemony could be achieved only through the growth of proletarian literature to a commanding position in both ideological content and artistic form;[17] and it must, moreover, gain for itself the predominant influence on the reading masses.[18] This doctrine of eventual proletarian hegemony through the superiority of the proletarian product would seem to have been reasonable enough.

However, the leaders of VAPP displayed in their contacts with fellow-travelers in the newly organized Federation an arrogance which should surprise no one in view of the official designation of VAPP as the "future hope" of Soviet literature. Believing themselves the special guardians of ideological purity, they were hindered by no political or moral qualm in their efforts to dominate the Federation. Their method was to rig the votes on the executive bodies of the Federation in such a way that VAPP was assured at all times of a two-thirds majority. This activity was exposed by Voronskii in a series of articles in *Red Virgin Soil*, and though Averbakh attempted to answer him he could not deny that his group had quite mechanically appropriated the "leading voice" in the Federation. Voronskii's outspoken articles reveal that the tactics of the proletarian writers had earned them the silent but deep contempt of other groups. That the Central Committee of the Party, however, supported VAPP in its activities became increasingly clear as time went on.[19]

3. The New Attitude toward Proletarian Letters: Study, Creation, Self-criticism

We have seen that the new leadership promised to concern itself more with literature and less with politics. The reform was an answer to the demand of Bukharin and many others that the proletarian writers give up the writing of manifestoes and declarations and instead produce literature. The new orientation which it exhibited in the early issues of *On Literary Guard* was welcomed not only by supporters of proletarian literature, but by those who had been opposed to it. The critic Polonskii reported that under the impact of the Party resolution the new leaders had shown a disposition to avoid copying the behavior and repeating the "mistakes" of the old On Guard group.[20]

In the first issues of the new magazine a number of articles appeared which were obviously inspired by the directive of the Central Committee to overcome "Communist conceit."[21] There are frequent references to the mistakes of the old leadership and to the intention of the On Literary Guardists not to repeat them. The new slogan, "Study, Creation, Self-criticism," is the keynote of most of these articles. The proletarians speak of their own shortcomings, especially those of a literary nature, with considerable frequency and rather insistent protestation. They are willing to admit that their proletarian product is still a very crude literature. The question of improving its quality is given first place:

> At the present time when the Party in all branches of our enormous socialist construction brings forward the slogan of *quality* . . . we must emphasize that in our sector of cultural construction, in the field of proletarian literature, the improvement of quality has not been satisfactory.
>
> There was a time when the demands of the moment called upon us to oppose to fellow-traveler . . . literature something of *our own:* "Though it may be ugly, yet it's *ours.*" Now a new slogan is required: "Ours, but not ugly."[22]

Libedinskii in a number of articles emphasizes the need for study. Taking the Party resolution as his point of departure, he gives special attention to the poverty of proletarian letters and the need for prolonged study and "hard work" in order to win the "right to hegemony." Libedinskii, as we shall presently see, became the chief theoretician of the proletarian literary method propagandized by RAPP.[23]

In spite of what may well have been a real intention to raise the quality of its critical and literary work, *On Literary Guard*, in part because it lacked a complement of fully educated people, and in part also because within the Communist Party there was no tradition of sober, fair, realistic, and liberal criticism of opponents, soon began to exhibit some of the worst critical habits of the old On Guard group. Polonskii, writing again in 1928, after *On Literary Guard* had been in existence for about two years, characterizes it in the following terms:

The latest period of activity of *On Literary Guard* indicates that they have forgotten nothing and learned nothing. Those scandalous critical devices and inadmissible methods of literary dispute which were condemned by the resolution of the Politburo have been renewed in this magazine in an even less acceptable form than before. . . . A low level of literary literacy, together with boastful arrogance and indifference to the real interests of proletarian literature, has at last alienated a large number of proletarian literary men.[24]

Polonskii's view of VAPP and its organ *On Literary Guard* may be somewhat jaundiced, since he himself was one of the most frequent targets of the kind of criticism he describes. But the VAPP leaders and critics were indeed addicted to criticism which might be characterized as "exposing the class enemy" in an opponent. A good example of this tendency and one which is typical of many is an editorial on the opposition to VAPP which appeared in *On Literary Guard* early in 1928. The author (probably Averbakh) explains the opposition to VAPP, much of which came from Communist literary figures, as simply an evidence of the continuation of the class struggle in the country: "As long as there is a class struggle in our country, VAPP will be attacked, and these attacks have nothing to do with the merits or demerits of the VAPP leadership." The editorial quotes a speech of Stalin to the effect that the class struggle inside the country is growing, cleverly tying this idea to the increase in opposition to VAPP. Stalin's remarks on the Shakhty trial and the "plots of international capital" are brought into the same context. Thus it is against the background of the class struggle and international plots against the existence of the Soviet Union that Averbakh would have his proletarian readers understand the criticism of VAPP. The critics he refers to are Polonskii, who is simply "resurrecting the old and buried ideas of Voronskii," Gorbov, a Communist whose articles appeared more than once in *Izvestiia*, and the magazine *Chitatel' i pisatel'* (Reader and Writer) to which he refers as "the Soviet philistine."[25]

Examples of such criticism could be multiplied. It consists

largely in the irresponsible and repetitive application to an opponent of politically opprobrious labels. This device became a permanent characteristic of VAPP literary criticism and dispute. It is a polemical device which anyone familiar with the writings of Soviet leaders will immediately recognize. The VAPP polemics were not much below the general level of political dispute of their time, though it is sometimes startling to find labels borrowed from the political arena mechanically applied to literary phenomena. Ironically enough, the VAPP leaders themselves about a decade later became the victims of just such polemics as this, though on an infinitely lower moral level, and with fatal consequences.

4. The All-Union Congress of April, 1928—Reorganization of VAPP

The first clear evidence of strong support to VAPP from the Central Committee of the Communist Party appears in the course of the All-Union Congress of Proletarian writers held in Moscow in April, 1928. The *Literary Encyclopedia* in its long and for the most part accurate article on RAPP points out that it was after this Congress in 1928 that the organization began to grow in numbers and prestige.[26] This Congress was a landmark in the history of VAPP.

A new executive of VAPP, elected shortly before the Congress was called, was made up of the following persons: Averbakh, Gorbatov, Gladkov, Ermilov, Zharov, Zonin, Kirshon, Libedinskii, Luzgin, Polosikhin, Panskii, Raskolnikov, Serafimovich, Surkov, Fadeev, Chumandrin. This group, with occasional defections and some additions, was from that time on the recognized leadership of the proletarian literary movement.[27]

Certain changes of a purely organizational nature were effected at the Congress. VAPP (All-Russian Association of Proletarian Writers) became RAPP (Russian Association of Proletarian Writers), and the designation VAPP fell into disuse after the Congress. In the All-Union Organization of Associations of Proletarian Writers (VOAPP) were now joined a number of regional organizations: VUKAPP (All-Ukrainian Association), SKAPP (North Caucasus Association), SibAPP (Siberian

Association), and other "APP's" representing separate republics or outlying regions. The most important of these was RAPP. In a short time the designation RAPP came to be used in reference to the whole movement of proletarian literature. That designation will hereafter be so used in this work, except where it is necessary to be specific as to the activity of a particular regional APP.[28]

Averbakh explained that this organizational change was effected because prior to the Congress, VAPP was not an all-Union association. It did not include, for example, the Ukrainian Association. The new organizational forms made it possible not only to include such a separate national organization as the Ukrainian APP, but also other proletarian literary organizations.[29]

In addition to the important changes of an organizational nature which it effected, the Congress of 1928 is important for evidence it provides of direct support to RAPP from the Central Committee of the Party. Three responsible members of the Communist Party and the Soviet government appeared at the Congress and delivered strong speeches in support of the proletarian literary movement in its present form. The three were Lunacharskii, People's Commissar of Education; Krinitskii, for the Central Committee of the Communist Party; and Lazian, secretary of the Moscow Committee of the Party.

Lunacharskii's remarks are especially interesting in that they suggest a rather recent change of attitude toward RAPP on the part of some leading figures who were not at first inclined to be friendly. He places himself squarely behind the idea of a proletarian literature, the RAPP leadership, and the RAPP program. He does, in fact, deplore some of the characteristics of the RAPP leadership—their youth, their inordinate zeal in polemical dispute, and the consequent sharp tone of their attacks on opponents. But his final judgment is that they are in the main an organization useful to the Party in its work. Their chief virtue, he says, is their "hundred-percent willingness" to carry out the directives of the Party. He continues:

Of course these two qualities—the readiness to lead a broad organization and to subordinate oneself to higher organizations—would not in themselves make the RAPP people worthy of all encouragement and all support. But after an attentive and at first not at all friendly investigation of this group, I cannot help coming to the conclusion that it includes a number of young people of outstanding talent—people who in spite of the fact that they are overloaded with Party tasks, are always working and studying.[30]

Krinitskii stressed especially the significant task of Soviet art and especially literature in the business of "remaking people":

All of our cultural work, all the tasks of the cultural revolution, are bound up with the one basic, decisive task, the reeducation, the "making over," of the masses.[31]

While pointing out that the hegemony of proletarian literature had not yet been achieved, he emphasizes that a change in the relationship of forces between proletarian and fellow-traveler literature had occurred in the last few years—to the advantage of the former. He indicates definite though not unqualified approval of the work of VAPP:

Speaking of the work and the literary creation of VAPP, as the major organization of proletarian literature, though there are a number of faults and errors to be overcome, yet one must at this First Congress admit that the total reckoning is on the credit side.[32]

He leaves no doubt in anyone's mind about the intention of the Party to support the literary organization which has shown itself so ready and willing to be the Party's support:

On its side the Party has aided, is aiding, and will continue to aid, the proletarian writers in the ranks of Soviet literature to "earn for themselves the right to hegemony."[33]

A new tone of confidence appears in the statements of Averbakh and other RAPP leaders after this First Congress. Although the Central Committee had not published a resolution on the subject, the definite impression is given that RAPP now thinks of itself as an official interpreter of the Party policy in the literary world. We shall see later that this version was not only never contradicted by the Central Committee, but was endorsed in a number of statements accepted as official by the whole literary world.[34]

Averbakh's statements at this time admit that the proletarian literary movement still has many "unfulfilled tasks" before it, but his writings breathe assurance that these can now be undertaken with good hope of success. Such tasks included the winning over of the reading masses for proletarian literature, increasing the social significance of its subject matter, and, finally, the development of its own superior literary method and style.[35]

The final point concerning artistic method was not neglected at the First Congress of Proletarian Writers. Indeed this Congress was a noteworthy event not only because of the evidence it provided of strong official support for RAPP and its leaders, but also because considerable attention was devoted in its sessions to questions of literary style and content. Proletarian conferences in the past had had little time for literary problems. But after this Congress RAPP emerged as a literary school with its own method and critical principles. The chief theoreticians of literary method were the novelists Libedinskii and Fadeev, whose lengthy reports at this Congress, together with other articles and extensive studies of the question published at this time, furnished the chief source of a theoretical approach to the problems of literary creation which, until the liquidation of RAPP, underwent only minor modification.

5. Conclusion

What, then, was the status and outlook of proletarian literature and its organization, RAPP, in the year 1928? A new leadership had been provided for it with the help and support of the Party, a leadership which declared itself fully in favor of the policy of the 1925 Resolution. This leadership recognized in theory the rights of the nonproletarian writers, though in practice it used the Federation of Writers and other means to advance the interests of the proletarians, and its methods were often neither fair nor admirable. Proletarian literature was the object of special favor from the Party and its most trusted support "on the cultural front." A consciousness of importance is obvious in the speeches and articles of the proletarian leaders. Since 1925 a number of important works by proletarian authors had helped to increase the prestige of the movement. Among these were Furmanov's *Chapaev*, Sholokhov's *Silent Don*, Gladkov's *Cement*, Fadeev's *The Rout*, Bakhmet'ev's *The Crime of Martin Baimakov*, Semënov's *Natalia Tarpova*, and a number of others. We shall soon see that such works served as models and guides in the development of proletarian literary theory in RAPP.

The promise of the Party that the future would be theirs seemed to the young proletarians fully realizable. And in order to chart their path more surely they now developed a theory of literature which they maintained was "Marxist" and a method of literary creation which they called "dialectical materialist."

Chapter V

The Theory of Literature, 1928

1. Introduction

We have seen that Voronskii and the proletarians had long been at odds on a number of issues. Voronskii regarded without enthusiasm the prospects of proletarian literature, and was scornful of its claim to hegemony. He admired, praised, and gave eager support to many non-Communist writers whose work he liked. He was sharp and direct in identifying the political and literary faults of the proletarian leaders.[1] At this point, however, when we come to investigate the literary theories current among the proletarians, we find, with a certain surprise, that they seem to have learned much about the nature of literature and literary criticism in the course of their long and embittered polemic with Voronskii. In fact, they had appropriated his most important ideas and consciously used formulas characteristic of him.

The RAPP leaders of course denied that they were "Voronskyites," though his influence upon them was eagerly pointed out by their enemies.[2] The difference between RAPP theory and the ideas of Voronskii which influenced it consisted in this, that RAPP placed greater emphasis on conscious Marxism and on the primacy of the proletarian writers. This difference seemed to the proletarians far more important than any similarity in general approach, literary evaluation or criticism.

There is no doubt that the RAPP theorists consciously assimilated Voronskii's ideas. Libedinskii's articles, as we shall see, offer evidence that the proletarians had learned basic truths from their antagonist. But it should be emphasized that the general agreement between the ideas of RAPP and the ideas of Voronskii also arises from the circumstance that both drew upon a common source, the Marxist philosopher G. V. Plekhanov. We have already noted that Voronskii used and developed the leading ideas of Plekhanov on literature; and in the course of this and later chapters, it will, I hope, become clear that the RAPP theoreticians themselves were heavily indebted to Plekhanov. In this they were quite orthodox, for in Soviet philosophical and literary circles Plekhanov was accepted as a source of doctrine until, in the early thirties, the Central Committee of the Party supported a movement to replace his authority in philosophical and literary questions with that of Lenin.[3]

In Averbakh's earliest contributions to the Soviet discussion of literature during the twenties he made an effort to find a middle ground between the description of literature as "cognition of life" and the Proletcult and On Guard understanding of all art as a "class" instrument, a means for organizing the psyche of the working mass. At the height of the controversy with Voronskii he wrote:

It is unquestionable that art is a means for the specific cognition of life. But it is no less unquestionable that art is a means of emotional infection. . . . By cognition art serves to transform life. Thus cognition of life on the one hand and emotional infection on the other are inextricably and immutably joined in a work of art.[4]

His compromise position is stated more definitely in the following quotation from an important discussion of literary theory:

We look upon art as a specific form for the cognition of life, distinct from other forms of cognition of reality, as an instrument of the class struggle and as a handmaiden in the social activity of a given class. By the same token we look upon art not only as a means for cognition, but also as a means for changing social reality.[5]

This attempt to find a compromise position between the "extreme right," which tended to regard art as pure cognition of life, and the "extreme left," which minimized its cognitive function in favor of a view of art as a class instrument, is characteristic of the RAPP approach. And Libedinskii gives full credit to Voronskii for drawing the proletarians away from the crude simplicity of their early views on art and literature.

In attempting to describe the RAPP theory of literature, we shall rely rather heavily on direct quotation of the theorists themselves. This may at times be painful to the reader, for the philosophers of RAPP express themselves in a Russian not always clear and smooth, and they speak in a ritual idiom which is strange to the non-Marxist ear. No attempt has been made to alter in translation the idiom and style of the originals. The purpose has been to give the authentic accent of time and place.

2. What Is Proletarian Literature?

The works of Averbakh and the official statements of the leadership of RAPP make frequent reference to the necessity for a "cultural revolution." The political revolution and the reorganization of industry and agriculture will be meaningless, they indicate, unless these developments are accompanied by a rise in the cultural level of the working masses. The term "culture" is used in a very broad sense to include not only an increase in the popular utilization of literature and art in all its forms, but most of all a rise in general literacy, in education, and in standards of health and sanitation.[6]

Averbakh's main thesis would appear to be that "the productivity of labor depends not only on the industrialization of the country, but also upon raising the educational and cultural level of the masses." This statement in itself would seem to be fairly obvious and to raise no serious political issues: such a program was, at least in its broad outlines, included in the Party program. But the question is one of emphasis. Averbakh's idea is that industrialization at the tempos contemplated by the program of the Party will be impossible without a continuous and concomitant rise in the cultural level of the masses.[7]

Averbakh was in 1928 extremely dissatisfied with the results so far achieved in this realm. He adduces figures to show that only very little had been done to liquidate illiteracy, to broaden educational services, to improve health, and to extend medical care. From the figures he gives the conclusion is inescapable that the USSR was not only far behind the nations of

Central and Eastern Europe, but had not even been able to make significant strides beyond the achievements of tsarist Russia.[8]

He stresses the extreme cultural backwardness of the country by comparison with western nations.[9] Apparently in answer to anticipated arguments, he emphasizes that funds expended for such things as education and health care will also contribute to the rise in production figures, for they will improve the quality of the workers.[10]

He quotes speeches made at the Fifteenth Congress of the Party (1927) by Rykov[11] and Bukharin[12] to the effect that further growth in industrialization must be accompanied by a corresponding rise in the cultural level of the masses. He quotes a speech given at the Moscow Party Conference, at which Bukharin had called for an increase in the funds allocated to cultural work. Averbakh concludes:

It is clear, then, that we are lagging behind culturally and that we must give special attention to the . . . financing of the cultural revolution.[13]

The cultural revolution, as Averbakh understood it, involved deep changes in human beings. Such changes of course presupposed the liquidation of illiteracy and the traditional "darkness" of pre-1917 Russia.[14] But they must go much further:

The cultural revolution is a lengthy epoch during which human material will be transformed, the toiling masses themselves will be reeducated, and a new type of man produced. In this work a great and serious task falls to the lot of art, with its specific means of influencing the whole human psyche.[15]

Echoing the conclusions of Averbakh in the brochure quoted above, the resolutions of the RAPP executive emphasize that this cultural work cannot wait for the consolidation of a firm material base for the new society, but must go hand in hand with it. A leading article in one of the early issues of *On Literary Guard*, printed in large type and apparently designed as a major statement of editorial policy, emphasizes that the Party and the government cannot wait for the outcome of "socialist construction" and the raising of the material level of the workers before interesting themselves in cultural matters. Cultural progress must go hand in hand with construction, or else the latter will be hampered.[16]

The theoreticians and practitioners of proletarian literature believed that their product should be an important agency of this "cultural revolution." The resolution adopted by the First Congress of Proletarian Writers in 1928 sets forth such ideas in the Marxist jargon of the day:

> Being one of the means for the cognition of social life and of the whole world which surrounds man, art organizes the feelings and thoughts by means of images influencing the psyche of the reader, listener, etc., through "emotional infection." In the conditions of a class society art is a mighty weapon of the class struggle. In actively influencing all ideological fields, the proletariat makes no exception of art. Therefore one of the main tasks of the cultural revolution is to aid the development of proletarian art and its advanced detachment, proletarian literature.[17]

"To aid the development of . . . proletarian literature," such is the important task of the "cultural revolution." What exactly was understood by the term "proletarian literature"? There is never any question in the statements of RAPP theoreticians on this subject that the term must include not only the literary product of people who are proletarian in origin but also that of nonproletarians who sympathize with—"take the viewpoint of"—the proletariat. And indeed it could not be otherwise, for the leadership of RAPP and a large proportion of its membership were made up of writers and critics who were not of working-class origin. Averbakh, Libedinskii, Fadeev, Panfërov, Kirshon, Gladkov, and most of the people active in RAPP, were in their family origins *petit-bourgeois* intellectuals. This was true not only of RAPP but also of the early On Guard group. Unlike the Proletcult, whose tendency was to accept as proletarian only works directly expressing the life of the "labor collective," On Guard and RAPP had a much broader understanding of the term:

> Proletarian literature we understand as that literature which comprehends the world from the viewpoint of the proletariat and influences the reader in accord with the tasks of the working class. . . .

Only from the point of view of the world outlook of the proletariat —Marxism—can social reality be perceived by the artist with maximum objectivity.[18]

Averbakh at one point clearly underlines the idea that the term "proletarian" has no necessary reference to the class origin of the writer:

> Proletarian art is not a form of art which must necessarily be created by a proletarian. Proletarian art is such art as aids the proletariat in the building of socialism, and organizes our feelings and thoughts in the direction of the building of a communist society.[19]

The spokesmen of RAPP were acutely aware of the fact that the "worker nucleus" of their organization was especially weak, and that their most prized authors were not proletarians. The need to correct this situation and to strengthen the worker nucleus is a frequent theme of their articles, and seems to have occupied much of the time devoted to organizational matters. The chief means for "proletarianizing" the ranks of RAPP existed in the literary circles, organized in connection with factories and sometimes on a regional basis. For the most part these circles were inherited from the old On Guard organization, and their prototype, as we have already seen, was the literary studios set up by the Proletcult in the early days of the revolution. Their importance is stressed by Fadeev in the following statement:

> We will orient ourselves not upon the "supermen" but upon those colossal layers of the population which are rising to the tasks of literature, and whom no one can ever take away from us. For only we, not fearing humble tasks, have approached them—the most advanced and the most backward of peasants and workers—who are learning to write "with a piece of charcoal on a wall," and only we are attempting to make them part of our general movement. . . . Our organization is raising up colossal layers of workers and peasants, for whom, in the past, every step in the direction of culture was, as Lenin said, beset with difficulties.[20]

The "humble task" of educating from the ranks of the working class new and "genuinely proletarian" forces occupied the attention not only of Fadeev, but of Libedinskii and Kirshon, whose special province it later became.

3. The "Social Demand"

The idea that RAPP was a kind of semiofficial censorship body regimenting the ranks of Soviet literature has become so widespread since RAPP's dissolution in 1932 that we must give some space to discussion of the concept "social demand." The attitude toward literary creation symbolized by this phrase was never congenial to the RAPP critics, nor does it figure prominently in their literary platforms. It was, however, one of the phrases current in the literary discussions of the time, and a correct understanding of RAPP's attitude toward it helps to define the general position of the RAPP leadership.

The term "social demand" originated not with the proletarian current in Soviet literature, but among the futurists and formalist critics organized in Novy LEF (New LEF).[21] It had a very narrow and highly specialized meaning derived from their general theory of literature "in the epoch of socialism." Reduced to its simplest terms, their notion was that the writer is simply a craftsman of words; that the highest form of literary creation is factual reporting: sketches, biographies, diaries, etc.; and that the activity of the craftsman-writer should be determined by the *demand* of his client, the proletariat. "Literary production is by its nature no different from other kinds of production," and therefore the writer, whatever his class origin or orientation, is simply a producer who is able to satisfy the demand of his client for clear, factual, objective materials.

Although this general approach is ascribed to the RAPP leaders in some Soviet studies written in the middle thirties, it is alien to their whole concept of literature in general and proletarian literature in particular. As a matter of fact, the RAPP theoreticians carried on an extremely violent controversy with New LEF as a group whose literary program meant the "liquidation" of art and literature.[22]

Averbakh in his report at the First Congress takes direct issue with those who would import LEF ideas into the criticism of proletarian literature. He describes and flatly rejects a notion which certain literary men had propounded to the effect that Party and Soviet bodies, when adopting a resolution on cooperatives, for instance, should add a final point ordering a certain number of poems and short stories on the given topic. He continues:

> Is it possible to give the writer a "task"? This is a question widely discussed at the moment. . . . The class position of the writer dictates immediately to him the choice of themes and their treatment. . . . The writer is not a kind of "otherworldly" being but is just such a man as you or I. . . . If he is like everyone else then he comes within the purview of Marx's formula: "The essence of man is the sum of his social relations."
>
> . . . .
>
> Yet the writer is conditionally free in his choice of themes and in his treatment of them. . . . But we must insist that this very freedom is conditioned. The fact that the writer is conditioned in his free choice of themes is in large part the real content of the term "social demand." I have been obliged to dispute rather frequently with those who maintain that the "social demand" is simply an order to the writer to "write on such and such a theme."

To give direct commands to the writer, Averbakh felt, was quite impossible; yet the critic should "help" the writer to be conscious of the "social demand." And for Averbakh this meant simply to be conscious of the fact that in producing a work of art he is taking part in social life.[23]

While Averbakh did admit the term "social demand" in the attenuated meaning "social conditioning," he was actually opposed to the assignment of definite themes to writers. It is passing strange that so many students have treated the idea of the social demand in its crude form as characteristic of RAPP.[24] It was not. The viewpoint of the RAPP leadership was so definite on this point that Libedinskii felt obliged to reverse the ideas on this subject which he had advanced earlier in his article on "Themes Which Await Their Authors."[25] He admits that the position he took in that early article was mistaken and agrees with Averbakh that "tasks" cannot be assigned to an author. An artist cannot be told that he must write on such and such a theme.[26]

Libedinskii develops this idea further in his programmatic statement on the "artistic platform" of RAPP, presented at the First Congress of Proletarian Writers in 1928. What is most important for both Libedinskii and Averbakh is not the writer's choice of themes, but his view of the world. That literature "answering the needs of the socialist epoch" will be produced by those writers whose view of the world is based on Marxist dialectical materialism, was Libedinskii's considered view. The assignment of "themes" never entered into it.[27]

4. "Study the Classics"

One of the constant themes of the RAPP theoreticians is that they have outgrown the early excesses of the proletarian literary movement and no longer "undervalue the cultural heritage." Citing the authority of Lenin, they point out that it is the task of the proletariat to "master" the cultural heritage of past ages and that it is therefore the duty of proletarian literature to "learn from the classics."[28] Yet their view of the classics was an extremely limited one. It was, in effect, limited to Tolstoy.[29] They did give some attention to Flaubert, Balzac, and other great realists, and the works of Gogol are occasionally mentioned. Yet the overpowering influence of Tolstoy on the style and content of proletarian literature at this time is a striking phenomenon.

Libedinskii, in his definition of the "artistic platform" of RAPP, which was planned as a major contribution to the RAPP theory of literature, draws his concrete examples of literary method from one author only: Tolstoy. And he refers only to two works of that author: *War and Peace* and *Anna Karenina*.[30]

Averbakh, in a report at a conference of MAPP in 1927, discussed his idea of study in the following terms: "First of all . . . we must learn from Tolstoy. A slice of life in Tolstoy is like a still from a motion picture film. It is part of a general process."[31]

In the last sentence we see already a hint of what was meant by the "dialectical-materialist method": that life must be portrayed as a developing process. In underlining the great value of Tolstoy as a literary teacher, Averbakh makes a comparison between Tolstoy and Dostoyevsky. Both, he says, are concerned with probing the human psyche, but for Dostoyevsky "it is a mystery" whose operations have no rational explanation. Tolstoy, on the other hand, has a rational approach to psychological phenomena: he *explains* the behavior of his characters in terms of environment, first impressions, memories, feelings, hidden motives and desires. Averbakh quotes Chernyshevskii: "Tolstoy is a dialectician of the human psyche."[32] As such he is regarded as the most fitting model for proletarian writers, who try to cultivate a rational and materialist view of the world.

Fadeev, in an article which became a banner of the On Literary Guardists and a frequent object of attack by their enemies, again emphasizes the primary importance of the realistic school for proletarian literature. The article in question bears the rather surprising title "Down with Schiller!" and it contrasts the romantic current in world literature, represented here by Schiller, with the realistic movement, the representatives of which are Flaubert, Stendhal, Balzac, and Zola.[33]

Fadeev gives some attention to Gogol in comparing the classics of Russian literature with the achievements to date of proletarian literature:

> The task of winning hegemony . . . involves studying and gradually mastering the classics. . . .
>
> In Gogol's *Dead Souls* there are characters such as Pliushkin, Sobakevich, even the names of whom suggest living, breathing human beings. They are types which we at once recognize. They still exist. . . . If we consider from this point of view all our classical literature, we must admit that it has reached the heights. . . . In every image there is a concentration of the characteristics of a certain individual concrete human being, and at the same time generalized characteristics, peculiar to a whole category of people.[34]

Libedinskii provides us with a glimpse of the proletarian writer's workshop in which the practical work of "studying the classics" (Tolstoy) is revealed:

> Before attempting to write my *Commissars,* I sat down and reread *War and Peace* and some Turgenev. Fadeev did the same before writing *The Rout.* . . .
>
> Tolstoy is especially valuable in that his development of character is very good, and he can teach us by what means to do this ourselves.[35]

Libedinskii recommends Tolstoy as a master of the literary devices by which a character is made sympathetic or repugnant to the reader. He recalls the famous passage in *War and*

Peace in which Nikolai Rostov subdues the rebellious peasants and rescues Maria. Tolstoy's superb description of the incident brings it about that we sympathize, not with the rebellious peasants, but with the young hero Rostov.

> That is why we are attracted particularly by Tolstoy. He shows us the devices which we must master so as to portray characters in such a way as to make the reader feel hatred for one and sympathy for another.[36]

The effect upon proletarian literature of the late twenties of this inordinate zeal for study and imitation of Tolstoy is obvious even to the casual reader of Soviet literature. Fadeev's *Razgrom* (The Rout), regarded as a model of the RAPP literary method, is striking for its close imitation of Tolstoy's manner of characterization and psychological analysis. *Tikhii Don* (The Silent Don), written by Mikhail Sholokhov, a member of RAPP and an editor of their "fat journal" *October*, was regarded as an outstanding example of the RAPP literary method in practice.[37] And Sholokhov's imitation of Tolstoy has often been commented upon.

We have seen that Libedinskii quite deliberately selected Tolstoy as a model when preparing to write his *Commissars*. The influence of Tolstoy is even more obvious in the novel which he himself prized above all his others.[38] *Rozhdeniia Geroia* (The Birth of a Hero) follows Tolstoy not only in its constant probing of individual psychology but even in its style, vocabulary, and sentence structure.

The preoccupation of the leading RAPP writers and theorists with the method and approach of Tolstoy and other representatives of the school of "psychological realism" invited attack from the left opposition, finally attracting the unfavorable attention of *Pravda* and other Party organs and even Communist organizations. The critic G. Gorbachëv, a member of the left opposition, complains that the RAPP theoreticians give primacy in all their writings to "the type of realism represented by Tolstoy and Chekhov," while ignoring almost all the other classics of world literature and completely ignoring the great revolutionary classics of Russian literature for the sake of "their method," and "their teacher" Leo Tolstoy.

"Thus everything that contradicts the contemplative-objective, individual-psychological method of Tolstoy, Chekhov, Flaubert, Maupassant is treated as harmful and reactionary," said Gorbachëv.[39]

The reason for this emphasis on Tolstoy as the most fitting teacher of the proletarian writers is to be found not only in the tastes and preferences of the RAPP critics, but in the literary bent of the most important RAPP writers. No doubt the fact that Lenin gave so much favorable attention to Tolstoy also contributed to the interest of the proletarians in him.[40] Furthermore, their understanding of the nature and function of literature, as we shall presently see, inclined them to embrace as their masters writers of the realist school, and among them to give a special place to those who sought to reveal individual character in all its complexity.

We have now, it is hoped, cleared the ground of a number of the more common misconceptions regarding the RAPP leaders. It should be apparent that in their understanding "proletarian literature" did not exclude the product of writers so unfortunate as to be born of the "*bourgeoisie*," that they were not the source of the social demand theory, and that they were far from indifferent to the classics of world literature.

What, then, was their positive program? What kind of literary doctrine did they propagate, and what exactly did they mean by "the dialectical-materialist method"?

5. The RAPP Dialectical-Materialist Method in Art

A. *The theorists and their problem.* The youthful leaders of proletarian literature were not without intellectual ambition. They approached without trepidation, and found neat solutions for, problems in the philosophy of aesthetics which still tease the mind of man. Yet they were ill-equipped for such an undertaking. They were not widely conversant with literature or philosophy. They did know the classics of Marxism and could find in them apposite quotations; they had studied Belinskii, Plekhanov, and Voronskii, and it would appear that they consulted frequently with a leader of Marxist philosophical thought of the day, the editor of the journal *Under the*

Banner of Marxism, Deborin. Their writings are studded with quotations from these authorities, and even from intellectual figures of lesser significance. Averbakh, for instance, in the course of a few articles quotes Spengler, Merezhkovskii, Bukharin, Stalin, Marx, Engels, Lenin, Voronskii (without credit), Victor Serge, and his colleague Ermilov. Fadeev establishes authority for his ideas by quotations from Plekhanov, Marx, Zola, Deborin, and Libedinskii. Libedinskii himself, the most interesting of the group, acknowledges that he is indebted to Voronskii, Plekhanov, and Belinskii.

The RAPP thinkers were, therefore, quite derivative. Moreover, they were narrowly derivative. For their most important aesthetic ideas they were largely dependent on Plekhanov and Voronskii. They were scarcely able, in their treatment of these ideas, to organize and elucidate them clearly, or to throw new light of their own on aesthetic problems. For very little literature had developed in their proletarian milieu, and they were not widely acquainted with the classics of Russian and world literature. We have seen that Tolstoy largely overshadowed other writers in the experience of Libedinskii, and while Fadeev mentions Gogol, Flaubert, Zola, and some others, he betrays no intimate knowledge of their literary product, and his remarks about them are confined to commonplaces. Ermilov, one of the theoretical leaders of the movement, once pontificated on Rudyard Kipling as a "representative of the American imperialist *bourgeoisie*."[41] Indeed the slogan of the proletarians, "study!" was a recognition of a very serious weakness—lack of education—and should perhaps have taken precedence over all other slogans. But the needs of the day in proletarian literature would not wait, and so the RAPP writers and critics applied themselves with energy to the solution of pressing problems.

It would be a mistake to dismiss their work as unworthy of attention. It is true that they were narrow and dogmatic and that they made only a minuscule contribution to the theory of literature. Yet, they must be credited with having attempted to solve a vital problem: the relationship of literature to their own proletarian state. The solutions they provided for their proletarian "writing cadres" are significant, not in themselves, but because they represent an effort to reconcile genuine literature with the inexorable demand of a monolithic state that all departments of life serve its interest and no other. Iurii Libedinskii, who seems to have given much thought to the problem, said: "Before explaining how literature must be an active class force, we should first explain that it must really be literature."[42]

Their writings are interesting also as an attempt to fill in a rather wide hiatus in the Marxist world view, that is, to apply the principles of dialectical materialism to the criticism and production of literature. An aesthetic theory in harmony with those principles was never worked out by Marx or Engels, whose views on literature and art were never given in any final, definitive form. Plekhanov and Voronskii had, as we have already seen, attempted to supply this deficiency, and their work was freely used by the RAPP theoreticians in developing their "dialectical-materialist creative method."

Before attempting the formidable task of setting forth the salient features of that method it would perhaps be well to state briefly the basic tenets of dialectical materialism itself, as they are understood in the Soviet Union.[43] The specifically *materialist* tenets are: (1) that matter is an objective reality existing outside and independent of our mind; (2) that our knowledge of the laws of nature, tested by experiment and practice, is objective truth. The *dialectical* aspect of the doctrine maintains that: (1) the world is in a state of continuous movement and flux; (2) internal contradictions are inherent in all things, for all things have a negative and a positive side: something dying away and something developing. The process of change and development results from these contradictions. These principles, applied to society, yield a number of ideas which are known as *historical* materialism.

Such was the philosophical basis of the RAPP method in literature. This method, too, had its *materialist* side. The world is real and knowable: it is the primary function of literature to provide knowledge of reality. Like philosophy and science, literature is a means of "cognition of the world." Literature differs from the former in that it *portrays* reality in sensible images, while philosophy and science arrive at truth through logical procedures. Of course there was nothing original in all this. We have seen how Voronskii developed these ideas, and that he had found them in the writings of Plekhanov.

Libedinskii did not hesitate to acknowledge the debt of the proletarians to Voronskii:

> In our old platform there was one essential omission: we never posed the question of the relationship between art and reality. Comrade Voronskii, when he criticized us for this omission, was largely correct, and he himself always gave proper emphasis to the question of the relationship between art and life. But we, in our struggle with the errors of Voronskii, fell into an oversimplification of these problems. . . . However, when the question was posed it was, in the main, answered correctly. Comrade Averbakh, for instance . . . defines literature as an "instrument for the cognition of reality."[44]

The idea of literature as cognition of life was, then, well established in RAPP theoretical literature by 1928, the date of the above quotation. We have seen that Averbakh emphasized also the somewhat more practical function of literature as an instrument for changing the world.

The idea that the distinguishing characteristic of art is the "concrete," sensible *image* rather than the abstract idea or concept is one which is taken for granted in RAPP literature.[45] The influence of Plekhanov and Voronskii is again quite clear. The RAPP leader Luzgin attempted very early in this period to examine the cognitive function of proletarian art, and his tentative and rather confused answer was that art gives us the "feelings" of people in the form of "concrete images," but conditioned by the "class nature" of the artist.[46] Libedinskii was at one point gently chided by a colleague for failing to develop the idea that the distinguishing characteristic of art is "not thought or feeling, but the *image*."[47] And in their last public statement, which was, as we shall see, in effect an answer to the dissolution of their organization by the Politburo in 1932, the RAPP leaders insisted that concrete images of the real world rather than publicistic or propagandist ideas constituted the material of literature.[48]

The proletarian theorists did add to these ideas something of their own on the *materialist* nature of literature. They added the notion that realism is the literary expression of the materialist philosophy. We have already seen that some of the best proletarian writers were realists of the Tolstoy school, or at least humble imitators of the master. In this they received support from Marx and Engels, both of whom had expressed a preference for writers of that persuasion. In a much-quoted passage Engels declared that he had "learned more [about the history of French society] from Balzac's *Comédie Humaine* than from all the professional economists, historians, and statisticians of the period together."[49] And Marx in a letter to Ferdinand Lasalle concerning the play *Franz von Sickingen* advised his friend to study not Schiller but Shakespeare: "Not to forget the realistic element in favor of the idealistic, not to overlook Shakespeare for Schiller."[50] Upon this the proletarians based a clarion call for the liquidation of Schillerism and the romantic-idealistic tendency in Soviet literature.[51]

Indeed the RAPP theoreticians went far beyond these modest statements of Marx and Engels. The preference of the latter for realism they erected into an absolute and arbitrary tenet of dialectical materialism in literature. If the proletarian writer was a materialist in his philosophical views he must also be a realist in his literary creation. "Materialism and idealism are not only two different schools of philosophical thought, they are two different creative methods," said Averbakh, who concluded that "realism is that literary school which is closest to a materialistic artistic method."[52] In 1929 Fadeev's article "Down with Schiller!" served as a kind of programmatic statement of the official RAPP position that realism is particularly suited to the proletarian writers, and that they must learn from writers such as Stendhal, Balzac, Flaubert, Zola, and Tolstoy. These great bourgeois realists, in spite of their ideological limitations, revealed the real world of social relations, said Fadeev, while romanticists only cultivate flattering illusions about the world.[53] This rather narrow doctrine was propagated for many years by the leading lights of proletarian literary theory.

The world is knowable; literature is cognition; literature must be realistic. Such were the *materialist* tenets of the doctrine. The *dialectical* requirement meant that life should be shown as in movement, and that literature should discover and reveal the inherent contradictions in society and in man himself. The writer must see the beginnings of tomorrow in the reality of today, and reveal the new arising from the old.

B. *"Immediate impressions" and "world view."* Iurii Libedinskii contributed in 1928 an important statement called the Artistic Platform of RAPP.[54] From the viewpoint of his career as a Soviet writer this ambitious study was one of the most unfortunate things Libedinskii ever wrote, for it became a fertile source of quotations indicating the presence of literary and philosophical "errors" in the theory of RAPP. On the basis of the ideas in these articles Libedinskii was accused at various times of Freudism, Bergsonism, menshevising idealism, Deborinism, cultivation of the erroneous views of Plekhanov—in fact, Plekhanovism—and Voronskyism. Libedinskii's position as a Soviet citizen never deteriorated to the point where he could be accused of "Trotskyism," though many of his colleagues were so accused. It should be emphasized now that the position Libedinskii took in 1928 is one which, from the point of view of Party spokesmen, he never thereafter "satisfactorily criticized." In other words, though later he formally rejected his own ideas under pressure, he never condemned them with sufficient conviction and vigor.[55]

Libedinskii asserts in this study of 1928 that "immediate impressions" of the real world are the basis of art. The "knowledge" characteristically used by the artist, is, he maintains, best defined by the Russian philosopher Belinskii, who wrote that "art is thinking in images, or the immediate contemplation of truth."[56] And the most important element of this definition is the word "immediate." Belinskii is quoted at length on the greater reliability of our "immediate impressions" as compared to "rational judgments." Speaking of the way an opinion is formed of an individual human being: "Our reason approves of his words, takes them for material on which a judgment of him can be made, but the immediate impression which he produces awakens skepticism concerning his words, and alienates us from the man."[57]

Though he thus accepts the idea that immediate, direct impressions of the world are the material of art, Libedinskii rejects any suggestion that artistic creation must take place independently of the conscious reason, or, on the other hand, that it can only be conscious. The production of art is neither wholly rational nor wholly irrational, and both the conscious and the subconscious part of man are admitted as participants in artistic creation.[58]

Moreover, immediate impressions of the world are not solely the possession of the artist. Every man has a multitude of impressions of the world which have nothing to do with his conscious, deliberate thoughts in any given situation: "Men know far more about the world than they think they know. And it is just such knowledge as this that art uses as its building material."[59]

What, then, is the function of the artist? In order to elucidate this, Libedinskii compares the artist's activity with that of the scientist, who also strives to reveal the true nature of things. The average man, says our theorist, receives a multitude of more or less disorganized impressions of the outside world; he observes events which he may ascribe to chance or fate. But science, provided it is the science of a "progressive class," reveals to a greater or less degree the causal relations which exist in the world. And art does the very same thing. It rejects chance. It tries to portray the world as it is and to reveal the hidden laws of its movement. The artist, however, accomplishes this through the selection of meaningful material from his own storehouse of "immediate impressions." He selects "typical phenomena": he fixes the attention on such concrete images as will enable him to show the connection of one event with another, and generalize the phenomena of the real world.[60]

Libedinskii, however, repeatedly cautions the proletarian artist that the method of art is not that of science: "The causal connection is not shown by way of abstraction from the concrete; no—the phenomenon of reality in art remains concrete, but it reveals its causal connection with other phenomena. . . . Art does not operate by the same method as science; it does not deal in abstractions, as does philosophy, but through immediate impressions it shows concrete phenomena in their interconnection, and this calls forth what is known as the 'aesthetic feeling.' "[61]

It is at this point that the decisive role of the artist's "world view" enters. For in order to select the really important phenomena from a multitude of "immediate impressions," one must look upon reality from a definite point of view; otherwise the result will be chaotic and meaningless. The artist who observes reality from the vantage point of a definite philosophy is able to present it in organized and meaningful form. Libedinskii calls the attention of his readers to the following description of the Napoleonic War, which is to be found in Tolstoy's *War and Peace:*

> The first fifteen years of the nineteenth century present the spectacle of an extraordinary movement of millions of men. Men leave their habitual pursuits; rush from one side of Europe to the other; plunder, slaughter one another, triumph and despair; and the whole current of life is transformed and presents a quickened activity, first moving at a growing speed and then slowly slackening again. . . . [62]

Libedinskii offers this as a magnificent example of the artist presenting the world in terms of "immediate impressions." And in order to penetrate the mass of patriotic prejudices which had grown up around the "Great War of Liberation" and to reveal it thus in its naked reality, Tolstoy had to shift his viewpoint and to look upon those events in the light of his own developing philosophy. Libedinskii concludes from all this:

> In order to accomplish the generalizing work of art one must possess a deeply felt philosophy (world view). Only such a philosophy permits man to free his immediate impressions of reality from their place of concealment under the casing of philistine judgment.[63]

This of course leads Libedinskii to the next important step: that the proletarian writer must cultivate the "world view" of Marxism, dialectical materialism, and that an important part of his activity must be "study" and general political education. Fadeev is even more explicit on the need for developing within oneself the Marxist view of the world. For he asks the question, "How, then, is a man to acquire the all-important world view which will enable him to understand and portray human character according to the dialectical-materialist method?" And he answers it as follows:

I cannot imagine how if not by way of the most conscious, intense, and prolonged labor of the writer upon himself, in the direction of developing his own world view, which, being deeply understood, will become part of his habitual feelings. This can be done only through active participation in our social life, which is developing in the same direction.[64]

Fadeev, too, exhorts the proletarians to "study." To realize the aims of the "dialectical-materialist school" in literature requires, he says, "fierce study."[65]

The general idea that literary men must be inspired by the Marxist ideology and show it forth in their writing runs like a red thread through all the theorizing of the RAPP leaders. A corollary of this was the demand that literary men must not "isolate themselves" from the real world but develop in active contact with it. This notion appears frequently in the articles and talks of Averbakh,[66] and was emphasized by Kirshon in his speech at the Sixteenth Congress of the Communist Party in 1930.[67]

6. *Diamat* (Dialectical Materialism) in Practice

A. *The "living man."* The RAPP leaders not only gave time and effort to the consideration of problems in aesthetics. They also devised slogans to guide and inspire the proletarian writer. Perhaps the most characteristic of these slogans was: "for the living man." The origin of the term "living man" can be traced to the beginnings of the On Guard movement: it figured prominently in the disputes between the Smithy and the young guard of proletarian writers who seceded from it in 1922. The latter group regarded the production of the Smithy writers as too abstract and too far removed from realistic portrayal of actual people. The dissenters, of whom the most articulate were Rodov and Bezymenskii, demanded, among other things, realism in the development of character. They proposed to create, not cosmic songs about the "iron proletarian" but proletarians as they really were.[68]

The new men who took over the guidance of proletarian literature in 1926 from the On Guard group added something of their own to these ideas. The new thing which they added can perhaps best be summed up in the term "psychological realism," though they themselves rebuffed such a designation. They maintained that the "living man" should not be treated superficially, but that the proletarian writer must probe his psychology, lay bare the conflicts and contradictions which take place in him, and understand these contradictions as part of a "dialectical" process of development. The "living man" slogan, then, represented the *dialectical* aspect of their dialectical-materialist method.

Among the resolutions of the First Congress of Proletarian Writers we find the following authoritative statement on the "living man" slogan:

> The slogan for the presentation of the "living man" . . . on the one hand correctly orients proletarian literature toward the reflection of contemporaneity, and on the other hand expresses the necessity of struggle with stereotypes, with schematic portrayal, with "bare poster art," and of development in the direction of showing forth the complex human psyche, with all its contradictions, elements of the past and seeds of the future, both conscious and subconscious.[69]

This "psychological" interest of the proletarians was the result of a number of influences, and perhaps most important among them was the influence of Tolstoy. And it should not be forgotten that in the twenties the ideas of Freud no doubt affected developing minds in the Soviet Union, both proletarian and "bourgeois."[70] For in those days the intellectual "window on Europe" was not yet closed.

Fadeev, moreover, was able to quote excellent Marxist authority in defense of the "living man" approach, the authority of Plekhanov. In an eloquent defense of the proletarian slogan he quotes Plekhanov as follows: "The psychology of characters acquires great importance in our eyes because it is the psychology of whole social classes, or at least of social groups, and because, therefore, the processes taking place in the souls of individual characters are a reflection of historical movement."[71]

It is from this point of view that the portrayal of the "living man" must be considered, and Fadeev goes on to point out the complexity of the problem which the proletarian writer has undertaken to solve:

> To portray the "living man" means in the last analysis to show the whole historical process of movement and development. And since the reflection of social processes in each individual does not take place in a straight line, mechanically, and since there is a complex process of dialectical interaction between the individual and his social environment; and since we must take into account the fact that man is exposed to the simultaneous influence of thoroughly opposed classes, a fact reflected in his psyche; and since the human psyche is in itself exceedingly varied, having impulses both conscious and subconscious . . . [72]

The task of the proletarian writer would seem to be unbearably complex; finally Fadeev concludes: "It is devilishly hard to portray human nature, especially since no one has ever tried to do it in this way until now."

It is a commonplace of RAPP theoretical literature that the slogan "living man" arose as a reaction to the crude tendentiousness of early proletarian literature, and that it is a mark of the proletarian writer's "maturity." The poverty of that early literature is the leading theme of those critics and government figures who, at the Press Section Conference in May, 1924, spoke against the position of the On Guardists.[73] And the leading Communist critics were generally in agreement that the proletarian product was little but "newspaper reportage in the form of belles-lettres."[74]

Libedinskii pointed out that it was not only on matters of literary politics that the new leadership of RAPP in 1926 and 1927 criticized the old leadership; other disagreements with the "left" soon appeared. The most important of them involved the evaluation of proletarian literature. The right wing—the On Literary Guardists—considered that the chief fault of proletarian literature was its fondness for the stereotyped character and for mechanically tendentious plots. In a report at an early conference of VAPP Libedinskii said:

> We concentrate more attention on the psychology of personality, while heretofore people were presented in our literature in the following way: here you have a certain commissar; he must possess

certain definite traits. And then you have a bourgeois, and he must possess certain *other* definite traits. And likewise for the intellectual. Themes were developed like geometrical problems. This tendency to oversimplify is a symptom of the first stages of our revolution, when the writer could grasp the facts of social relationship in their broad outline only.[75]

Libedinskii and others had been inclined to believe that at the height of the revolutionary struggle the simple communist morality tale answered the needs of the moment, and he asserted that with such material the proletarian writer had "won the reader." But now, apparently, both the reader and the writer had grown up, for Libedinskii feels that above all individuality and concreteness in characterization are required. Readers are no longer moved by thoroughly good and noble characters, nor by complete and unmitigated villains. For they realize now that the "living man" is a complex of many qualities, and that his psychology is the product of conflicting social and "class" forces.[76]

Libedinskii provides us with some insight into this process of rediscovering the alphabet of literary creation. In a speech at an assembly of "worker-writers" he gives us an interesting glimpse into the proletarian literary workshop and a hint as to the problem which the "living man" approach was expected to solve. In his discussion with the workers Libedinskii was forced to face squarely the problem of tendentiousness in literature. For it was found that the new world view of communism had not deeply penetrated his proletarian comrades, and that when they tried to express their new "communistic" feelings in literature they "lost everything."[77] One of the literary comrades complained that proletarian writers were "inhibited by the necessity of writing ideologically."[78] And he continued:

You have to write: "The factory whistle sang out and I arose, cheerful, full of strength, and went to my work at the factory bench." But just take a look at what happens in real life and you'll see that it's nothing like that: the whistle blows and you curse the damn thing, you get up and you go, yawning, and you don't feel any particular cheerfulness. But if you don't say "cheerfully" then its ideologically unseasoned. And if you do write "cheerfully" what you get is not true to life: it's political agitation.[79]

Libedinskii admits the seriousness of this problem, and insists that the answer to it is to be found in really mastering the "dialectical-materialist method" and, particularly, in understanding the "dialectic" of the human character, with its conflicting and contradictory urges, moods, and thoughts.[80]

This means, reduced to simple terms, that there are no absolutes in the world of characters; but that all living men are mixtures of "good" and "bad," or as Libedinskii expresses it in "Marxist" terms, every man is a battleground of the class struggle. To reveal the class enemy *within us* is one of the functions of a genuine literature, said the RAPP theoreticians.[81] It should deeply reveal the struggle of the new with the "old": with laziness, superstition, cruelty, ignorance, selfishness. In this way Libedinskii attempts to reconcile tendency with truth, and a way is found for the worker-writer to be ideologically sound and at the same time to be himself.

The propositions of the RAPP literary leadership underwent searching and severe criticism. Far from the dictatorship and monopoly of literature which RAPP is supposed to have enjoyed during this period, the common rule in the years 1928–32 was not passive acceptance of authority, but animated, enthusiastic, and often bitter disagreement. It should be remembered, of course, that these controversies took place within the dogmatic framework of Marxist doctrine, and that only a very limited range of speculation on literary and aesthetic problems was possible for the disputants.

The leaders in the criticism of the "living man" idea were, of course, the "left opposition," the minority within RAPP itself. Lydia Toom, a theorist and critic aligned with the left, objected to the approach of the leading proletarians on the ground that the writer would find no fertile field for his psychological probing in the simple and uncomplicated Russian worker. The method being recommended to the proletarian writer was one suited to the portrayal of "intellectuals" who were, indeed, a confused mixture of psychological conflicts. Not the psychological experiences of individual workers, but the life of the collective itself should occupy the attention of the new, proletarian writer. With that approach Libedinskii had no sympathy; for he believed that workers too, as members of a social group with conflicting tendencies and sharp contradictions, would reflect in themselves as individuals those conflicts and contradictions.[82]

Other dissidents advanced the view that literature should present the proletarian with positive "heroes" capable of inspiring and guiding him. After the liquidation of RAPP this became one of the leading ideas of Soviet literature; but it was contemptuously rejected by Libedinskii, Fadeev, Averbakh, and other leading RAPP figures.[83] What proletarian writers must *not* do, said Libedinskii, is simplify, idealize, and romanticize their heroes, for writers must not try to improve on reality.[84]

Before leaving this discussion of the "living man" slogan, it should be pointed out that the ideas on that subject expressed by the RAPP critics are to be found in the earlier writings of Voronskii. He had expressed these ideas with greater clarity and less verbiage than we find in the RAPP documents.[85] Here again we see the curious dependence of the proletarian literary theorists on their literary "enemy."

B. *"Tear off the masks!"* The RAPP slogan which is recalled with special horror in later Soviet statements on its role is one which occurred in Averbakh's report at the First Congress: "for the removal of any and all masks" or "tear off the masks!" The idea contained in it is a corollary of the RAPP doctrine of the "living man" as a complex of contradictory qualities, both good, from a Marxist class viewpoint, and bad. The effect of realistic literary creation would be to "remove the masks" from the "bad" in men wherever it occurred, in workers, Communists, and bureaucrats, as well as in representatives of the "old" classes. For remnants of the "old" psychology existed even in Party men and "developed" workers, and should be revealed by the proletarian writer.

The Party representatives who later made so much of the "evil" and "harmful" slogan "tear off the masks" were quite right in pointing to it as an important item in RAPP's literary creed. In fact Selivanovskii, a RAPP poet, critic, and administrator, maintained that it was the central point in their literary doctrine, and he quoted Fadeev on its significance: "The new style of proletarian literature is a stranger to any and all adornment of the truth; it is a stranger to all 'illusions which exalt us'; it must and will be a style involving the most resolute, consistent, and merciless removal of all masks."[86]

This phrase was not invented by Averbakh, but was used by Lenin in one of his articles on Tolstoy. Lenin in that article commented on the surpassing genius of Tolstoy in revealing the real social relationships which lie hidden beneath the "masks" of convention. The phrase occurs in a slightly different form in a famous passage from Tolstoy's *Anna Karenina*, where the artist Mikhailov is described at work. Tolstoy characterizes the process of artistic creation as "removing the coverings" which prevent an object from being distinctly seen. Voronskii hit upon this image as expressing the essential activity of the artist's special faculty: intuition. By virtue of this faculty, said he, the artist is able to perceive the truth; in moments of freedom from the control of his rational self, when he is susceptible to "direct, childlike impressions," the artist "removes the coverings" from the real world and sees it as it is.[87]

The image used by Tolstoy and Voronskii to characterize creative work was taken up by Averbakh and the RAPP theorists and critics. Here, too, the influence of Voronskii on proletarian literary theory is evident. But the RAPP spokesmen used the wording of this idea preferred by Lenin: "tearing off of masks," rather than "removal of coverings." The proletarians claimed that they had eliminated from Voronskii's theory its "idealistic" content, that is, its emphasis on the irrational and the subconscious. The meaning of this slogan for the proletarian littérateur was supposed to be quite different, for his "tearing off of masks" was to proceed from a knowledge of the class nature of society and his understanding of social relationships. Fadeev thus sets forth the function of the proletarian artist working according to the "tear off the masks" slogan:

It means that our proletarian artist, who has mastered the world view of dialectical materialism, is in a better position than any other artist to sweep away the accidental and superficial; to remove the coverings from the essence of things. . . . It means that we need such an art as will enable us to perceive objective reality in its movement and development, in order to change it in the interests of the proletariat.[88]

The slogan "for the removal of any and all masks," though it is implicit in the RAPP doctrine concerning the "living man," received no special emphasis as a separate slogan until rather late in the history of RAPP. We shall see that during 1930 and 1931 RAPP was fighting for a realistic treatment of Soviet reality and against what it described as a rather prevalent tendency in literature to "varnish reality." Early in 1931, the RAPP secretariat incorporated the slogan in an official resolution:

The Leninist characterization of Tolstoy's creation, "the tearing off of all masks," has a tremendous significance for writers who are working out their own artistic method. Such a slogan opposes the tendency to "varnish" reality . . . and is directed at a Bolshevik *cognition* of that reality. . . . For, "Since when do Bolsheviks fear the truth?" says Comrade Stalin.[89]

The point will be developed later that under the influence of this slogan RAPP writers, in treating the phenomena of Soviet reality, often drew censure on themselves for the consistency with which they exposed its dark side. This honest presentation of reality the RAPP critics defended as one of the basic requirements of genuine literature.

7. Conclusion

What, then, was the effect of the RAPP literary preachment on Russian literature? The evidence so far presented does not warrant a final answer to that question. It does give us a clear picture of the literary and artistic bent of the RAPP leadership and of their approach to the problems of a Marxist theory of literature. We not only can see how that theory developed out of "practice" in guiding the work of proletarian writers, but we have had some very clear indications of the Marxist sources upon whom the leading theoreticians relied for the formulation of their ideas. Of these Plekhanov was the most important;

many of Voronskii's ideas were quite frankly used in a modified and more class-conscious form; the philosopher Deborin is quoted frequently as an authority; Marx and Engels are not neglected, though apart from the justification they offer for cultivating the realistic style, it does not appear that anything specifically literary can be traced to their casual, occasional, and very infrequent remarks about literature. Lenin is very little used in the discussion of purely literary problems: the one important exception is the "tear off the masks" slogan, which comes from one of Lenin's articles on Tolstoy.

There emerged from this attempt to apply Marxism to literary theory and criticism a body of ideas some of which were not without objective merit. The emphasis on realism and against direct propaganda and obvious tendentiousness was the result of elementary lessons learned at the feet of Voronskii, and confirmed by the reading of Plekhanov. The notion that reality is complex, unstable, and even a little mysterious, and that the "psyche" develops on more than one level and under influences not completely understood was an idea that the proletarians seem to have been groping for in their lengthy disquisitions on the "living man" and "immediate impressions." These ideas were of course woven into the fabric of "dialectical materialism," and the writer was required to portray reality from the viewpoint of the Marxist ideology. That this requirement did inhibit many writers, especially those in whom Marxism was not organic, could easily have been foreseen, and was in fact admitted by Averbakh and Libedinskii. If demanded mechanically of all writers its effect might be to discourage serious literary production. But as a viewpoint elected by a group of writers intent on exploring and perhaps explaining the world, it was capable of producing good results; and the proletarians did produce some works of genuine merit: we may mention Sholokhov's *The Silent Don*, Libedinskii's *Birth of a Hero*, Mitrofanov's *June-July*, and the early chapters of Panfërov's *Brusski*.

Yet there was a fatal flaw inherent in the nature of RAPP. The literary ideas of the leading group became articles of faith to which all writers within the organization were required to subscribe. The literary attitudes and habits of opposition groups were not granted autonomy. The fictitious and oppressive authority bestowed upon RAPP by the Party during these years tended to vitiate literary life, even within its own organization. Just how this happened we shall presently see.

Even if we grant the harmful effect of the "authority" given RAPP by the Party, there would still seem to be something missing from this account of the RAPP theory of proletarian literature. It is often said that literature was regimented severely during the period of the Five-Year Plan, given "tasks," and told to carry them out. We have heard also that the reflection in literature of industrialization and collectivization was the one supreme task for which the whole literary world was mobilized. It is said that RAPP was the Party's own organization, entrusted with the job of carrying out this "line." Clearly the ideas outlined above as characteristic of the RAPP approach to proletarian literature and literature in general cannot easily be fitted into such a picture. The evidence indicates that RAPP was neither the author nor the willing executor of the program for literature which is usually associated with its name. It indicates further that the RAPP leadership actually resisted the intrusion of Party spokesmen in the affairs of the literary world, and that it rejected as unsound and unworkable their program for literature during the period of the first Five-Year Plan. We shall see that this recalcitrance of the leading group of proletarian literature, the "representative of the Party in the literary field," can be convincingly demonstrated, and that it is the key to an understanding of the fierce "literary" struggles which occupied the attention of Communist literary men in late 1930 and 1931.

Chapter VI

The Party and Its Instrument

1. Literature As Propaganda

We have now seen who the proletarians of RAPP were, what they thought proletarian literature should be, and the manner in which they expressed their ideas. It has also been indicated that they were a favored group with many advantages and privileges arising from their intimacy with the Party and their announced devotion to its program. Yet their organization was liquidated by that same Party only a few years later and its leaders publicly castigated for "errors" and "distortions" of the Party line. Their literary theory and their slogans and much of their output were soon to be condemned as heretical. What was the reason for this strange turn of events?

With the adoption of the first Five-Year Plan in 1928 the Party had undertaken a program which called for the maximum efforts in the direction of overcoming the industrial backwardness of the Soviet Union. Its program called for tremendous sacrifice and constant exertion. All forces were quite frankly "mobilized" for the task, and no exception was made for the forces of literature and art. Literary men, too, were expected to help in the colossal job of "overtaking and surpassing" the advanced countries; they were expected, in plain words, to devote their talents as writers to the humble task of publicizing and propagandizing the Plan. The idea that belles-lettres are an "instrument" in the hands of the dominant class—always the contention of the extreme left in Soviet theory—was now adopted by the Party in its simplest and crudest form.

With this change in the Party's attitude toward literature,

the RAPP theory and practice began to lose favor; for the leaders of RAPP were slow, reluctant, and ineffectual in carrying out the direct "social demand" of the Party. Under the pressure of its own program, the Party moved gradually but surely into a position of direct antagonism to the announced literary principles of RAPP, as set forth in the last chapter.

In the summer of 1928 the Central Committee of the Party called an all-Union conference on questions of agitation, propaganda, and cultural work. Among the resolutions adopted in the course of this discussion we find the following:

Literature, the theater, and the cinema should all be brought forward and into contact with the widest circles of the population, and should be utilized in the fight for a new cultural outlook, a new way of life, against bourgeois and *petit-bourgeois* ideology, against vodka, philistinism . . . against the resurrection of bourgeois ideology under new labels, and against a slavish imitation of bourgeois culture.[1]

In December, 1928, the conclusions of this conference were embodied in a formal resolution of the Central Committee of the Communist Party. This resolution is the central document on the literary policy of the Communist Party during the period of the Five-Year Plan. It is not a resolution devoted exclusively to belles-lettres, but a directive to publishing houses on the emphasis which they are to give in selecting books for publication, and further, on how they are to proceed in selecting writers and assigning them their tasks. It lays down a publishing policy motivated by simple utilitarian considerations, and based on the theoretical assumption that belles-lettres can and should be employed as a directed instrument of policy. It makes no distinction between belles-lettres and propaganda brochures; between belles-lettres and educational works; between belles-lettres and works on Marxist theory. All types of writing are included in a general directive to the publishers to give emphasis to writings of a socially useful character.[2] The resolution is regarded by authoritative Soviet critics today as a "landmark" in the history of Soviet literature,[3] and one of the most important of all Party directives to literary men.

Without specifically mentioning the tolerant policy of 1925, it departs from that policy decisively and finally. The very fact that belles-lettres are mentioned only in section *d* of point 2 of the resolution, and that their publication is treated on the same level with that of agitation and propaganda pieces, Marxist-Leninist brochures, popular scientific works and the like, is eloquent of the new orientation. It is significant also that the resolution is addressed, not to literary organizations, but directly to the publishing houses, which in the Soviet Union as in other countries assert the "social demand" in practice. It directs the emphasis which they are to give in selecting books for publication. This emphasis determined the character of so-called "Five-Year-Plan literature." Specifications for the mass book including belles-lettres provide the background we need to explain that period:

1. The publication of belles-lettres is to be increased, especially of works developing present-day themes and directed against bourgeois influences, philistinism, decadence, etc.
2. The book intended for mass circulation must be intelligible and accessible to the masses.
3. Such books should be an instrument for the mobilization of the workers around the tasks of industrialization and agricultural collectivization.
4. Publishers should depend for the most part on Communist authors, who are to be drawn into this work through the writers' organizations.
5. In addition they are to recruit new writers from the working class and the peasantry.
6. The publishers are to proceed systematically in the matter of determining the tastes and preferences of the workers and peasants through worker and peasant criticism.

The six points given above provide a blueprint for literature of the Five-Year-Plan period. It is also important to realize that this resolution involves a departure from the policy enunciated in 1925 of not favoring any one group. For publishers are to depend in the first instance on Communist writers, and they are to utilize the writers' organizations. Moreover, they are to recruit new writers from the proletariat and the peasantry and give them special attention. This explains in part the reason for the leadership in the literary field which RAPP acquired in the following years. It was an organization made to order for the purposes of the Central Committee; it was composed mainly of Communists willing to undertake social tasks; it was organized and disciplined; it was already actively engaged in developing new writers from the working class; it announced as its chief virtue devotion in carrying out the policy of the Central Committee.

RAPP was the organization to which the Party would naturally turn as the chief support of its policy in the field of literary organization, literary production, and literary criticism. And while there is no statement of the Central Committee which definitely names RAPP as the spokesman of the Central Committee, yet it soon became clear that the Party depended upon RAPP to consolidate all Communist literary forces, to fight against "deviations" in the literary field, and to aid in carrying out literary directives.[4]

2. The "Social Demand" of the Central Committee

There is evidence of a continuing interest in the literary field on the part of the Central Committee, and of an increasing emphasis on literature as an aid in the accomplishment of political and economic ends, especially after the first Five-Year Plan was well under way.

Pravda, the official organ of the Central Committee, began with its issue of February 17, 1930, to publish a special literary page which appeared regularly thereafter, about every ten to fifteen days. The literary page was given over to stories, sketches, essays, and poems, on the problems of the day: chiefly construction and collectivization. It also printed occasional articles devoted to the problems of Soviet literature. Upon the first appearance of this Literary Page, an editorial appeared on it with the title "New Tasks." It said that one of the chief failings of proletarian literature was its backwardness in meeting the demands of the day. The rapid industrialization of the country, collectivization, etc., were still but poorly represented in literature, and proletarian literature must liquidate that backwardness.[5] The editorial goes on to say that the Literary Page of *Pravda* should be a "sharp weapon" in the fight for socialist culture, and calls for "more proletarian vigilance" and "more Party leadership!"

This is the continuing emphasis of the *Pravda* editorial policy. The clearest statement of it is perhaps the following from an editorial printed one year later:

> We must educate a type of literary man who can write for the newspapers, who can give a vital, gripping description of our socialist construction, of all its gigantic achievements, and of all its failings. We need a fighting literature on contemporary themes, one which will react to the burning questions of socialist construction and which will daily mobilize the masses around the task of carrying out the general line of the Party.[6]

The activity of *Pravda* (and *Izvestiia*) in directly promoting such literary work as is here described was a constant factor in the production of Five-Year-Plan literature. Not only was such work encouraged editorially by both newspapers, but individual writers and sometimes groups of writers were organized by the editorial boards of *Pravda* or *Izvestiia* to carry out definite tasks. Thus the prominent novelist Leonov reports that his trip to Turkistan in the company of Vsevolod Ivanov and other prominent Soviet writers was undertaken as the result of a "mission" given him by *Izvestiia*.[7] Bezymenskii, whose literary activity during this period was to a large extent devoted to the production of poems (and one play) on the problems of industrialization,[8] declared at one point that his "comradely work with the editorial board and collective of *Pravda*" made him realize his own responsibility.[9] It was *Izvestiia* in the person of its editor, Gronskii, that sent Pil'niak on a tour of Central Asia, the result of which was his book *Tadzhikistan; Sed'maia Sovetskaia* (Tadzhikistan; Soviet Seventh).[10] Gronskii was also responsible for the rehabilitation of Pantaleimon Romanov after his book *Comrade Kisliakov* had been severely criticized. Romanov reported that Gronskii had "brought him out of his isolation" by sending him around to visit farms and factories.[11]

"Production conferences" of writers, poets, and sketchers were sponsored by the editorial college of the Central Organ, *Pravda*. One of these was presided over by the secretary of the *Pravda* editorial board, L. Mekhlis, who said:

Writers should provide such sketches as will offer material for the coming All-Union Party Conference. Writers and sketchers should help the Party in the working out of the national economic plan for 1932. A group of sketchers might, for instance, go out for a lengthy trip to the collective farms and work out in detail the production plans of one or another collective farm for 1932. The attention of writers must also be directed to such an important matter as the second Five-Year Plan.[12]

So much for the activity and policies of the two authoritative publications, *Pravda* and *Izvestiia*. Even more revealing than their activity is the evidence of direct guidance of literary development which is provided by additional resolutions of the Central Committee on publishing. A resolution of the Central Committee "On Publishing Work" was published on August 15, 1931. It lists the "successes" of Soviet publishing, pointing to the increase in number of titles issued, especially in the field of theory (the works of Lenin) and industrial technique. It goes on to point out what, in general, is expected of "the book":

The content and character of the book should in every way respond to the demands of socialist reconstruction; it should be militant and deal with political themes of the present day; it should arm the broad masses of the builders of socialism with Marxist-Leninist theory and with technical knowledge. The book should be the mightiest means of educating, mobilizing, and organizing the masses for the tasks of economic and cultural building.[13]

Such is the Central Committee's description of what literature generally is expected to accomplish. On the subject of belles-lettres the resolution is no less definite as to the utilitarian aims to be pursued:

Imaginative literature, which plays such a huge educational role, should reflect far more deeply and fully the heroism of socialist construction and of the class struggle, the transformation of social relations and the growth of new people—the heroes of socialist construction. The publication of imaginative literature should be to a certain extent specialized by the GIKHL [State Publishing House for Belles-Lettres][14] into different sectors (for example, there should be, alongside synthetic imaginative works, historical literature, agricultural belles-lettres, industrial belles-lettres, classical literature, etc).[15]

It should be clear that in the view of the Central Committee there was no question of eliminating entirely the production of literary works on historical subjects, or of such as are described as "synthetic," a term which apparently refers to fictional works having no immediate relation to the realities of socialist construction. It is clearly a question of emphasis. The Party policy is to increase the weight and relative importance of literature serving the ends of "socialist construction." And the Central Committee gave writers a material incentive for the production of such literature:

> In view of the fact that the system of payment of authors has considerable importance in improving the quality of the printed work, it is necessary to differentiate payments, *and to set up such a scale of honorariums as will stimulate the promotion of the most talented authors; that is especially necessary in the case of those forms of literary production which have special importance for the present period.*[16]

Thus it was the policy of the Central Committee in literature as in other sectors of "the economy" to use the incentive of higher pay in order to increase the production of "better quality" works, and by this they meant works answering the "needs of the day." It has not been possible to get reliable information on the scale of payments for literary works during this period; but it is reasonable to assume that more would be paid for a novel on the Dneprostroi construction than for a novel dealing with the "sufferings of mind" of an intellectual at odds with the epoch. It seems fairly certain on the basis of this official directive that there was, in fact, a wide differential in payments to authors, based in part on the importance of the subjects chosen in promoting the aims of "socialist reconstruction." This assumption is borne out, further, by the fact that Soviet writers generally gave themselves with a will to the depiction and stimulation of the labors of the Five-Year Plan.[17] Thus the incentive of material success was added to the administrative directives, editorial propaganda, resolutions, and enterprises of the Central Committee, all aimed at producing a literature for and about the Five-Year Plan. In addition, there was undoubtedly present in many writers a genuine sympathy for the aims of the industrialization program and a real interest in the transformation of the country which was going on around them.

The Central Committee did not confine itself to the issuance of resolutions and general directives. It carefully followed up the performance of the publishing houses. A special meeting of the Press Section (Central Committee) was held in December, 1931, to examine the work of the publishing house Molodaia Gvardiia (Young Guard). The result of the meeting was a special resolution censuring Young Guard for its failure to carry out adequately the directives in the resolution of August 15, 1931, and specifically, for its failure to publish works showing "the heroism of socialist construction, and the participation in it of the youth."[18]

Such an emphasis could hardly help affecting the policy and activity of all literary organizations, and most of all of RAPP. The latter reacted immediately to the resolution of August, 1931:

> With complete contempt for the reproaches of the right-wing fellow-travelers, and not in the least embarrassed by the cheap accusations that it is forcing on the Soviet writer ideological tasks and 100 percent themes, GIKHL should come forth in the role of conscious transmitter of the "social demand" of the epoch.[19]

This article goes on to point out that RAPP and the section of Literature and Language in the Communist Academy should aid the publishers in carrying out this task.[20]

The leaders of RAPP had no course open to them except to support, at least in words, the decisions of the Central Committee on publishing. But it should be pointed out immediately that in this article there is to be observed a lack of clarity and directness in support of the program for a literature dealing with contemporary themes. The "social demand of the epoch" need not mean a demand for Five-Year-Plan literature; indeed, the phrase is not entirely clear as to the subject matter of literature. We shall have occasion to notice more than once that RAPP statements on this subject are characterized by ambiguity.

In addition to its directives, propaganda, and direct guidance of literary development through the "social demand" of the publishing houses, the Central Committee initiated on its own authority a number of special literary projects involving not only the publishing houses, but also literary organizations and individual writers. Among these should be mentioned a new magazine called *Nashi dostizheniia* (Our Achievements), devoted entirely to sketches on socialist construction, the first number of which appeared in December, 1930, under the editorship of Maxim Gorky.[21] A special resolution of the Central Committee called for the issuance of a series of collections called *Istoriia zavodov* (History of Factories):

> These collections should give a picture of the development of old factories and the rise of new ones, their role in the economy of the country, the condition of the workers before the revolution, forms and methods of exploitation in the old factories, the struggle of workers with owners, living conditions . . . shock work, socialist competition, and the rise of production in recent years.[22]

The editorial college of the *History of Factories* consisted of Gorky, Averbakh, Bukharin, Enukidze, Postyshev, Piatakov, Ivanov, Libedinskii, Chumandrin, and many others.

Perhaps the most interesting and revealing of these "projects" of the Central Committee, and the one which most strikingly affected the activity of RAPP, was its movement to involve literary men in the "portrayal of heroes," the heroes, that is, of socialist construction. The initiative for the portrayal of heroes came directly from the Party. A resolution of the Sixteenth Conference of the Party had the following to say: "The names of the best workers, specialists, and agronomists, of factories and mines, and of the best collective and state farms should be known to the whole country."[23]

Pravda in an editorial put the matter quite simply:

> Have all the levers in the hands of the proletarian state been used; have the newspapers, magazines, belles-lettres, the movies, the theater, etc., been used for the portrayal of positive models of the militant initiative and enthusiasm of the millions? . . . It is quite clear that we have before us the task of rapidly reorganizing our work, of taking advantage of the most powerful levers for influencing the masses: the press, radio, movies, theater, etc., for the portrayal of positive models of labor, for the portrayal of heroes and creators.[24]

Shortly thereafter nearly every number of *Pravda* came out with a page of sketches of workers and collective farmers—the heroes of labor. This page was entitled "The Country

Should Know Its Heroes." We shall see in good time how the leadership of RAPP reacted to this project.

3. RAPP and the Party

What was the role of RAPP in the production of such literature? At this point, investigation encounters what is perhaps the strangest anomaly in the history of the period. There is ample evidence that RAPP was intended by the Party to be a center for the organization of Communist literary forces and the purveyor of the Party line in the field of literary criticism and theory. It was expected, under strict guidance from the Party, to combat "hostile" ideological and literary tendencies, and to develop a sound approach in theory and criticism. It was expected also to mobilize proletarian literature in support of the literary policy laid down by the Central Committee of the Party in its resolutions and day-to-day activity.[25] The anomaly consists in the fact that, though RAPP was admittedly successful to some extent in combating political "deviation," yet the theory of proletarian literature developed by its leadership involved a basic disagreement with the simple utilitarian approach of the Central Committee, and led to continual disputes over literary theory and method, disputes which were finally settled by the Party in such a way as to discredit and punish the RAPP leadership. This anomaly need cause no surprise; for the Communist Party of the Soviet Union throughout this period was engaged in a struggle—sometimes open but more often concealed—with an opposition to Stalin's policies which included a large proportion of the Bolshevik leaders who had participated in the revolution and the civil war. The leadership of RAPP was undoubtedly a part of the concealed opposition.[26]

Estimates of RAPP's role and importance written soon after its dissolution in 1932 emphasize that with all its "errors" and its many serious faults from the Party viewpoint, RAPP under the leadership of Averbakh performed satisfactorily in fighting literary "Trotskyism" and "Voronskyism," and in exposing the "errors" of Pereverzev. Such services are admitted by the *Literary Encyclopedia* article on RAPP written shortly after its dissolution.[27] They are emphasized by authoritative spokesmen in the discussion of literary organization which took place late in 1932. Fadeev in his defense of RAPP claimed that RAPP had fought a number of "harmful" phenomena: proletcultism, Trotsky and "his agent" Voronskii, the "left opposition" within RAPP, the right opposition in the Party.[28] The possibility that some of his associates may themselves have been oppositionists was either not known to Fadeev at this time or was deliberately concealed by him. It would seem, then, that RAPP was considered useful to the Party in these years (1928–32) chiefly as the scourge of certain opposition groups in politics and in literature.

The "left" in literature was represented principally by the New LEF, survivals of the Proletcult, and remnants of the early On Guard group. The "right" in literary criticism and policy included Trotsky, Voronskii, the critics of the Pereval group and those associated with them, the Pereverzev school, the critic Polonskii, and numerous fellow-travelers. During the twenties a voluminous discussion of literary questions went on in an atmosphere of relative freedom; in this discussion all of the groups mentioned had something to contribute. Though the part which RAPP played in this controversy is important in its history, the limitation of space makes it impossible to describe this aspect of its activity in all its bewildering and various ramifications. It is possible, however, to generalize briefly regarding the points at issue, the significance of the controversy, and its end result.[29]

The basic cleavage was between those who believed that literature and art were special provinces immune to the direct influence of the Party, and those, on the other hand, who regarded them as instruments of propaganda or education to be used by the Party in the interest of the "class." Voronskii and those associated with him were opposed to the deadening influence of official censorship and directive on the ground that the production of literature involved subconscious factors not amenable to external directive. The spokesmen of the "left" denied the importance of specifically literary factors, whether subconscious or not, insisting on the view that literature was no different from other kinds of production and that Soviet literature could be organized and regulated so as to serve its master, the proletariat.

Any attempt to generalize where great variety exists is foredoomed to partial failure at the least, and in any case to oversimplification. Such a criticism might be made of the generalization given here. It should be remembered, for instance, that the New LEF group possessed a theory which differed in many respects from the ideas of the On Guard group, and that the "right-wing" thinkers differed among themselves on many points. However, a single thread of disagreement can be observed in every twist and turn of the long dispute: one side believed in the primacy of the rational, utilitarian, and social component of literature; the other side emphasized the emotional, aesthetic, and individual element.[30] The critical activity of RAPP during the years of the first Five-Year Plan was a fairly consistent though finally unsuccessful effort to find a middle ground in this dispute.

However the dispute itself proved to be an unwholesome thing in the eyes of the Party. The top leadership wanted to bring about uniformity in the treatment of literary questions: there are frequent complaints in *Pravda* and other organs about the state of internecine warfare prevailing among Communist critics. What the Party desired was a "consolidation of forces" in Marxist theory and criticism. As we have already seen, RAPP was intended as the rallying point for this consolidation. By the end of the period of the first Five-Year Plan the relative freedom in the discussion of literary questions which we observed at its start had largely come to an end. In a series of ignorant and oppressive resolutions the Communist Academy had condemned the "errors" of several schools of thought. Bukharin's policy of encouraging competition among many groups and tendencies had been abandoned, and the number of organizations in the literary field had been sharply reduced. Pereverzev's pupils renounced all of their teacher's works in 1930 and joined RAPP. Maiakovskii, Aseev, and other leaders of New LEF (which had become REF, the Revolutionary Front of Art) abandoned that group and joined RAPP at about the same time. The constructivists had disbanded their literary "Brigade." And only one important organization was left in the literary field: RAPP.

The leaders of RAPP were not behindhand in taking advantage of the position they were given. We have already seen how narrow and how doctrinaire they were with their "dialectical-materialist" approach to literary questions. We have observed their tendency to make of their own literary tastes and preferences arbitrary tenets of Marxist literary criticism. Yet the RAPP literary theorists and critics, relying as they did on a relatively limited arsenal of literary slogans, were neither narrow nor limited enough to suit the demands and the needs of the Party leadership in the critical period of the first Five-Year Plan.

As the events of 1930 and 1931, together with the final dissolution of RAPP in 1932, demonstrate beyond any doubt, RAPP's own literary doctrine and the practice arising from it were themselves sources of deviation from the simple utilitarian approach then prevailing in most editorial boards and publishing houses and clearly supported by the resolutions and activities in the literary field of the Central Committee of the Communist Party. The most important fact of RAPP's history is that it resisted the type of regimentation which the Party itself desired to effect. Evidence of this will be given.

It is a commonplace of both Soviet and non-Soviet histories of this period that literary men were given the most humble utilitarian tasks; that the "forces" of literature were mobilized behind the campaign for industrialization and collectivization, organized into brigades for the accomplishment of assigned tasks, and ordered to portray, inspire, and glorify the great work of the Five-Year Plan. Literary men were enlisted in campaigns of every conceivable kind: against vodka,[31] against wrecking, for the completion of the spring sowing in a particular region,[32] for the liquidation of illiteracy, and so on. They left the "isolation of their studies" in order to observe, take part in, and describe the erection of industrial giants.[33] They were urged to speed up their "tempo" to keep pace with industrialization.[34] They were directly "used" for immediate ends.

It was of course inevitable that the new emphasis of the Party in the literary field and the express demands made upon literary men should affect the behavior of RAPP. For instance, in connection with the campaign for the "portrayal of heroes" of socialist construction, the RAPP secretariat handed out a direct command to its lower echelon writers to engage upon this task immediately. Through the agency of RAPP, proletarian writers almost without exception were drawn into this work. The RAPP secretariat issued the following resolution on May 4, 1931:

Resolved, That each association and every proletarian writer individually be given the task of undertaking immediately the artistic portrayal of the heroes of the Five-Year Plan . . . ; That this task be considered obligatory upon all, and its fulfillment be scrutinized within two weeks.[35]

Reports "from the field" appearing in subsequent issues of *On Literary Guard* indicate that the proletarian literary detachment was working almost to a man on the portrayal of heroes. Reports from both Moscow and Leningrad were received to the effect that their most important members were engaged in fulfilling the RAPP directive to describe the "heroes of labor": individuals, factories, kolkhozes. LAPP reported that the worker-writer group Zakal (Tempering) had entered unanimously into this work, and had challenged the group Napostovskaia Smena (On Guard Relief) to a socialist competition in describing the best shock workers. *On Literary Guard* gives detailed reports on the localities, factories, and kolkhozes being covered by proletarian writers.[36] In the work of RAPP on this task there is clearly observable an almost anxious insistence on the importance of the directive for proletarian literature as a whole, and the statement is specifically made that in this project the proletarian literary movement—that is, RAPP—is on trial before the Party.[37] The latter apparently expected it to carry out the directive enthusiastically and successfully.

This was a "social demand" in practice which seemed to contradict the announced liberalism of RAPP in the matter of choice of themes. But RAPP as an organization supported by the Party in the literary field could not fail to carry out its policy and its directives.

The slogans and ideas announced in the RAPP documents of 1928, though they were not withdrawn until much later, were supplemented by new slogans more in harmony with the "demands" of the period. It was at the second plenum of RAPP, held in the middle of 1929, that the new emphasis was particularly observable. It is significant, however, that at that plenum the new note was struck not by Averbakh, Libedinskii, or Fadeev, the chief theoreticians of the movement, but by a little-known writer of peasant origin named Stavskii, a man later to become prominent as the secretary of the Union of Writers in the middle thirties.[38]

The report of Averbakh at this meeting deals in rather general terms with the problems of the reconstruction period: the fight against "the right danger" and the rebirth of proletcultist tendencies. It gives few concrete directives. The report of Stavskii, on the other hand, is direct, unmistakable, and down to earth. The slogan raised in it is "RAPP at the Works,"[39] and by this slogan is understood not only emphasis on the themes of socialist construction, but also the strengthening of the working-class element in RAPP's own ranks. The idea of applying the methods of "socialist competition" to literature and of emphasizing themes of the reconstruction period appears also in a resolution submitted by Stavskii:

> Competition between individual circles in factories should embrace all aspects of work, and in the first place . . . service to the workers and their organizations. At the same time the whole progress of competition should be given space in the press. . . . It is necessary that the proletarian literary organization be included in the general system of competition in the factories and workers' organizations. The plenum also considers competition in creative work necessary, particularly in those types of literary production which reflect the problems of the reconstruction of the country.[40]

Averbakh, the leader of RAPP, of course sanctioned this approach and a little later quoted with considerable complacency these "RAPP slogans," but in his interpretation of them he dulls their edge and blunts their significance. The slogan

"RAPP at the works," for instance, he interprets as meaning "RAPP, face to the works." There would seem to be little real distinction, but Averbakh offers one: "A writer can be a proletarian no matter what themes he chooses."[41] In other words, proletarian literature need not concern itself *only* with themes of the reconstruction period.

It is an extremely curious fact that even when Averbakh appears to be saying the kind of thing that one would expect him to say as the "dictator" of Soviet letters during the reconstruction period, he yet manages to introduce a note of ambiguity and confusion into the Five-Year-Plan directives. This can hardly be explained as due to his lack of skill in the expression of ideas, although he did lack such skill. The ideas one would expect him to express were very simple and could be found in their rawest form in a series of Party resolutions and *Pravda* editorials. There was no need for confusion.

For instance, in his report at the second plenum of RAPP he points out that "the difficulties of the cultural revolution are reflected in literature," and that "we have failed by 20 percent to fulfill the cultural Five-Year Plan." Now this might be taken as a call to literary men to work harder on books dealing with the reconstruction period, but it simply does not say that in so many words.

Again he says: "In addition to the industrial and agricultural *piatiletka*," (five-year plan) "we have a '*piatiletka* for people,' " and he emphasizes that the "transformation of people is one of the tasks of proletarian literature." There follows a rather dull disquisition on the "superstructure" and the "base" and the influence of the former upon the latter in a workers' state. But he does not give clear, simple, and unmistakable directives in the spirit of the Central Committee resolutions on literature and the frequent *Pravda* editorials. He is ambiguous, and it would seem intentionally so.[42]

In a somewhat clearer statement of the matter, he calls upon proletarian writers to give more attention to "working-class themes."[43] On the question of "tempo" he agrees that tempos should be increased, but points out that there are limits to the speed with which a writer can react to the events of the day.

"You cannot write a novel about the Fifteenth Congress immediately after it has opened."[44] He advises writers to overcome their prejudice against "sketches," and applauds the new school of "sketchers" which has grown up in RAPP. Yet the authors of sketches should not forget the basic literary doctrine: they must not be content with externals but should give a "psychological portrayal" of people.[45] For the novelist the question of tempo cannot be stated simply, according to Averbakh, because a novel will have greater "importance for the present day" the more saturated it is with ideology. Real "importance for the present day" rests in the philosophical depth of the novel.[46] And, might one add, regardless of subject? We shall see that Averbakh said just that, more than once. Thus in the speeches and statements of Averbakh the Party emphasis of the period on the production of a "utilitarian" literature does appear, but in blunted, ambiguous terms. And until late in 1930, he hardly ever fails to emphasize the correctness of the already established RAPP literary doctrine, and to refer with pride to the RAPP slogan "living man" and the RAPP emphasis on "psychological truth."[47]

Though its leaders and chief theoreticians reacted slowly and reluctantly to the new demands, RAPP as a whole did participate in the organized and directed literary work of the period. There are fairly frequent news items in *On Literary Guard* which reveal the activity of the proletarians on the production front. We learn, for instance, that in September, 1929, V. Stavskii, Anna Karavaeva, the poet Surkov, and other members of RAPP were to be found at work in a number of factories and plants producing sketches on "socialist competition."[48] The widespread local proletarian Associations affiliated with RAPP were engaged in similar work. We read that Azerbaijan proletarian writers had challenged all Soviet writers of Azerbaijan to a socialist competition in the production of literary works serving factories and enterprises, and that it had sent several groups of writers to the collective farms of the area and to the plants in the city of Baku.[49]

Although the emphasis on tempo in the production of literary works was deplored, as we shall see, by the leading authorities of RAPP, that organization did not escape the pressure to write "so as to keep up with the tempo of socialist construction." The poet Surkov, addressing the Moscow Oblast' Conference of Proletarian Writers, urged that all work be organized so that "in the field of developing new cadres of proletarian writers we may achieve those tempos which the proletariat has already mastered in the economy."[50]

The secretariat of RAPP was directly involved in the organization of "literary shock-workers" and writers' brigades. There is some reason to believe that the leadership had been behindhand in organizing such projects, for the statement was made that local Associations had already taken the initiative in promoting them. However, the secretariat threw its influence behind such activities, and dispatched a letter to all local organizations giving instructions for the organization of "shock brigades" which were to include the most outstanding writers, whose job would be to participate directly in socialist reconstruction and to aid the farms and factories directly by their artistic work.[51] Such work would take the form of organizing literary clubs, writing wall-newspapers, and doing other "cultural" work. The secretariat at one point published a list of "assignments" for proletarian writers, some of whom were to be sent to the collective farms and some to factories.[52] Serafimovich, at the Sixteenth Party Congress, stressed the widespread participation of Soviet writers in "socialist construction."[53]

The tardiness and reluctance of the RAPP literary leadership to take up this new form of activity is illustrated again, however, by the fact that on a number of occasions initiative is taken by the lower echelon or by the workers of a particular factory addressing demands and challenges to the proletarian writers. We find the workers of the factory "Il'ich" calling upon proletarian literature to concern itself with working-class themes and to organize its work so as to aid the workers.[54] Averbakh himself sometimes discouraged the current forms of literary activity, and at one point he bluntly remarked to a meeting of the Union of Writers that though a great deal of fuss had been made about writers' brigades their work was often insignificant. The leader of RAPP even permitted himself to take a sly dig at the rage for "socialist competition" among writers. The proletarian literary movement, he said, believes in creating "a great art of Bolshevism," and is really in competition with the great writers of the past, Shakespeare, Goethe, and Tolstoy. The problem of developing a "new type of writer," a writer who is also a dialectical materialist, is a complicated one for which there are no easy and obvious solutions. "Ideological depth" rather than topicality of themes was the important thing for Averbakh.[55]

It is clear that RAPP as the mass organization of Soviet literature and the one whose line was "closest to the line of the Party" did participate in the general movement to publicize the Five-Year Plan. It is, I believe, equally clear that the leaders of RAPP did it reluctantly and half-heartedly. The "demands" for a utilitarian literature appear in the statements of the leaders in ambiguous terms. They continued to favor their own literary approach, even though it was clearly out of tune with the current literary demand. And the product of the leading RAPP writers, as we shall now see, conformed not so much to the literary demand of the Party as to the precepts of the RAPP leadership.

Chapter VII

October: the Proletarian Writers

1. The Proletarian Journal

THE MOST CONVINCING EVIDENCE that the leaders of RAPP were not the source of the utilitarian emphasis described in the last chapter and that they tried to maintain their own literary principles in spite of it is to be found in their literary magazine, *October*. This publication, which bore the subtitle "A Literary-Artistic and Social-Political Journal," was published monthly by the Russian and Moscow Associations of Proletarian Writers. From 1928 until the July issue of 1931 it was controlled by the leadership of RAPP, and from January to June, 1931, its editor-in-chief was Leopol'd Averbakh. Other members of the editorial board at various times from 1928 to 1932 included the writers Anna Karavaeva, Mikhail Sholokhov, author of *The Silent Don*, A. Serafimovich, whose most famous book was the civil war novel *The Iron Flood*, and A. Fadeev, author of *The Rout* and *The Last of the Udegs*.

A typical issue of this magazine included a rather large literary department devoted to stories and poems and to novels published serially. There was a department called "Experiences," in which autobiographies (usually of workers or revolutionaries) and notes on historical events appeared. A third department, "Life in Progress," was devoted to sketches and commentary on the events of the day, and nearly every issue contained a "critical" section in which literary questions or controversial books were discussed. In addition, there was a department called "Bibliography," given over to reviews of current literary production. The largest section was invariably the literary section, accounting for about two-thirds of the total pages in most issues. *October* was printed on paper of good quality; both its binding and its typography were well above the average for the Soviet Union; it carried fairly clear photographs and was printed in an edition of about twelve thousand copies.

The great majority of the writers contributing to its pages were proletarians either by orientation or in social background, yet it published a substantial number of plays, poems, and stories by fellow-travelers. Iurii Olesha published in it scenes from his famous play *The Conspiracy of Feelings*,[1] and Valentin Kataev's play *Vanguard* appeared in *October*.[2] The poets Aseev and Bagritskii were occasional contributors. It cannot be charged, therefore, that the leaders of RAPP were completely sectarian in their policy toward the nonproletarian littérateurs.

The well-established stereotype of RAPP as an organization which dictated industrialization and collectivization themes to literary men will not withstand a careful examination of *October* for the years of the first Five-Year Plan. Had RAPP been extremist and uncompromising in its demand for a journalistic literature on contemporary themes, surely the results of such a "social demand" would appear in the stories, plays, and poems selected by the editors of *October* for publication. Yet we find that they gave little space and relatively weak support to the literature of industrialization and collectivization.

In order to reconstruct a somewhat more credible portrait of RAPP's artistic face, we shall now examine some of the most important literary works published in *October* during the most critical years of the first Five-Year Plan, from 1929 to 1931. The selection of stories and novels for study has been governed by a number of considerations. Only works by members of RAPP in good standing who enjoyed the favor and support of its leaders have been selected, since these provide a sure indication of the direction in which RAPP sought to influence the production of literature. Furthermore, only works of some importance —those which provoked favorable or unfavorable comment from sources outside of RAPP—have been included. As a matter of fact, we shall find that several of the literary works considered here have acquired a considerable reputation, and that one of them, *The Silent Don*, was an international success. Finally, a rigid requirement was that the material selected be typical of the *October* product.

2. The Party and the Workers

In examining the issues of *October* for this period as a whole, we find that though the thematic content was indeed varied, the editors exhibited a tendency to encourage writing on proletarian and Party subjects. For the proletarian and Communist writers of RAPP such subjects held special interest.

One of the most successful of such works was the story "Chatter," by L. Ovalov.[3] It is cast in the form of casual notes containing a record of the quite ordinary activities of a middle-aged typographical worker named Morozov. The style is offhand, racy, and humorous. The author of the notes is a kind of undiscovered literary man with a flair for lively self-expression. He sets down his observations, his unremarkable day-to-day adventures, his opinions and feelings with complete lack of inhibition and no discoverable ulterior motive. His "notes" provide one outlet for a largely unrecognized artistic urge; a second outlet for creative energy is his work as a compositor, to which he is completely devoted and which furnishes him on occasion with real aesthetic pleasure. A third source of aesthetic pleasure is more or less accidentally revealed to him in the classics of Russian literature when he decides he must read Turgenev's *Mumu* in order to help his little daughter write a composition about it. For the contemporary proletarian writers Morozov has a hearty and frankly expressed contempt. He feels that with all their ideology they should learn to write from such a master as Turgenev.

On the job Morozov is recognized as an excellent worker and respected by the men around him. Yet he has no particular ambition for advancement. He has a young son who is a veteran of the civil war, and a Party member. Because of his good Party connections the son has been promoted to the managership of a printing trust far ahead of "workers who have lost their lungs and their eyes on the job." Though he has a tolerant affection for his son and is more in favor of the Bolsheviks than of anyone else, Morozov tells himself that his son "does not take after me." The local authorities have tried more than once to get him to join the Party, and he is sick and tired of hearing their endless persuasions. He finally tells the leader of the Party cell in his plant that he will on no account join the Party because then he would "lose prestige among the workers," for Party men were regularly promoted ahead of workers with long records of service.

The notes are full of sharp and penetrating comments on contemporary Russian life, and the characters evoked in the shrewd and humorous observations of Morozov are people of flesh and blood. Prominent in Morozov's experience are the local Party leaders, who are shown as inefficient and prattling bureaucrats for whom the workers feel and express a sincere contempt. There is a brief but unforgettable portrait of a Soviet librarian conscientiously discharging her duties. When Morozov comes in to get a book she overwhelms him with conventional newspaper editorial phrases and Soviet clichés: "So, a genuine worker from the bench, and you are in search of culture. Excellent, comrade. Well, now, a proletarian should read proletarian novels, maybe something on socialist construction: take Gladkov's *Cement*. . . . " To Morozov's request for Turgenev's *Mumu* she replies with the usual stock phrases regarding the "cultural heritage" and the "movement to the classics." But she has a very difficult time locating *Mumu*.

Morozov, the honest Soviet worker, reveals to his diary that he is repelled by the godlessness of the youth. Though not himself a believer in any religion he feels that the young Communists in their attacks on it violate natural human feelings. "Why tamper with God? So there is no God! All right, then there isn't one. Excellent. But why do you have to shout about it all the time?"

Like so much of the literature produced in the Soviet Union, the product of RAPP did not escape the urge to didacticism, and the writer Ovalov seems to have felt it necessary to include in the notes an event which conveys a message; and the message conveyed in one section of "Chatter" is a not infrequent one in Soviet literature: the high merit of social motives and social behavior as opposed to individualism. Morozov joins with his fellow-workers to build a collective apartment house. When it is just about finished he decides that though he has contributed far more work than anyone else, and is therefore entitled to an apartment, yet he will give up his own rights to other members of the collective who have large and young families and whose need is far greater than his. Could it be that in this little piece of didacticism the writer Ovalov is commenting on the already well-advanced Soviet policy of basing rewards on service rather than on need? In any case this part of the story is the least successful artistically and the least convincing as an actual picture of the behavior of "living men." It is a clear demonstration of how literary workmanship is crippled by the effort to inculcate social or political doctrine.

Yet the total effect of the story "Chatter" is one of a more or less consistent artistic honesty. Ovalov the proletarian writer was actually trying to show us what life was really like for the printer Morozov, who lived in the Soviet Union in the year 1929. To reveal this life for us is the writer's primary aim; from this was derived the real pleasure of creation.

A second story by Ovalov was far less successful. "Hunters of Doubts"[4] is about life within the Communist Party, and it deals with the activities of the Trotskyite opposition in the year 1927. In this story Ovalov seems to have lost his sense of reality and to be presenting, not the Trotskyite movement as it really was, but a judgment upon it. The reader is given no sense of the motivation of the main characters, nor is there a clear realization of elements in contemporary life against which they were reacting. It must be set down as a piece of "thesis-writing" in which "living men" do not appear. There are three main theses: (1) The underground Trotskyite opposition was made up to a large extent of sentimental, romantic, and ineffectual people emotionally attached to the idea of rebellion against authority. (2) The logic of their antigovernment position led them into alliance with kulak and criminal elements. (3) "Decent" people who happened into the movement, when they saw the error of their ways, denounced it and informed on their comrades. This has the sound of an official pronouncement on the Trotskyite movement, yet the story deals less violently with the members of the opposition than one would expect, and it is valuable to us as a document giving some insight into the political discussions, the secret meetings, the plotting, and the political repression of the times.

A more successful attempt to penetrate the sources of opposition and discontent within the Party and to portray honestly the bearers of such moods were the stories "June-July,"[5] by Mitrofanov, and "Once There Were Two Comrades," by B. Levin.[6] The first story, "June-July," contains frequent echoes of a controversy which took place late in 1929, and in which some of the RAPP leaders were on the "wrong" side, that is, the opposition side. A prominent Soviet journalist named Sten had published in the *Young Communist Pravda* an appeal to the Party youth in which he deplored the development of "ideological cowardice," by which he meant the growing tendency to accept as doctrine the pronouncements of authorities and to avoid the obligation of thinking for oneself. He pointed out that the mechanical repetition of dogmas handed out by authorities did not make useful Party members and he urged the youth to think for themselves on all topics. The words he used were: "Criticize and verify, on the basis of your own experience, the whole policy of the Party."[7]

It should not be difficult to imagine the reaction of the authorities to the appearance of such preachments in the youth organ. The official press joined in indignant refutation of Sten's idea, stigmatizing it as "an apology for Trotskyite leanings." Averbakh proposed a resolution to the RAPP secretariat, and his resolution was at first accepted by them, but later criticized as too sympathetic to the Sten viewpoint.[8] This incident, which occurred in the fall of 1929, argues that there was at least a modicum of sympathy and support for Sten in the RAPP leaders at this point, and indeed this was reflected from time to time in the stories they accepted for publication. One such story was "June-July."

The two central characters in "June-July" are active Party

members and old comrades of the civil war days. One of them, Olshanin, is at least outwardly in complete sympathy with the Party program of the day, has thrown himself into the work of the labor brigades, and is attempting to organize shock work and competition among the workers in his plant. In this he meets some opposition from "backward" workers. Stremiannikov, his close friend, is also a veteran of the civil war, but a thoroughly disillusioned character. He frequently complains of the rigid orthodoxy he sees around him, and of the desire to solve all problems in terms of authority and to carry on argument in terms of appropriate citations from the classics of Marxism. At one point he says: "I don't believe in anything, and I criticize everything on the basis of my own experience. I don't omit anything from my criticism—not the building of the kolkhozes, nor the Five-Year Plan in general."

Stremiannikov is especially disturbed at the evidence he sees around him of a developing conservatism even among Communists, and of a tendency on the part of the proletarian state to become a solid and staid government on the model of the bourgeois state. He says: "You know the hammer and sickle has already acquired a kind of heraldic heftiness. No one doubts that Marx was correct, and so far he has not been refuted. But has there ever been a young state in which there were not . . . coats of arms, legends, and the signs of beginning old age?"

Another bitter reference to the rising theoreticians of Marxist dogma for whom all problems were already solved or susceptible of easy solution is contained in the following interesting observation. Stremiannikov is strolling about Moscow on a summer day: "The day was confused, vast, and senseless. But that's just the way Stremiannikov wanted it. He was no Gerta. He was sick and tired of attempting to translate this magnificent tongue-tied life into the poor Marxian dialect."

The growing complacency of his Party comrades, their attachment to the established order, and their developing acquisitive sense, are a source of pain to Stremiannikov, who remains a revolutionary:

It's interesting to observe how people gradually are taken captive. One of them gets himself some furniture on credit, then begins to think about the pattern of his wallpaper; he pays off the money slowly, in installments; and when the huge and ugly furniture becomes his own property, he even casts his anchor deeper. . . . Just try to move such a fellow; even with rifle in hand he will still be glancing back at the trunk where his bonds are kept.

To one of the rising generation of young Communist girls Stremiannikov makes the following observation:

It will be interesting to see what you will do with the country in five years. . . . In my opinion you will make a very good wife of some parliamentarian, here in this country. Take Ionich, for instance. . . . He goes into the colonnaded hall of the House of Soviets as though he were going into his own room. But the House of Soviets was once the Nobles' Hall and blood was shed for it in October. Ionich doesn't give a damn for any of that.

Of a rising young Communist bureaucrat his opinion is no less negative: "He comes from his Party meeting like a village deacon coming from the archbishop's service—he simply venerates it, the worm. And there are too many like him."

On the other hand, Stremiannikov does not favor a return to the days of War Communism: "I don't regret the days of War Communism—that would be too stupid. But one thing makes me melancholy, that is, that we've taken the wrong direction."

Of course all of Stremiannikov's discouraged observations are answered by his friend Olshanin in terms of the accepted Party line. Olshanin is at last outraged by Stremiannikov's deviations, and he demands that he leave the Party, calling him an "enemy." The following exchange occurs:

"Give me your Party card," demanded Olshanin.
"Since when is a man not allowed to express his opinion?"
"Give me your Party card."
"You mean I can't express my opinion in a comrade's room—but I came to you for help. . . . "

Stremiannikov, having lost his faith in the revolution, and also his best friend, finally commits suicide. Olshanin himself is deeply shaken by his old comrade's death and he remarks that "the new times did not set Stremiannikov on his feet; they crushed him."

Pictures of disillusioned Communists unable to accept or adjust to the new social organization which they felt had already begun to harden in the Soviet Union and to develop its own hierarchy of values, its own shibboleths and conventions—such pictures are not infrequent in RAPP literature. A short story describing such disillusionment and a deep indifference to the slogans and attitudes of the Five-Year Plan was Boris Levin's "Once There Were Two Comrades." It tells in episodic style of the experiences of two civil war veterans and Communists as they attempt an adjustment to the changes which were occurring in the Party and in the country generally as a result of industrialization and collectivization policies. It is a story containing many convincing characters, and though it is not particularly strong in plot construction, its episodic shifting of scenes and impressionistic treatment of character and action communicate a real sense of what life was like and what people felt and said—at least in a certain milieu—during the period of the first Five-Year Plan in Russia.

The keynote of the story is struck in the first few lines, where we learn that the hero's favorite book is John Reed's *Ten Days That Shook the World.* This stirring, romantic, and highly literary account of the Bolshevik seizure of power in 1917 Korchagin carried about with him at all times, and he knew whole passages from it by heart, and could at the slightest provocation reel off the exciting descriptions of the struggle for power in Petrograd. This inordinate fondness for John Reed's book is the key to Korchagin's character, for he is a Communist who has never outgrown the romance and the excitement of the revolution: he is not at home in the Russia of 1931. Like Stremiannikov in "June-July" and like many another character in RAPP fiction, Korchagin and his friend Debets are depressed and discouraged by the development in the Soviet Union of solid, comfortable bourgeois characteristics: the tendency to accept things as they are; the attachment to one's possessions and one's position in life; and above all the tendency to forget the thing which meant most to them, the world revolution.

Korchagin, true to his romantic nature, has a rather shallow love affair with an American girl, the daughter of an American engineer hired to superintend the building of a factory. Her name is Noel, and she too has a romantic attitude toward the Bolshevik revolution; John Reed's book is her favorite also; she wants to paint pictures about the revolution—even plans one entitled "Ten Days That Shook the World"; and at one point she asks to be shown a genuine Russian worker. The love affair between Noel and Korchagin is not to the liking of the latter's comrades of the factory, and he is called before a meeting of the local Party cell. There follows a priceless scene in which the local Party leaders inquire into his love life and finally demand that he give up the girl, "because his activities are interfering with production in the factory":

> This is causing a break in production. The engineer is nervous about his daughter; you can see he isn't himself. He's lonely and sad, and all that shows up in production figures. . . . It's absolutely not in our interests to excite this man and irritate him.

The comrades are not at all impressed by Korchagin's defense that he is in love with Noel; their only concern is with the practical problems of production in the factory: "The devil with her. . . . Give her up, you'll fall in love with someone else."

Korchagin at one point grows furious at his comrades for their prying into his private affairs; he accuses them of spying, and they quite easily admit that they have been spying on him: "We would be poor managers if we didn't know what was happening in our plant."

Korchagin, however, is intransigent, refuses to tolerate the Party's interference with what he considers his private life, and announces his intention to marry Noel. This he does, in the rather informal way accepted in Russia at that time. He takes her home with him, where Noel promptly falls in love with his best friend, Debets. Debets, too, is a cynically disillusioned Communist, but he has less sentimentality than Korchagin and soon tires of Noel.

There are many extremely persuasive scenes of contemporary Russian life. One revealing episode is a party at the house of Debets at which a rather large group assembles for the purpose of drinking and talking. One of the guests is a certain Poliarkin, a successful writer, whose favorite subject of conversation is the size of his royalties: "Last month," he says, "I made 400 rubles; however, I'll make 500 this month. This month my piece on the Pope of Rome brought me 150 rubles;

my study of socialist competition brought 175, of the collective farms 80, and of the Chinese events 100 rubles." He is a popular writer of the journalist type—the type which the RAPP leadership did *not* favor. Of the RAPP writer Sholokhov, author of *The Silent Don*, he says: "His novel is too long; there's no time to read it. One should write shorter pieces. One should write so that every word, every period, every comma, agitates for the revolution, for the Soviet Power." Korchagin's contemptuous answer to this is a quotation from Lenin: "You sell your souls, and not only from need, but from love of art. We have too many like you; just pay them, they'll write about anything you like."

An old comrade of the civil war days visits Korchagin and tells him that he has been purged from the Party because his wife was a Seventh-Day Adventist and had used his apartment to hold underground religious meetings.

Korchagin, walking about the streets, meets another old comrade, Shvetsov, who when he was fighting in the civil war kept two diaries, in one of which on every page he declared his loyalty to the Tsar and faith in the White cause, and in the other of which he described himself as a convinced Red. When questioned he replied that he kept the White diary in case of capture by the Whites, and the Red diary in case the White one should be discovered. Korchagin finds that Shvetsov has developed in twelve years into a fat, important, self-confident bureaucrat, equipped with urgent business and a brief case.

There are constant reminiscences of the civil war, and a clear note of discouragement, disappointment, and disillusionment runs through the story. Korchagin receives the following letter from his father:

The younger generation looks upon us as so much rubbish. They are sure that they are smarter than we are and know more. I'm sick of that attitude. I want to have my own room, with a desk and books. I want to drink strong tea, read Pushkin, and smoke. But what have I got: bedbugs and a divan with the springs sticking out. We have to stand in line to get bread—such are our accomplishments. And everybody's always talking about the class enemy. Where is the class enemy? I can't see him. They deprived eighteen men in the village soviet of their voting rights, and then it turned out that only twelve of them were rightly deprived, and the other six were restored. But what do you suppose they suffered during all that time? What do you suppose it did to their circulation, to their nervous systems? And here's why it happens: Today they send an official and they say, "Deprive them of their rights, punish them." The officer wants to do his best so he disfranchises as many as possible. What he wants is quantity.

I've been a revolutionary, but I'm tired; I just want to live quietly. Don't I have that right?

In a discussion of the prospects of building up industry under the Five-Year-Plan program, one of our heroes says to the other:

So we're building factories and reconstructing the country. But what is there to be enthusiastic about? I can't be enthusiastic about working up to our knees in mud and with no protection against the cold. Let others shout about it.

There is an account of a Party purge which is the best thing of its kind I know of, literary or nonliterary. It is proposed to purge Debets from the Party, and a session of his cell is called for this purpose. At first Debets is given the platform and charged to tell all about himself, his virtues, his faults, his mistakes, and anything else that might interest the avid comrades. Debets makes a long speech, telling quite frankly about his past, admitting that he got into the Red Army and the Party only as a kind of accident, that he was of foreign birth, that his father was a landlord, and that he had attended Trotskyite opposition meetings some years before. He had killed his father in the civil war, but though that would have helped his cause, he did not mention it, for it seemed "in bad taste." Then the assembled comrades asked him questions:

"How much land did your father have?"
"What have you done since the civil war?"
"Is it true you are an anti-Semite?"

Afterwards several comrades accused him of various faults and deviations, among them having had a father who was a landlord and having once said that he was glad he was not a Jew.

His best friend, Korchagin, attempts to defend him in the following terms: "Debets is the kind of man we need. He is the kind of man who is willing to fight and die for the revolution."

But even as he said this Korchagin felt that it was insincere, that he could not really defend the sad and disillusioned Debets as a useful person, and that his remarks could not convince the comrades.

Debets finally kills himself, and Korchagin, after a mood of frustration and near despair, leaves for the wilds of Siberia to take part in the building of a factory, though without any of the official enthusiasm attested to by journalistic reports and novels about the Five-Year-Plan period.

3. Religion and the Ultimate Things

Certain topics of more or less permanent interest in all ages, religion and death for instance, were not neglected by the proletarian littérateurs. There were two noteworthy stories dealing with such transcendental problems published in *October* during 1929. One of these is called "The Garden of Father Arsenii,"[9] and it is an exceptionally clear and moving picture of the struggle between the new and the old, between the church with its dogma, its practices, and its social life, and the new communal organizations which were taking its place. The story is not told as propaganda, nor is any message explicitly delivered in the process of telling. It is not in any obvious sense an attack on religion. It is rather brief, involves hardly any plot or action, and relies for its effect on the impressionistic juxtaposition of two simultaneous events. Father Arsenii is working in his garden and patiently waiting for the faithful who had promised to come and help him with the digging. The picture of the priest is rather sympathetic; he is a fine figure of a man, good-natured, with an excellent voice. As he digs at the ground he sings hymns and thinks of ways to organize his work so as to interest more people. He plans changes in the services and improvements that may hold his dwindling flock; it would be a good thing, for instance, to do away with the pulpit and move among the people while delivering his sermons. At the same time there is a meeting in progress at a communal apartment house next door to Father Arsenii's church and garden. It is a noisy meeting with many loud acrimonious speeches; and one speaker is particularly exercised at the behavior of the cultural committee. He maintains that not enough is being done for the cultural advancement of the workers. "The cultural counterrevolution is raising its head," he says. "The cultural committee visits Father Arsenii's church to hear his choir." There is discussion also of the improvement in the communal house, and how much better the workers are living now.

Meanwhile Father Arsenii goes on working. The parishioners who promised to help him finally arrive—a few rather ill-favored ladies. They have forgotten to bring shovels, and only hover around him picking up twigs and stones. Father Arsenii is furious with them but does not reproach them. His anger and frustration find their outlet in vigorous digging and in loud, full-throated and lusty religious song.

Another story dealing with religious problems was called "Death."[10] It tells of the last days of a peasant Communist. There is an attempt to realize the fact of approaching death in the experience of the old man, to convey his thoughts and feelings as he nears his end. Most prominent is his feeling of utter loneliness and of terror at the thought of the *darkness* and *coldness* of the grave. But then there is an added terror. He cannot face the fact that he, as a Communist, will be the first man in the village to die without the priest. His terror at this thought is so intense that he cannot endure it; he orders the ikon to be brought, and candles to be lit, and tells his wife to call the priest. The priest is afraid, however, to visit a member of the local Communist cell, and he pays a visit first to the secretary of the cell, who says to him: "If you go near him we'll tear your head off." The secretary is adamant on this point, for the prestige of the local Communists is at stake. He pays a visit to his old friend to help keep up his courage. On his way to the dying man's house the peasants follow him at a distance, and one of them abuses him cautiously: "You want him to die without a priest; but just wait till your time comes. It won't be so easy."

At first he is able to give his comrade courage, reminding

him of the civil war, the great days, the revolution; but when he leaves, the dying man again sends his wife for the priest. Finally the secretary organizes all the Communists in the village to take turns sitting with their comrade to keep his spirits up and keep the priest at a distance. At last the dying man can stand it no longer: "After I'm dead do what you like with me, but now. . . ."

They hand him the ikon and he holds it, waiting for the priest. Then his eye falls on an old mustard glass which he had used for an ink bottle when he learned to read and write. He reaches for that, too, and he meets death clutching the ikon in one hand and the ink bottle, the instrument of enlightenment, in the other.

4. The Psychology of Classes in Individual Experience

There are a number of stories dealing with the social and psychological problems of the young Communists, and I have selected two of these as perhaps the best. A story called "Individual Education"[11] relates the experiences among the workers of a young girl student, a Communist, who is assigned to "educational" work. She is not herself of a pure proletarian family, and, conscious of this, is under constant strain in her effort to act, feel, and look like a proletarian. At a meeting of factory-workers where she is speaking, she looks over the drawn, ugly faces of the women, and firmly refuses to be repelled by them. Instead she decides to select the dirtiest and ugliest of the lot and make a special friend of that one. She finally finds one unlettered and ignorant worker who becomes the object of her educational efforts. Nina, the young Communist, is full of self-admiration, and rather superficial, frothy class-conscious attitudes. She is quite sure that this "genuine" proletarian must have great admiration for her as a young Communist. Being concerned with the workingwoman's cultural development, she takes her to the theater where an operetta is playing. Nina is much surprised to find that her workingwoman protégé is moved to tears by the piece. She had thought that a genuine worker would be repelled by anything so *petit bourgeois* as an operetta. Nina is also shocked by the workingwoman's interest in money, and her concern for her poor belongings; such interests seem to Nina *petit bourgeois.* Nina is of course well stocked up with Marxist-sounding phrases which carry her through life and seem to provide answers for such problems as the ugly worker. Yet her real disillusionment, and, as is suggested, the beginning of her education, comes when Nina learns that the poor proletarian on whom she has lavished so much attention actually despises her. In the course of a speech for which Nina has carefully coached her, Avdotia departs from her prepared text and complains bitterly to the other women: "How poor we are, how high the cost of living is, yet they waste money educating the youth, and they're *stupid, stupid.*"

A story called "Sisters"[12] gives us still another aspect of the psychological problems which developed in some persons as a result of their efforts to adjust to a radically new and terribly difficult social situation. It tells of two people, one a young Communist girl and the other a rather elderly seamstress, each of whom is attempting, in her own peculiar way, to lose her "class" identity. The young Communist girl, Tonia, is the daughter of a priest and by that token a hopeless bourgeois. But she has renounced her religion and her family, joined the proletariat by getting a job as a dishwasher, and become a member of the Komsomol (Young Communist League). She displays pride in her callouses, her cracked hands, in the dingy room she has, and in her simple workingwoman's clothes. Tonia, in the course of her travels, meets a seamstress named Adelaida Terëkhina. The old lady Terëkhina has the outward appearance of an aristocrat of the old regime. She wears clothes that were in the best fashion in 1914, has cultivated accents which mark her off from the proletarians, and loses no opportunity to refer proudly to her "aristocratic" background. In the Soviet Union in 1929 she would, of course, suffer for such a thing. She has to wash staircases out of turn in the communal apartment house and is forced to pay double for everything. She complains of this treatment, but rather philosophically: "You can't blame such as them for hating a woman of my birth and background." Tonia and Adelaida, strangely enough, become good friends. Something about Adelaida irresistibly reminds Tonia of her own family and friends, and she is not convinced that her renunciation of the past is complete. Tonia soon discovers, however, that her seamstress friend is really of proletarian birth and, in fact, a close relative of one of her fellow-workers. Yet Adelaida has persuaded other people, and even to some extent herself, that she is made of finer stuff than the simple proletarians who, in theory, rule the state. And she maintains the fiction at great cost to herself. A dialogue such as the following transpires between Tonia, the priest's daughter, and Adelaida the proletarian. Tonia: "I am a worker and I'm proud of it." Adelaida: "We must all accept the lot that is destined for us. . . . All my life I danced quadrilles and mazurkas, and others have had a dark and humble fate." Tonia: "But I would never exchange my labor for your idiotic mazurkas. See how my fingers are cut? That's my lot," and Tonia gaily stretches out her hands to the old woman, hands covered with black cracks and scratches.

Tonia became very sick as the result of overwork, and Adelaida, warmly concerned about her welfare, told the girl's family about her condition. Her father, the priest, paid a visit to his daughter, bringing her some religious gifts in the form of traditional foods. There follows a poignant scene in which the priest tries to persuade his daughter to partake of the food for her health's sake, forgetting about its religious significance. But Tonia, frightened at this threat to her social position, coldly orders her father to leave and to take his gifts with him. However her comrades of the Young Communist League have learned of his visit, and before she is out of bed have passed a resolution expelling her from the organization:

> Comrade Antonina Palisadova has all the time been passing herself off as a worker, as though that was her social position, and many workers were against the Komsomol on her account, because she could not appropriate for herself this social position. . . . Palisadova has all the time kept up her connections with the priestly rabble, not considering the fact that when she was taken into the Komsomol she renounced her birth. . . . This is evidence of what kind of a proletarian she is, and it is evidence that she has been our secret class enemy and was only waiting for her hour.

Tonia, furious at being thus deprived of her social position, seeks out the old seamstress as the one person who can testify in her favor and whose testimony will prove that she had had no bond with her family. When she finds Adelaida in the slum quarter where the latter is living, it turns out that she too is in the process of being deprived of *her* social position, for the proletarians in her house have called an informal session in the courtyard and are trying to force the unyielding Adelaida to admit the truth, that she is not of noble birth. But Adelaida firmly insists that she is of better stuff than the shoemakers and factory-workers among whom she lives. Noticing Tonia in the crowd, she calls her friend as a witness that she is a noblewoman accustomed to the best, and that her sons were Guardsmen. Tonia gives up in despair. Yet she cannot help feeling a warm kinship for the old woman, who, like Tonia herself, only wanted to belong to the best and the finest people.

5. *The Birth of a Hero*

We now turn to one of the most important, interesting, and at the same time one of the most puzzling novels of the whole Five-Year-Plan period: Iurii Libedinskii's *Birth of a Hero.*[13] Published early in 1930, it almost immediately became the center of a violent and prolonged controversy which ended in an official condemnation of the work through a *Pravda* editorial which had the force of a directive. *The Birth of a Hero* was written by a prominent and popular leader of RAPP; it had been warmly received and highly praised by the leading RAPP critics and had been presented to the public as an outstanding example of the dialectical-materialist literary method in practice. Libedinskii himself thought it was his most successful attempt to present an "idea" in a work of art. Yet the enemies of RAPP, and finally higher authority in the Party itself, condemned the novel and castigated its author. The reason given officially was that it represented an evasion of the important problems of the reconstruction period: in other words, that it was out of touch with the official literary line of the day.

The novel is indeed a difficult one to interpret, for its plot is meager, its action is slow, and its meaning is not easily understood. There is much psychological probing of human motives in the manner of Tolstoy, and there are lengthy investigations of the sex life of the main characters. Accident, mood, and subconscious impulse play a large part in the behavior of these characters, a circumstance which amazed and outraged some of the solidly Marxist critics who reviewed the book. At every turn there is some indication that the author wishes to suggest many things which he perhaps dared not express openly. It is extremely tempting to engage in allegorical interpretation of many passages, and some of the contemporary critics did speculate that the whole novel had an allegorical meaning, though none of them put his finger on it.

The Birth of a Hero is a deliberate and conscious protest against the developing conservatism of the Party and also against already visible evidences of timidity, conformity, and stagnation in its intellectual life. It is one more literary echo of the Sten letter warning the youth against "intellectual cowardice." It is, further, an eloquent defense of the revolutionary attitude, and a plea for radical evaluation of all established things, including even the Soviet state. For Libedinskii emphasizes the inevitability of change and development, of distant revolutions, and warns, as did Stremiannikov in "June-July," against the comfortable feeling that any system of values is finally established and safe. Libedinskii in this novel defends the idea of a "continually developing revolution," against which the comfortable, the conservative, and especially the practitioners of power and authority in any state will always array themselves.

The main character is an old revolutionary named Shorokhov, presented as an intelligent, sympathetic, and basically attractive character. He is a Party man and Soviet functionary, but one of what might be called "the old school," and the structural basis of the novel is his conflict with a new generation of Bolsheviks whose attitudes and standards he feels are inimical to his. These include his young wife Liuba, a beautiful and strongly sexed woman whom he has married in a moment of carnal abstraction; his daughter by an earlier marriage; and his assistant, an efficient and proper young Communist named Eidnunen. The last is completely prosaic and thoroughly conventional: an efficient administrator and conscientious organizer for whom all problems are susceptible of patterned, symmetrical solutions. Shorokhov has come to depend on Eidnunen because of the latter's absolute devotion to order, efficiency, and the hierarchical world of things. Yet in the conduct of his job Eidnunen, conscientious though he is, lacks any sense of the complexities of human nature, and attempts to solve all problems in terms of cold, rational formulas, especially those that are supported by established Communist authority. The deepest things in the old Bolshevik Shorokhov rebel against the cold, patterned, and unoriginal mind of Eidnunen; and he feels at the same time that Eidnunen is a threat to him: not so much to his position in life as to his own inner integrity.

The other antagonists of Shorokhov are all reflections or facets of the character Eidnunen, the bureaucrat. Shorokhov, in the course of his Party work, is called upon to send a man to Turkistan to combat certain harmful ideological developments there. A young ambitious Communist named Gorlin is highly recommended to him by many people, including his assistant, Eidnunen. Upon Gorlin's first appearance the reader can recognize in him the literary prototype of a whole series of Communist bureaucrats whose influence has, over the years, had a deadening effect on Russian intellectual life, especially in literature and the arts, but lately even in biological science. He talks and behaves like Pavel Iudin, the literary lawgiver, like Mitin and Ral'tsevich, the heresy-hunters of Soviet philosophy, like Elena Usievich, whose brochure against RAPP bore the title "For the Purity of Leninism in Marxist Theory," or even like Trofim Lysenko, who recently drove out the dissident heretics in the biological field. It is to the credit of Libedinskii that he identified and portrayed this type in powerfully negative colors so many years ago.

Gorlin is revealed to us as a serious, grim young man. Humor has never touched his spirit. He enters Shorokhov's office reading a current brochure and deeply immersed in it. "What's this you're reading," asks Shorokhov. "Emmanuel Enchman . . . " said he. "A very harmful book, an oversimplified and pseudo-scientific heresy. But at the Red University some few people are carried away by him. We're waging war with them now, decisive warfare!"

Discussing the situation in Turkistan, Shorokhov remarks,

"What strange things they mix Marxism with there." And Gorlin immediately answers, "It makes no difference; we'll straighten them out. Now, as never before, we must struggle for the purity of Marxism." "As Gorlin said this his face was covered with a flush of inspiration and at the same time modesty. Shorokhov for some reason repeated all this to himself, as though examining it. But it was all said very well. These were correct words. . . . "

Yet Shorokhov vaguely feels that there is something wrong with Gorlin, something deeply and basically wrong, and his foreboding is borne out by certain events in Turkistan which followed Gorlin's arrival. For Gorlin proceeds in highhanded fashion to expel from the Party and deprive of their posts as heretics and traitors a score of native Turkistanians of whose value Shorokhov has no doubt. The situation created by Gorlin's highhanded methods is so serious that Shorokhov himself makes a trip to Turkistan in order to straighten things out. There he finds that his daughter Olga (also in Turkistan) and Gorlin have gotten married, and that they are an excellent match. In observing their behavior, their attitudes, their way of life, Shorokhov sees with sudden clarity that they, too, represent the forces of Eidnunen. He observes that Olga walks among the poor and ignorant peasants as a stranger, holding herself aloof from them, and that they look upon her with distrust. He hears Gorlin characterize with complete intolerance the native opposition as composed of "deviationists." He listens with profound contempt to Gorlin's talk about the future industrial strength of Turkistan, while they walk about in the midst of poverty, dirt, ignorance, and vice bred of centuries of oppression. Above all Shorokhov is disturbed at the picture of conventional red marital bliss which the young pair Olga and Gorlin display for his edification.

"This is all Eidnunen," he reflects, "this . . . isolation of themselves from Selim [one of the native leaders], this assertion of themselves within their own little family world, and this business of naming their child after Lenin. . . . All of this means lack of consciousness of that which exists, all of this is concealment and obfuscation."

Liuba, Shorokhov's youthful wife, is a third incarnation of Eidnunen, though on a much lower level. Her interests and her intelligence are limited, and her main pursuits are *petit bourgeois* in the extreme: they are limited, indeed, to home, family, and reproduction. In fact Shorokhov complains constantly of his inability to get enough sleep. And as Shorokhov's thoughts on the characteristics of the Eidnunen generation gain in clarity, as he grows to feel that his own radical nature can never live in harmony with it, the need to free himself is borne in upon him strongly. He leaves his wife, who marries a young university student but soon gives birth to a child of Shorokhov's. She tells Shorokhov about this, and he goes to see her and his child. As he observes Liuba's room he reflects:

> And suddenly he felt himself a new and youthful creature by comparison with her. . . . And in the desolation . . . of this large room he sensed the barely visible elements of Liuba's family world: the varicolored embroidery on the window sill; a quite new meat grinder glistening in the corner, and her comfortable worn slippers under the bed. And he looked upon all this, which had before been so sweet to him, as a new manifestation of the old enemy, as the elemental repetition of immemorial and hateful forms of life. He had fought with them all his life, all his life he had exposed them, tearing the hypocritical masks from them; and now he had even found them inside himself: his own inner Eidnunen had been covering them up. And never before had he been so deeply . . . armed against them as now, and he looked sharply and coldly at Liuba—as one looks at an enemy.

Liuba, feeling his elemental hostility, is prepared to put up a struggle for the child. She announces that she will never give him up. The novel ends on the following note, as two worlds stand over the cradle of the next generation, prepared to fight to the death for its allegiance: "And they stood on either side of his cradle, concentrated in their hostility to one another, and ready for new struggles."

The Birth of a Hero, in spite of many and obvious artistic shortcomings, holds great interest as a muffled and deliberately enigmatic protest against the growing bureaucracy of the Party, with its cold-blooded, purely logical approach to the development of socialism. The labored style and the lack of clarity are the result, partly, of the difficult situation in which Libedinskii worked—he could not make his meaning perfectly clear—and of the fact that he himself had not fully realized the idea he was trying to convey. We have seen that as a literary theorist Libedinskii inclined to the position of Voronskii that artistic creation is the result of subconscious processes inaccessible to the logical part of man. Part of his not fully realized idea in *The Birth of a Hero* is that reason and logic unaided cannot successfully plan human life, for they leave out important though intangible factors in the human soul (Libedinskii would not have used that word). The protest against dogmatic rationalism and the complacency which is its concomitant in the character of Eidnunen, Gorlin, and Olga runs like a red thread through Libedinskii's novel. Like Stremiannikov in "June-July," Libedinskii will not attempt to reduce "this magnificent tongue-tied life to the terms of a poor Marxist dialect."

The main action of the novel develops as the result of an accident: Shorokhov just happens to see Liuba at a moment in which her womanly beauty is displayed to advantage, and it is emphasized that his whole love affair with her was casual, unplanned, and impossible to explain or justify according to any of the usual rational formulas. In another scene a man who has attempted to kill his wife in a fit of jealousy is shown explaining the circumstances of his action and as he talks the man's hands idly play with objects on a desk, and he attempts absent-mindedly to arrange these objects in a symmetrical fashion. Shorokhov, watching him, feels that "the shot he fired at his wife had indeed been the result of just such a symmetrical organization of objects." The idea is that this man had tried too hard to reduce his relations with his wife to a well-ordered, rational system according to the best Communist morality, and his shot at her was a sudden assertion of his own nature against a rigid pattern of behavior. Perhaps the best statement of Libedinskii's idea is put into the mind of a ten-year-old child, doing his homework. Little Valka, the young pioneer, is making up arithmetical problems which he works out and demonstrates with matches.

Then Valka tried to make up a problem for some young pioneers. But the problem wouldn't work out. For he couldn't treat the pioneers as he handled the matches. With matches it was simple: you have 52 and you add 36; how many are there? Or you lay the matches out in 12 rows and the total is 240—how many in each row? But the young pioneers were different somehow: they were always doing something.

And Valka was distracted from his arithmetic problem because he just could not think of the pioneers as so many units; he kept remembering them as living beings and thinking about what each one would do.

He remembered something which had happened while the pioneers were at camp: some pioneers went to bathe and left some others to guard the camp. But here they are playing leapfrog, and there are so many of them: the problem wouldn't work out. All the pioneers were interested in their own affairs, each one had his own face, his own name, his own voice—and Valka's arithmetical problem just melted away into life.

Perhaps even more important than its protest against the rational organization of life is Libedinskii's affirmation of the "permanent" and continuing nature of the revolution. The character of Shorokhov is an expression of restlessness, of change, of radicalism in the best sense of the word, and it is a negation of the static, the established, and the essentially conservative forces represented by Eidnunen, Gorlin, Liuba, and Olga. At one point in his musings Shorokhov realizes that with age he has found his own nature:

And it was as though he had climbed upon a mountain peak. . . . And here he stood already at the highest point and he could see ahead of him the far-off golden-warm . . . mist which hid new peaks rising before him. "I shall never see them . . . " he thought. . . . And with unusual strength he felt that those guiding thoughts which had been with him all his life not only were a part of his life, but he himself was part and parcel of a wave of new thoughts yet to enter the world, and though he must perish, yet these thoughts would come to fruition far off on those distant heights which now could only be dimly discerned.

6. Sholokhov and Panfërov

It should never be forgotten in estimating RAPP as a literary influence that the novel which is often considered the best product of the Soviet period, *The Silent Don*, was published first in the journal *October* and was written by one of its editors, Mikhail Sholokhov. *The Silent Don* is perhaps the best example of the RAPP literary principles in practice. It is a long panoramic novel of the First World War, the revolution, and the civil war, done in conscious imitation of Tolstoy's *War and Peace*. The workers, Cossacks, Communists, and soldiers who enliven its pages are believable characters. They are presented with objective detachment and, according to the RAPP recipe, both good and bad traits are featured in the Communists as well as in their enemies. The hero, Gregory Melekhov, is a young Cossack torn by conflicting loyalties who sides at one time with the Reds, and then again with the Whites, and in the end is shown as a lost and defeated individual; yet the author, on the whole, refrains from drawing any moral, or teaching any Marxist lesson in setting forth his hero's tragic fate. *The Silent Don* is an example of what the RAPP ideas meant in the work of a superior writer.

The early chapters of Panfërov's *Brusski*, dealing with the early years of collectivization, treat a topical issue but with strict attention to RAPP creative principles. The hero, Zhdarkin, is a young peasant who returns from the wars intent on developing his own plot of ground. His peasant individualism is at odds with another side of his character, which is strongly drawn to the collective. *Brusski*, an incredibly long and at times unspeakably dull novel, is the story of Zhdarkin's gradual conversion to the idea of collective farming. The later chapters are frankly propagandist, and the novel in its final form is a dull reflection of official doctrine.

There are, indeed, other novels and stories dealing with strictly Five-Year-Plan subjects: Stavskii's *Stanitsa*, an account of collectivization in the Cossack communities; Chumandrin's *Leningrad;* and some few others. Il'enkov's novel of wrecking and reconstruction, *The Driving Axle*, was published in *October*, though it was criticized by the RAPP leadership. But the idea that the leaders of RAPP and the editors of *October* wished to confine Soviet literature to such things is a very mistaken one.

The examples of prose fiction which we have examined here

would indicate that the RAPP leadership did not dictate directly any particular type of literary content, though it favored works which dealt with the life of the working class, the Communist youth, and the Party itself. There is no uniformity as to the time of the action in the novels selected by the editors, though the period of the civil war and the early years of reconstruction seem to have been favored. Yet A. Vesëlyi's *Guliai Volga*, an experimental novel dealing with the Cossack invasion of Siberia, was published in *October* in 1930, and a number of autobiographical novels dealing with the period before the revolution or immediately after it appeared in the section of the magazine devoted to "Experiences."

The literary works featured and favored by the editors of *October* did not conform to any strict pattern of propaganda. The viewpoint of their authors was Marxist; but that did not at all times interfere with their main function as literary men: to reveal the real world. The material which we find in *October* is rich with the reality of Soviet life, both its positive and negative features, though it was perhaps weighted in favor of the latter. Living men do inhabit its pages, and their doubts, conflicts, and weaknesses are neither concealed nor spared. The "masks" were torn from hypocrites, sycophants, and prattlers, both proletarian and bourgeois. The ignorant and backward worker was as prominent in these stories as were the models of sobriety and industry. The literary tastes and theories, and no doubt also the political bent, of the leading RAPP writers inclined them to resist the expressed demand that they offer the proletarian a literature which would directly inspire in him the kind of attitude and behavior demanded by the Party. For this reason *October* became a rich source of direct knowledge or, if you like, of "immediate impressions" of Soviet life, not inferior in its aesthetic standards to anything which has followed it.

Chapter VIII

On Literary Guard: the Proletarian Critics

We have seen how the embattled slogans of RAPP—"learning from the classics," the "living man," the "tearing off of masks," the "dialectical-materialist method"—worked out in the production of literature. These slogans were also the property of the proletarian critics, who used them as reference points in evaluating the current literary product. In order to complete the picture of RAPP as a literary influence close attention should be given to the behavior of these critics.

The best of their critical articles, together with lengthy disquisitions on literary theory and literary-political action, appeared in the magazine *On Literary Guard*, the editor and leading light of which was the secretary-general of RAPP, Leopol'd Averbakh. Associated with him on its editorial board were the writers V. Ermilov, V. Kirshon, Iu. Libedinskii, A. Fadeev, V. Sutyrin, and N. Shushkanov.

On Literary Guard was peculiarly the property of the RAPP leadership, who were often called the "On Literary Guardists." The statements appearing in it were regarded by the whole literary world as expressing the views of that particular group. If we examine a representative section of its criticism, therefore, we shall be able to generalize with some confidence regarding their "social" and literary demand.

1. RAPP and the Heroes of Labor

We have seen that the Party at its Sixteenth Congress in 1930 and *Pravda* in its news and editorial columns thereafter had called for the concentration of literary forces on the portrayal of the heroes of socialist labor. The RAPP administrators swung into this project with system and thoroughness, yet without abandoning their literary precepts. Their basic demand was that the authors of sketches avoid the superficial and the stereotyped, and that they portray heroes as living people. It was emphasized again and again that the portraits should be true to the real character of the shock-workers. The "varnishers of reality" are repeatedly castigated by the RAPP spokesmen. A resolution of the RAPP plenum on this subject had the following to say:

> Many sketches are characterized by stereotype and the inability to show the advanced shock-worker of socialist construction as a living man. In the case of many sketches this means that all the complications in the remaking of man which take place in reality are replaced by the worst kind of schematism. In some sketches the authors are carried away by mere industrial technique—technique obscures the living people—a technique, moreover, which has no connection with social facts. . . . All these faults are due to deviation from the method of dialectical materialism.[1]

Fadeev says on the same subject:

> Take the mass of sketches which we have. In many of them you do not find the most elementary things: you don't find, for example, a natural conversation of two workers upon entering the shock brigade, and becoming shock-workers; what has changed inside them, in their relations with others, in their way of life, is not shown. . . . People changing the world change themselves also, but we do not see this very well, and we are very weak in describing it.[2]

The publication of a collection of hero sketches by Molodaia Gvardiia[3] was the occasion of an article criticizing certain chronic tendencies observable in them. The article makes the general point that oversimplification must not obscure the general task of showing people as living beings who are developing new attitudes toward one another and toward labor. Authors represented in the collection were criticized because they confined their description to externals or to purely subjective enthusiasm and unconvincing declamation in description of character. "Problems of the social growth of the people shown are not even entered into."[4]

Alteration of sketches by overenthusiastic editors in the interest of a mechanical Marxism is mentioned as a common phenomenon by Makar'ev, secretary of VOAPP. He cites several instances of the application of a ritual Marxism in correcting sketches submitted to publishers. Such a practice is to be discouraged, he says. For instance, a shock-worker, describing his experience in the First World War, wrote: "And all the time I was thinking of my wife. What will she do? How can she live?" This was corrected by an editor to read: "Where are they driving me? Why? To defend that Tsar against whom I fought on the barricades?" Another example—shock-worker's version: "The train went on for several days, . . . rushing to where the cannon were groaning, shrapnel bursting, bullets whistling, blood flowing." Corrected version: " . . . where the blood of German and Russian workers was flowing by the will of their autocratic governments."[5]

Makar'ev gives a heavy and rather ominous emphasis to the doctrine that the portrayal of socialist heroes is now the one important theme of proletarian literature, and that in executing this task RAPP is undergoing a test as to its right to be called a "proletarian literary organization."[6] Yet he too insists on the need for genuine portraits free from stereotypes: the chief danger, he says, is superficiality. This arises from the inability of some writers to enter into and portray the process by which a worker becomes an *udarnik* (shock-worker). He gives several examples of a false, superficial approach: for instance, a poem by Minikh, in which an *udarnik* is killed putting out a fire in the oil fields, and dies while scribbling in the sand, "What a pity. I am dying without becoming a member of the Party."[7]

The efforts of the poets to distil enthusiasm into their verses on the heroes of labor are described and belabored by the RAPP critics. Beginning poets especially are criticized for the romanticism, exaggeration, and lack of individuality characteristic of most of their sketches of *udarniki*. Much of this material is compared to the verse of Gastev and the early Smithy poets, whose romantic deification of the abstract machine and impersonal worker was one of the things from which the young proletarians in 1922 sought to free themselves. An example of the type of work criticized:

Morning rises in its strength—
Time for work.
The collective comes forth
Gay and ruddy.

What characterizes this kind of work is superficiality, lack of attention to individual character, and lack of understanding of the real process of shock-work and socialist competition.[8]

At one point *On Literary Guard* offered a simple recipe for writers of "hero sketches" who know nothing about the heroes and who "in their hearts" have nothing to say about them. Along with this very funny article were included drawings of the objects which such a "sketcher" must have: (1) a rail or spike, for the hero's "iron sinews, iron heart, and iron nerves"; (2) a bit of chain lightning for the "flashes of class enthusiasm" observable in his eyes; (3) a thermometer to register the "heat" of his enthusiasm; (4) a glass of tears which he will shed over the "faults and failings" that we still have; (5) a comb and brush, eau de cologne, and powder for his appearance.[9]

2. Criticism of Current Literary Production

In his report at the second plenum of the RAPP executive in 1929, the same report which refers to the Five-Year Plan for people and the lag in carrying out the cultural revolution,[10] Averbakh touches briefly upon current literary production. His chief concern is, ostensibly, to maintain the quality of Soviet literature. He calls to task several of the publishing houses because they have failed in this respect and are carrying on, he says, a "veritable socialist competition" in the production of trash.[11] He recalls a dispute which had taken place earlier on the question of whether the proletariat is capable of producing or appreciating a great art and reaffirms his position that the aim of the proletarian literary movement should be to produce first-class works:[12]

Take Kibalchich's *Shoots.* This is an absolutely disgusting work in which reality is presented in false colors. . . . Such a work is, from my point of view, dishonest. And yet the novel is about a sovkhoz; the hero dies for the sake of building the sovkhoz, etc., etc. All such things are to be found in this book. . . . And there are many such productions—works pandering to the philistine taste with a Five-Year-Plan moral tacked on somewhere.[13]

A writer who dealt with themes of socialist construction even before the literary Five-Year Plan was Gladkov. His novel *Cement* (1926) enjoyed wide popularity and official approbation. Gladkov was a member of RAPP from 1926 to 1928, but left the organization in that year because of disagreement with the leadership. He reports that the RAPP critics rejected his novel *Cement* in its entirety, and declared it to be a production which could not be considered "literature."[14]

Indeed the literary style of Gladkov's novels had always been uncongenial to the spokesmen of RAPP. His works were regularly met with silence or censure. It is not entirely fair to say that they wholly rejected *Cement*, though Fadeev was especially sharp in his criticism of its influence on proletarian literature.

What character types have been drawn in our literature? In the first place you all know the type of the iron Communist in a leather jacket with an iron jaw. . . . I believe this type reached its highest artistic expression in Gladkov's *Cement*. . . . But the weakness of Gleb Chumalov[15] as a character is in this very quality. He is an incarnation of the mighty will of the working class for the building of socialism . . . but he is not shown as a real human being: that's the weakness of the book. And now an uncounted number of proletarian writers are producing characters on the Gleb Chumalov stereotype.[16]

Gladkov gives a second example of the negative attitude of RAPP criticism toward his work. He mentions that a sketch of his on Dneprostroi—one of the first in this genre—was published in 1928 and received the warm approval of Comrade Stalin, who ordered it published in an unlimited number of copies. Soon thereafter the RAPP critic El'sberg appeared in print with the declaration that it was a very poor piece of work. Gladkov reports that his book on the kolkhozes, *New Earth*, was declared by RAPP to be the product of a "class enemy."[17]

It must not be assumed from this that RAPP criticism at all

times rebuffed themes of reconstruction. Many novels and poems dealing with such subjects received their hearty approbation, but only if they lived up to certain RAPP standards of performance. Anna Karavaeva's *Krutaia stupen'* (Steep Grade),[18] a story dealing with the development of shock-work methods and socialist competition among the young Communists, was very warmly reviewed on the pages of *On Literary Guard:*

> In showing the growing consciousness among the youth of the demands of the reconstruction period, Karavaeva has not taken the path of superficially recording facts. . . . She has taken the line of *most resistance* and has portrayed the complex psychological experiences, feelings, and thoughts which perturb the young Communist. . . . This is not at all the method of opposing the "sharply positive" to the "sharply negative."[19]

A story by Medinskii, *Samstroi*, dealing with the construction of a factory, gets favorable mention because of its interesting portrayal of the old peasant character in all its savage selfishness, vindictiveness, individuality.[20] Gorbatov's *Nashgorod* is highly praised as a truthful presentation of the negative aspects of factory life in the period. Yet the critic finds that the "happy ending," in which the responsible elements take over and correct abuses, is "mechanical" and "unconvincing."[21]

A dramatist whose Five-Year-Plan plays were popular and officially approved was N. Pogodin. His plays, *Tempo* and *Poem about an Axe*, are often considered typical of the Five-Year-Plan emphasis in drama. The subject of the play *Poem about an Axe* is the search for a rust-proof steel, and in particular the contribution of individual workers to that search. According to the critic of *On Literary Guard*, it had "met with general approval." Considerable space was devoted in *On Literary Guard* to the discussion of the merits and demerits of this play, and the main emphasis of the articles contributed is on the negative side. "The fact is," said a writer in *On Literary Guard*, "that the demands we make upon art cannot be satisfied by attention to present-day themes alone." The critic's main objection to the play is that the characters are "elemental." The main character, for instance, makes his great discovery of rust-proof steel under the stimulus of a bet, and the psychological and rational factors in his development from a worker into a worker-inventor are not shown.[22]

An excellent example of the RAPP critical method at work was a criticism of Pogodin's play *Tempo*. The article in question found *Tempo* wanting in several important respects: (1) the working "mass" is shown as a solid, undifferentiated whole; (2) the change in the attitude and behavior of peasant seasonal workers who suddenly and unaccountably become shock-workers is not entirely convincing; (3) the psychology, motivation, and class position of the "wrecker" Goncharov are nowhere revealed: he is a wrecker in the abstract; (4) production problems, vital to the plot of the play, are neither thoroughly understood nor concretely presented. There is, moreover, an element of Slavic chauvinism in the treatment of the sudden rise in production norms far above American standards. A criticism made of both *Tempo* and the *Poem about an Axe* is that as the action develops the conscious and organizing role of the proletariat and its vanguard, the Party, are "nowhere clearly revealed."[23]

Pil'niak's effort to sew a Five-Year-Plan idea into his novel *Mahogany*, a clumsy effort in which the threads plainly show, resulted in the novel *The Volga Falls to the Caspian Sea*. This effort was contemptuously rejected by the critics of RAPP, who could never understand or appreciate Pil'niak. Averbakh points to this novel as an example of the fact that one could not meet the standards of RAPP merely by writing about present-day themes.[24]

Yet there is evidence that the fellow-traveler did not have to deal with "themes of the present day" in order to meet the demands of the RAPP critics. Iuri Olesha's play *A List of Good Deeds*,[25] which deals with the problems of the intelligentsia whose loyalties are divided and who cannot with complete certainty accept the new order, was found seriously wanting when viewed through the dialectical-materialist critical instrument of an On Literary Guardist. Yet his strictures upon the play are not all based on the author's selection of a theme:

Olesha must not be criticized because of his choice of subject. We must write about the intelligentsia (even that part of it which Olesha has chosen) just as about any other social group. Literature cannot and should not, in reflecting and perceiving contemporary reality, confine itself to any small slice of that reality.[26]

The play is criticized, however, because the intellectual's conflict with his environment is not presented in terms of a concrete, dialectical development in the direction of the proletarian viewpoint: a rather narrow and unreasonable demand.[27]

The importance of the "sketch" as a new and particularly significant genre is emphasized by many observers and critics of the period. Nor was it neglected by the RAPP theoreticians, who on many occasions and in official statements stressed its importance, while resisting the movement to make it the one and only important form of writing. The RAPP critical and ideological standards were applied to sketches as well as to novels and plays. These short pieces were expected to meet the requirements of literature as set forth in the RAPP creative program. At a conference of sketch-writers early in 1931 the RAPP critic Korabel'nikov rejected an idea proposed to the meeting that in the present era "publicism" and not genuine "art" was required, especially in sketches. Korabel'nikov maintained that it is possible to combine "real art" and "publicism," and that this combination will result if the writer thoroughly assimilates dialectical materialism and the ideas of the socialist epoch. Should the writer succeed in this, his ideas will emerge in living artistic images, and it will be unnecessary for him to prove, demonstrate, and propagandize.[28] Here again we may observe the efforts of the RAPP thinkers to reconcile their demand for the acceptance of a particular ideology with genuine art.

A volume of sketches about the workers at the Putilov factory by a writer-*udarnik* named V. Vinogradov was found worthy of a special article in *On Literary Guard*. The virtues and the faults of this book as pointed out by the critic give a good insight into what RAPP expected of the sketch: "The author is in general correct in striving dialectically to describe the life of the factory and the psychology of individuals, and to reveal the inner essence of the phenomena he reports." Yet the writer has faults, and these are: "stylistic imperfections . . . a tendency in the direction of the newspaper propaganda stereotype . . . weakness in the character-drawing, especially in the case of wreckers."[29]

The *New LEF* critic Pertsov devoted considerable attention to the problem of the sketch, and to the problem of working-class literature in general. In 1931 he published a discussion of such matters under the title *What and How Should a Worker-Writer Write?*[30] *On Literary Guard* reviewed this work and took sharp issue with what it described as the chief error of Pertsov: "that he narrows the subject matter of the working-class writer to the communication of his experience of socialist labor." Such a doctrine is labeled and pilloried as "LEFism," since it leaves out the most important ingredient of literature: the psychological experiences and changes of the individual worker.[31]

Poets of the Five-Year Plan in general fared badly at the hands of *On Literary Guard* criticism. S. Kirsanov, whose efforts to celebrate in verse the achievements of reconstruction constitute an interesting contribution to this genre,[32] was criticized without mercy by *On Literary Guard.* Upon the appearance of a collection of his political and agitational poems, an article appeared which said:

> The genre in which Kirsanov works is one of the most difficult, and many working in it forget the injunction of . . . the RAPP secretariat that "to write much and to write rapidly does not necessarily mean to aid the working class."

Such superficial and sloganized verse as Kirsanov's, it was felt, would be forgotten by posterity and had no effect at all on contemporaries.[33]

Bezymenskii, whose verse regularly appeared in *Pravda* during this period, is the target of some of Averbakh's sharpest barbs:

> Though I am not a partisan of Bezymenskii I must say that his poem *Tragic Night*[34] is a great step forward. But if he would stop hurry-

ing, if he would give up the effort to have a great poem ready for every anniversary and every event, his work would gain in artistry.[35]

And again:

Taking part in a brigade, making a five- or six-day trip to a factory or a kolkhoz, is not enough to make a writer's works good. What is needed is genuine participation in socialist construction. Bezymenskii's *Verses Make Steel* is poor for just this reason.[36]

Bezymenskii's poem *Socialism*,[37] the text for which is Stalin's statement, "We have entered upon the socialist epoch," is dealt with quite summarily by an *On Literary Guard* critic. In this poem Bezymenskii, says the critic, only succeeds in stringing out a lot of words (steel, Dneprostroi, tractor, etc.) which do not mean socialism at all; but he is not able to present a single concrete fact in an artistic image which would show the socialist nature of "our reality."[38]

Bezymenskii's *Tragic Night* was dealt with in a separate article, and quite favorably reviewed, though the reviewer emphasizes a number of serious faults in it: (1) romantic "varnishing" of reality, and romantic rhetoric; (2) neglect of psychological portrayal of changes in character: the conversion of workers to shock-work methods is "mechanical and unconvincing"; (3) an unrealistic attitude toward the machine as a thing of beauty in itself, apart from its effect on the lives of human beings; (4) lack of individuality in the characters: as in *The Shot*[39] the working mass is presented as a homogeneous, undifferentiated whole. It is concluded that Bezymenskii is still under the influence of the "intellectual" approach to the problems of socialist construction.[40]

Criticism of O. Minikh's book *Face of the Professions*[41] was so sharp that it caused a mild scandal in the literary world. The RAPP poet A. Surkov attacked this book of verse as an unprincipled and dangerous attempt to deal with "themes of the moment" in a "superficial and mechanical manner." Granted that all of the contemporary motifs are used: steel, machinery, *udarniki*, metal, smelting, etc., yet there are no convincing artistic images of real people or believable situations, says the implacable RAPP critic.[42]

A poet associated with the On Guard movement since its

earliest days and a favorite of the RAPP leadership was Demian Bednyi. Demian remained a favorite of the RAPP leaders, though one of his most popular topical poems, *Slezai s pechi!* (Get Off the Stove!), was heavily criticized by higher authority in the Party.[43] The controversy which arose over this poem is indeed most revealing as to the program and approach of the RAPP leaders and the meaning of the fierce struggle which was taking place at this time just below the surface of literary life, and which did rise to the surface occasionally in vicious polemics over particular works.

Bednyi's poem is a verse commentary on articles which had appeared in *Pravda* concerning the flight of workers from the Donbas fields on the one hand, and the ignorant, bureaucratic attitude of the "management" on the other. It is an eloquent indictment of all those faults which the Russians have inherited from pre-October days: indifference, sloth, ignorance, a slavish attitude toward labor. In one passage Bednyi avers that this ignorant folk "drove Lenin into an early grave—and will drive Stalin into the grave, too." Yet it strikes a positive note in the person of the main character Migaev, who personifies those "new" qualities which are to overcome the old "slave mentality" of Mother Russia.

Iurii Libedinskii praised this poem in the warmest terms as an outstanding example of the dialectical-materialist method in poetry:

> It is an artistic work outstanding in its power of mobilizing . . . the working class and the peasantry in the fight for communism. . . . Even the most advanced people of our movement have had a powerful experience of the cultural backwardness of our country, its poverty, sluggishness, and laziness on the one hand, its ignorant conceit and bureaucratism on the other . . . and all these defects are reflected in us also, and do hinder the building of socialism. . . . And in spite of what the conscious and unconscious theoreticians of "varnishing reality" may write about it, *Get Off the Stove!* has a tremendous mobilizing force, just because it embraces in all its real depth this negative aspect of our reality.[44]

And the poem, according to Libedinskii, is a perfect example of the RAPP-sponsored dialectical-materialist method because it presents faithfully not only the negative side of "our reality," but also:

> It overlays this negative reality with a new and greater force, the force of Bolshevik hatred. . . . It is just to this feeling of hatred for those elements of our pre-October way of life that the poem of Demian Bednyi appeals.[45]

Such was the opinion of Libedinskii on the poem in question, expressed in terms of unstinted praise soon after its publication in *Pravda*. His opinion was shared at that time by many people, for he reports that the poem was immediately printed in a mass edition and prepared for presentation on the stage.[46]

Yet individuals with greater authority than the RAPP theoreticians of proletarian literature had found Bednyi's outspoken and caustic verses a "harmful" and "slanderous" attack on the "great and noble" Russian folk who had already accomplished a social revolution and were engaged in the tremendous effort of the Five-Year Plan. Demian Bednyi himself recanted and rejected the poem.[47] The editors of *On Literary Guard* dissociated themselves from both Bednyi and Libedinskii in an editorial statement[48] criticizing the poem. Libedinskii himself withdrew absolutely and unconditionally his extremely favorable first reaction to it.[49] This he acknowledged as another of his many "mistakes."

This incident of literary life in the workers' republic during the period of the socialist advance exhibits in bold relief both the literary "demand" of the RAPP theoreticians and critics, and the way in which that demand buckled under the pressure of higher Party authority. It is now known that the Central Committee itself had intervened to condemn Bednyi's work as a "slander" on the Russian proletariat. Bednyi dispatched a letter to Stalin protesting that the attack on his poem was persecution, but received a reply in which Stalin laid down the literary law in flat, dogmatic terms, supported by a quotation from Lenin on the correctness of "national pride." Stalin's letter to Bednyi is a sharp-spoken, crude demand that the latter return to what he calls the "old Leninist line," and indulge in no further literary attacks on the Great-Russian folk.[50]

The actual demand asserted by the RAPP critics constantly emphasized literary quality as they understood it. These critics were, however, at the same time insistent in their demand that Soviet literature be imbued with the Marxist philosophy, and written according to the "dialectical-materialist method" outlined by them. They were impatient with directly propagandistic belles-lettres even in the so-called "lower genres" such as sketches of industrialization. Even in the work of the *udarniki* they expected some artistic quality, and Averbakh is on record against the policy of rushing them into print.[51] Shortly before the dissolution of RAPP he made a speech at a conference of poets in which he said: "The slogan 'fight for artistic quality' embodies the most important RAPP task; for the improvement of the artistic quality is a necessary condition for raising the political effectiveness of literature."[52]

The RAPP leaders demanded "artistic truth" as they understood it.[53] The steady reader of the magazine *On Literary Guard* was given the impression that the most serious fault to which Soviet writers were prone was the tendency to paint reality falsely, to de-emphasize its negative aspects and feature only its positive side, in short, to be a professional "varnisher of reality" (*lakirovshchik*). With writers who could be convicted of this offense Averbakh and his people were indeed merciless, and their censure no doubt went beyond the bounds of polite and cultivated literary criticism. The terms "sycophant," "class enemy," "dishonest writer," and others just as severe are often used in this connection.

The RAPP leaders insisted on individuality and psychological analysis in the treatment of character. Though the term "living man" was not used as a slogan after the Litfront controversy of 1930,[54] the critics continued to demand the revelation of individual character in all its complexity. It is true that this demand was complicated by the orthodox doctrine that such treatment would reveal the "dialectical" movement of the individual worker in the direction of socialism. But it is also true that any attempt to substitute for individual character analysis the leather-jacket and iron-jaw stereotype was pilloried without mercy.

The RAPP leadership was implacable in its demand that reality be the object of the proletarian writer, and that it be apprehended from the viewpoint of dialectical materialism. The writer was expected to master the "world view" of Marxism, make it organically his own, and with the aid of this ideological equipment describe the phenomena of real life in their dialectical development. A writer who succeeded, according to the RAPP critics, in taking this viewpoint was warmly welcomed as an "ally" of proletarian literature. Many fellow-travelers received such an accolade: Kataev, Shaginian, Tikhonov, Leonov, Slonimskii. Those who did not were often characterized as "enemies."

The RAPP theorists maintained that "all of reality" was the object of the proletarian writer, and not any "small slice of it." Libedinskii thus expressed the matter: "We have said that the object of artistic expression for the proletarian writer may be any part of reality."[55] They, too, emphasized the importance of themes of the reconstruction period, but they opposed the strong tendency to limit literature to such themes. Averbakh declared:

> The entrance upon the period of socialism requires that the proletarian writer reflect those more complicated problems which are being solved by the working class in practice: to reflect by dealing with reality, to reflect for the sake of operating on reality. This does not at all mean forbidding proletarian writers to treat themes other than those of the reconstruction period. . . . It is possible to write about the Pugachëv movement in such a way that it will become immediately clear that the writer is on the level of the theory and practice of the reconstruction period. And it is possible to write about shock brigades . . . in such a way as to reveal that the writer hasn't the slightest understanding of the reconstruction period.[56]

Fadeev was completely intolerant on this subject: "We must drive out those critics who do not understand that a writer taking as his theme *any* historical subject, but working it out in the light of and on the level of *our* time, fully merits the title 'writer of the reconstruction period.' " And again: "We should fight against the stupid and harmful identification of the 'tempos' of reconstruction with the tempo and character of literary development. . . . "[57]

The RAPP critical "apparatus" was not as oppressive nor as ignorant an organism as has been described in both Soviet and non-Soviet versions of the period. Yet one cannot fail to see its tragic limitations. The insistence upon ideology in the proletarian writer was necessarily narrowing and inhibiting to the writer himself, and inclined the critic to emphasize theory and politics in his evaluation of a given work. The apparent certainty of the critics that only one ideology was correct and that they themselves thoroughly understood how it must be applied in literature often led them into arrogant condemnation of excellent artistic works. On the lowest level their lack of education and their intellectual arrogance resulted in the substitution of formulas and easily handled labels for intelligent criticism. The RAPP leaders appear to have been aware of this fault in themselves and their movement, and in other Communist critics of the time. Late in 1931 they published in *On Literary Guard* a refreshing and humorous analysis of the Communist critic's addiction to citation from the classics of Marxism, his phrase-mongering, and his slavish acceptance of authority. The secretary of the *Pravda* editorial board was outraged at this "calumny" against Communist criticism, and *On Literary Guard* was obliged to print a statement admitting its mistake and expressing its "repentance" over the publication of the article. But in the course of two long pages of self-castigation and admission of error the editors managed to quote at length and thus publicize a second time the most devastating paragraphs from the offending article![58]

The demand that Marxist ideology inform and inspire the work of proletarians and that the fellow-travelers in their development "come ever closer" to that ideology in many cases had the effect of depriving the writer of the joy of creating in his own way. For this, let us again emphasize, the leadership of RAPP does not bear the sole blame: the "general line" of all Communist criticism at this time tended to emphasize ideological at the expense of artistic factors. Examples of this we have seen above in the RAPP criticism of plays by Olesha and Pogodin. The demand for a dialectical-materialist viewpoint often enough meant that the RAPP critics arbitrarily prescribed what the writer should "see" from that viewpoint. In the case of Olesha, the playwright was criticized for not "seeing" the movement of the intelligentsia in the direction of the proletariat, a movement which might or might not have existed in reality, and which Olesha might or might not have observed. And Pogodin was criticized for not portraying the leading role of the Party in the events of his play *Poem about an Axe.* Lydia Seifullina, a member of the fellow-traveler wing of literature, complained that a writer who portrayed social relations in a given area at a given time as they really were might easily be attacked for not showing them as the critic, viewing the world through his dialectical instrument, assumed that they ought to be.[59] Thus Marietta Shaginian's novel of reconstruction *Hydrocentral* was generally approved by a RAPP critic, but with reservations on the ground that she did not adequately "understand" the fundamentals of the class struggle, nor "see" that only the proletariat can build socialism.[60]

The fellow-traveler Lidin put the matter strongly and eloquently: "RAPP in its past activity dealt unjustly and cruelly with writers. But the heart of the matter is not in these former errors. The point is that those errors poisoned the joy of creative activity for the artist. And you know, what else do we live for, we writers?"[61]

The negative attitude of the leaders of RAPP toward Maiakovskii is the most glaring example of their failure to appreciate a genuine and original artist whose creative "line" did not happen to agree with their own. Maiakovskii had joined RAPP early in 1930, shortly before his suicide. After that tragic event the RAPP left wing and some Marxist stalwarts from the Communist Academy proceeded to glorify him as a great poet of the revolution from whom proletarian literature had much to learn.[62] The leaders of RAPP were not at all pleased with this development, and Averbakh soon published a brochure *To the Memory of Maiakovskii*[63] in which he stated the official RAPP estimate of the poet. This brochure, though its general tone is sympathetic to Maiakovskii, stands out as an example of the failure to appreciate an artist on his own terms and for his own sake, a failure for which RAPP must be called to account in the case of Maiakovskii, Pil'niak, Prishvin, Shishkov, Lidin, Alexey Tolstoy, and other nonproletarian or insufficiently dialectic writers.

I have said that the leadership of RAPP bears no peculiar blame for the situation on the "front" of Communist criticism, and I have indicated that their "line" was a relatively decent one, often free of the vulgarization characteristic of other Soviet criticism in these and later years. This was also the view of a number of contemporaries. At a meeting in 1932 the main purpose of which was to repent the errors of the recently liquidated RAPP, the chairman of the meeting, Gronskii, frankly admitted that he did not know whom to blame for the situation in literature, and that he could not blame the former leaders of RAPP.[64] At the same meeting Prishvin, a writer of nature sketches to whom RAPP was profoundly indifferent, said that he did not know whom to blame for the fact that ignorant and irresponsible people had called him a reactionary and a "mystic."[65] The playwright and novelist Olesha had a word of warm praise for the RAPP critics on this occasion,[66] and Andrey Belyi, a writer ideologically and artistically far removed from them, had the following to say:

> For the sake of objectivity I must remark (and I can do so without any suspicion of collusion with Averbakh, because only yesterday I was considered a representative of Soviet literature's *right* wing) that the magazine *On Literary Guard* published the best review of my novel *Moscow*. . . . What does that mean? It means that RAPP had its good qualities.[67]

Those good qualities, it is true, were more in evidence in the early period than they were in early 1931 and 1932, after successive waves of Party criticism had rolled over RAPP. We shall presently see this process at work. However, as a final example of a RAPP critic's labor on the task of appreciating an artist who is difficult, abstruse, highly literary, and remote from ideological or publicistic aims, let us examine this statement about the poet Pasternak, by the RAPP critic Zh. El'sberg, who until late 1930 was a regular contributor to *On Literary Guard:*

> Often the reading of Pasternak is a concentrated and difficult labor, calling for creative synthesis on the part of the reader, and none the

less often ending in questionable guesses and unresolved doubts. And yet however difficult may be the path to the heart of Pasternak's prose and verse, and though at times the reader is overcome by dull incomprehension, the conquest of difficulty sooner or later turns out to be highly profitable, for though Pasternak is miserly of elucidation, he is astoundingly rich in images, thoughts, emotions, and sensations which give knowledge of the world.[68]

At the same time El'sberg finds there is a dualism present in Pasternak's "world outlook," which can only be resolved through embracing the "one philosophy" which reconciles freedom and necessity.

Under the dictatorship of the proletariat, in a state acknowledging only one set of doctrines, during a period of forced liquidation of the "class enemy," the narrowness of Communist criticism and its indifference to aesthetic values was an almost inevitable phenomenon. But the unexpected and anomalous quality of RAPP is its attempt to find a way, within the confines of dogma, to appreciate literature.

Chapter IX

Dissension in RAPP: the Litfront Controversy

1. Proletarian "Backwardness"

A constant theme of literary journals and literary spokesmen in the years of the first Five-Year Plan is the deplorable failure of literature in general to keep up with the pace of socialist reconstruction. It is pointed out again and again that literature does not adequately reflect the events of the day, and that this "lag" of literature behind technical and industrial progress must be "liquidated." The fact that proletarian literature had been particularly slow to reflect such progress was a matter of some concern.[1]

Pravda itself at one point opened its editorial pages to one of the most radical critics of "literary backwardness," a former member of the Left Front of Art, Boris Kushner. His article, "Reasons for Backwardness," was published in *Pravda* October 4, 1930, and was the occasion of a bitter controversy, for it singled out as one of the chief causes of backwardness the literary slogans and policy of the RAPP leadership. Kushner's emphasis was on the supreme importance for the present day of the so-called "lower forms" of writing: sketches and reports, as opposed to imaginative works:

> We need not so much a historical chronicle of class battles and socialist building, but rather the participation of literature in these movements in the capacity of a mighty and active weapon in the hands of the proletariat. . . .

Those people writing sketches are to some degree taking part directly in political and economic work. Because of this the sketchers come closer to answering the real demands of the present day.[2]

He goes on to list the "harmful influences" which hinder the proper development of proletarian literature, and among them he gives special weight to the theory of "immediate impressions" and to the "living-man" approach. The latter is singled out by Kushner as a serious brake on proletarian literary class consciousness:

It is quite impossible to understand how the incorrect slogan of the "living man" could ever have taught anybody to write correctly. In essence it is a theory which places the writer above classes. . . . It teaches him to seek good in evil, to reveal the pangs of conscience in the renegade and the sparks of remorse in the traitor. The slogan tends to make the proletarian writer an objective observer and unprejudiced judge. . . . It hinders his participation in the class struggle. . . . The method of "psychological realism" leads writers to consider the problems of the day exclusively from the viewpoint of complicated individual psychology.[3]

At the Sixteenth Congress of the Communist Party in June, 1930, the backwardness of proletarian literature in reflecting the events of the day on the economic and political fronts had been given special emphasis in two statements, one made by Kirshon, a popular dramatist and a leader of RAPP, and the other contained in a poem read to the meeting by the poet-agitator Bezymenskii in which he ridiculed the literary slogans of the RAPP leadership and called for immediate participation of writers in the struggles of the reconstruction period. Kirshon, speaking for the leadership, claimed that since the last Party Congress proletarian literature had had many successes, and he read a list of sixty works by proletarian authors which, he said, testified to the growing strength of that detachment. Yet he does not venture to deny the backwardness of proletarian literature in the specific task of aiding "socialist building." He says: "We are not yet able to depict in our works the great events taking place in the country."[4]

The bitterly satirical attack of Bezymenskii on the RAPP leadership, an attack delivered before the assembled Party delegates, was one important incident in a deadly internecine struggle within the not-too-solid ranks of RAPP. As a matter of fact the literary program of the majority leadership was at this time (1930) under severe pressure from the "left opposition" as the factor chiefly responsible for proletarian backwardness. All elements of opposition to the leadership of RAPP had united in a bloc which called itself the Litfront. The nature of their criticism and the contrary slogans which they advanced are of the first importance for an understanding of the real nature of RAPP.

2. On the Literary Front

The Litfront, in spite of the fact that it quarreled violently with the leadership of RAPP, was made up of writers and critics almost all of whom were members of RAPP. The first clear evidence that a strong, vocal, and self-confident opposition to the policy of RAPP had developed within that organization itself appears in the *Literary Gazette* for March 24, 1930, the first issue of that periodical to be edited by B. Olkhovyi. In that issue an article attacking the literary program of RAPP is given prominent space on the first page.

The leaders of this group were members of the extreme left in RAPP, and their nucleus was a number of propagandist writers who had been prominent in the leadership of the old On Guard organization which had so stoutly opposed the activity of Voronskii from 1923 to 1926. Among these were the Party poets Bezymenskii and Rodov, the critic and administrator Zonin, and the teacher and theorist Gorbachëv. The Litfront campaign represented an attempted resurgence of the old On Guard leadership which had been in eclipse since 1926.[5]

They had important sponsorship within the Party. They had access to the literary-political press: the important and influential *Literary Gazette* under the editorship of Olkhovyi was their organ, as was the magazine *Press and Revolution*, later called *Literature and Art*.[6] Both of these publications specialized in attacking the RAPP leadership during the period of the Litfront's activity. Displeasure with the editorial policy of the *Literary Gazette* is a not infrequent subject of articles and editorials in the magazine *On Literary Guard*.[7]

The Litfront concentrated its critical fire on the "living-man" slogan and the emphasis on psychological analysis which it represented. The most representative product of this school was Iurii Libedinskii's novel *The Birth of a Hero*, published early in 1930, and the Litfront campaign against the On Literary Guardists opened with a bitter polemic against this novel, the work of Averbakh's chief lieutenant and the leading theorist of proletarian literary method.[8] It had been highly praised by the RAPP critics and presented to the public as an outstanding example of the RAPP dialectical-materialist method in practice. The *On Literary Guard* critic Ermilov and even Libedinskii himself spoke of it as a most successful example of the presentation of an idea in a work of art.[9] Therefore, in selecting *The Birth of a Hero* as the object of its displeasure the Litfront group was directly attacking the leadership of RAPP.

The storm which arose over this novel may at first appear to be a result without an adequate cause. But the meaning of the attacks upon it which culminated in an official Party condemnation of the work as a "mistake" can be understood if we bear in mind that it was a document illustrating the RAPP approach to literary creation, and that it was a literary echo of the 1929 Sten letter in *Young Communist Pravda:* the appeal to the Party youth to think for themselves.[10]

The main fault of the novel, according to its vociferous critics of the Litfront, was that it put too great emphasis on the "inner life" of its heroes; that it gave too great prominence to problems of the subconscious, to sex and family life, while deemphasizing the "tasks of the day," namely, socialist reconstruction. And such a book should not be presented to the proletarian writer as an example of the RAPP literary method, because it could only divert him from active participation in the job of building socialism, and get him to delving into his own and other people's subconscious. The Litfront critics saw in *The Birth of a Hero* the end result of all the mistaken emphasis and "false" slogans of the RAPP leadership: "imitation of Tolstoy" had led to preoccupation with the subconscious; the "living-man" approach had led to the portrayal of a Bolshevik not from the viewpoint of his activity, but from that of his sex life and subterraneous psychological conflicts; "the dialectical-materialist method" had only resulted in de-emphasizing today's reality in favor of a continuing and dialectically developing revolution.[11]

One of the most vigorous Litfront statements on *The Birth of a Hero* came from the critic Gorbachëv, a long-standing member of the RAPP left. He found the basic reason for the appearance of such a "harmful" novel to be the RAPP doctrine of the "living man,"[12] and the Litfront critic attempts to analyze the real political significance of the novel:

> Shorokhov, in *The Birth of a Hero*, represents a revolt against the disciplined and organized forces of the Communist Party, personified in the character Eidnunen, the forces that are *driving us* toward the future. . . . He represents a revolt against the Party demand that writers produce sketches and work on newspapers. . . .
>
> Shorokhov represents a revolt against the epoch, and like him those writers go against the epoch who have a desire to write psychological novels and consider the sketch a lower genre . . . who do not care to work on mass journals; who are contemptuous of present-day themes and refuse to submit to discipline; "supermen" who verify on the basis of their own experience, according to the advice of the left deviators, even the policy of the Party in Turkistan.[13]

A clear statement of the Litfront opposition to the literary ideas dominant in RAPP was given in an article by T. Kostrov in the *Literary Gazette*.[14] Kostrov criticizes the notion that proletarian literature must be realistic and the doctrine of RAPP critics that realism is the literary expression of materialism. This notion Kostrov believes to be philosophically unsound, for dialectical materialism presupposes man as an *active* agent, not as a passive contemplator of objective reality. The realism advocated by RAPP is a narrow, contemplative one, he says, and in their selection of models the RAPP critics have confined themselves to only a few realists: chiefly Tolstoy. Kostrov emphasizes the need for a literature which will play an active role in *changing reality*. He rejects as spurious Fadeev's distinction between romanticism and realism, "for in a revolutionary period and under the government of a new, struggling class, it is especially difficult to produce a pure realism unaffected by romantic influence." And the author cites the romantic element in bourgeois literature of the eighteenth century. Moreover, the RAPP doctrine of the "living man," according to Kostrov, had disoriented proletarian writers and was responsible for their neglect of social relations and their concentration on family and cultural problems, treated from the viewpoint of individual psychology. *October*, the literary journal of the proletarians, is, says Kostrov, "full of such things." His plea is for a literature actively engaged in real life, and romantic in its approach to the perspectives of the revolution.[15]

The idea that romanticism rather than realism is the proper orientation for proletarian writers appears in this statement by Gorbachëv:

> We say that a romanticism which foresees the future, such a romanticism as Gorky has mastered in *Mother* and *Enemies*, is necessary for literature. In this sense Bezymenskii's *The Shot*, where mighty social forces are given in concrete artistic form, is really dialectic, and *The Birth of a Hero* is a mistake.[16]

By "romanticism" Gorbachëv and other Litfront theorists seem to have had in mind a literature not primarily "objective" but permeated with the class feelings and revolutionary enthusiasm of the author. In a collective article written by Gorbachëv, Rodov, and Bezymenskii, Gorbachëv's idea is stated as follows:

> Gorbachëv affirms that an abstract idea by itself, utilized by the author as the basis of his production, is not so important as the general emotional effect of the latter, and that the decisive thing in a work of art is not so much the author's conscious view of the world, as the author's emotional reaction to the world.[17]

The *Literary Encyclopedia* article on Litfront, written by a partisan of RAPP in 1932 when the heat engendered by the controversy had not yet died down, has the following to say about its "subjectivism":

> The creative platform of Litfront consisted wholly of a purely formal demand for the active class viewpoint in art, quite separate from its objective cognitive function. Subjectivism was characteristic of the group. . . . This shows itself in their artificially contrasting the cognitive role of art and its affective role as an agency of a particular class. They were opposed to the "realistic" portrayal of the world as "naïve realism"; they were opposed to "verisimilitude." In fact

Bespalov declared war on "verisimilitude," opposing to it the class viewpoint, and class ideology. Thus Bespalov admired the "Chinese novellas" of Erdberg, not because they show us the Chinese revolution, but because they give us the viewpoint of the proletariat.[18]

We have seen that the RAPP literary theorists were devoted above all to what they called *realism*, to the production of a literature faithfully reflecting objective reality, of course from the viewpoint of dialectical materialism. They maintained and reaffirmed this position in their controversy with the Litfront. Ermilov, the *On Literary Guard* critic and authority on the "living man," takes the members of the bloc to task for their hostility to psychological realism. The Gorbachëv-Bespalov group, he says, feels that to study the emotional and intellectual experiences of a character, his home life, personal likes and dislikes, will inevitably awaken sympathy for class enemies in the proletarian reader; for example, the "renegade" Kautsky could be portrayed as a dangerous class enemy or as a good-natured old man who loves his family. And Ermilov's answer is that the only effective portrayal of character is one which is true to the character itself, which does not treat the "enemy" as a being with no attractive traits whatever, but draws a convincing picture of the whole man as a mixture of good and evil, with manifold and various motives. Otherwise, says Ermilov, the proletarian who gets his idea of the kulak or the *petit bourgeois* from oversimplified journalistic accounts of him as a hateful element will be confused when he meets his enemy in real life and finds him a human being with many attractive qualities.[19]

Ermilov has no patience with the subjectivism of the Litfronters. Their exclusive emphasis on the subjective element will only deprive proletarian literature of the possibility of influencing the development of reality, for in order to change the world "one must first of all have objective knowledge of it." Therefore the proletarian artist must first of all know and describe the real world *as it is*, and "living men" as they really are: mixtures of good and bad traits.[20]

An important reason for the Litfront objection to RAPP psychologism was the tendency they saw in it to represent the individual in isolation from social forces. Their chief emphasis was on the collective rather than the individual. The specific literary works which they opposed to the current product of the proletarians as represented by *Birth of a Hero* and Fadeev's *Last of the Udegs* were productions dealing with the struggles of the masses. The most important of them was Bezymenskii's verse play *Vystrel* (The Shot). Indeed the controversy between Litfront and the leadership of RAPP was to a large extent carried on in terms of the respective merits of two literary works: *The Birth of a Hero* and *The Shot.*

The Shot is a play dealing with the reconstruction period. It presents in episodic style a number of scenes from working-class life of the Five-Year-Plan period. All of the familiar ideas and jargon of Five-Year-Plan literature are in it. There are both positive and negative characters with no shades or gradations between them. The positive characters consist of shock-workers, dependable Party workers, and so on. The negative characters are easily recognizable saboteurs, wreckers, irresponsible careerists, inefficient managers. Bezymenskii is not interested in their psychology or motivation: they behave like "bad" puppets in a puppet show. The "enemies" unmask themselves in lengthy monologues that reveal only their evil designs and foul purposes. The *udarniki* (shock-workers) recite speeches full of class-conscious enthusiasm. It is said that *The Shot* was favorably received by audiences of the day, and it is quite possible that its rapid tempo, enthusiasm, and skillfully constructed verse dialogue would present a moving spectacle on the stage. But it can be classified as literature only in the broadest sense of that term.

The numerous articles and declarations of the Litfront show a decided preference for a utilitarian literature dealing with "present-day" themes and directed to the mass audience of the builders of socialism. Bezymenskii, for instance, records that when he realized that his poems influenced the workers, he knew that he had found the "right path." The Litfront declaration to Party and public announces that it will struggle for: (1) militant loyalty to the Party; (2) themes of the present day; (3) the many-sided portrayal of the experience of the working class; (4) the portrayal of the socialist transformation of the industrial-technical base; (5) the development of proletarian satire; (6) moving to the forefront of literary work those forms most useful in answering to the immediate demands of the political struggle of the proletariat: political poetry, novels and dramas of socialist construction, "perspective" (utopian) stories, the sketch, the *feuilleton*, and political pamphlets.[21]

The declaration goes on to say that the cultivation of just such a program is the condition for winning proletarian hegemony in the shortest possible time, and that the basic aim of their whole campaign will be to overcome proletarian backwardness, for which the present leadership of RAPP is held responsible:

> The basic aim of this struggle is the overcoming of the backwardness of proletarian literature in carrying out the tasks of the reconstruction period. . . . Such a struggle is impossible without a determined fight . . . against the right opportunist theories of Ermilov, Libedinskii, Selivanovskii, and the rest, which are protected and screened by the diplomatic phrasemongering of L. Averbakh and the whole On Literary Guard group which he leads.[22]

This declaration was signed by a number of literary figures, the most prominent of whom were former adherents of the On Guard group, and leaders of VAPP in the early twenties.[23] This group claimed that it was against the RAPP slogans so long as these were propagated as the *only* path for proletarian literature, for it considered such a doctrine to be responsible for the backwardness of that literature.

An editorial in the *Literary Gazette* insisted on the need for and the complete propriety of a debate between the competing groups on the points at issue. It emphasized that such a debate could be very important for Soviet literary development. The editors of the *Literary Gazette* maintained that the defense of psychological realism, the slogan of the "living man," the theory of "immediate impressions," and the foisting of *The Birth of a Hero* on writers as an example of the true path for proletarian literature "can only disorientate the rising cadres of young proletarian writers." And further:

> We [the Litfront] are for a conscious, militant, loyal literature . . . a literature which reacts immediately to the problems of the recon-

struction period and the struggle for the proletarian revolution in the whole world.[24]

The point is made with considerable acidity by Bezymenskii that the leadership of RAPP has used the Party statement that "RAPP is the organization closest to us" as grounds for propagating the idea that the leadership of RAPP *is* RAPP, and that the literary method dear to that leadership is also the method closest to the Party. He complains that they have converted RAPP into a kind of "literary Communist Party" in which there is no freedom of criticism and only the views of the leadership may be defended. Bezymenskii finds that the freedom of various groups and tendencies to develop within RAPP has been hampered by the doctrine that *only* the literary method of the leading *On Literary Guard* writers is approved by the Party.[25] The demand that various styles and tendencies be allowed to develop freely within RAPP is one of the cardinal points in the Litfront program.

3. Stimulus and Response

The reaction of the RAPP leadership to this criticism from the left appears to have been at first uncertain and confused. Undoubtedly the On Literary Guardists felt themselves in danger of being deposed at this time, even as they had deposed the old On Guard leadership in 1926. They must have detected in the behavior of the Litfront bloc the very same devices which they (Averbakh, Kirshon, and Libedinskii) had used earlier with such success in forcing Vardin, Lelevich, Rodov, and Bezymenskii out of their leading position in VAPP. In 1926 the On Literary Guardists had won Party favor by their complete and unqualified acceptance of the Party program for literature as expressed in the resolution of 1925 and by their vociferous readiness to carry out the demands of the Party. The tables were now turned. The resolution of 1925 had, in effect, been nullified by a number of resolutions of the Central Committee on the need for a literature militantly participating in socialist reconstruction. It was generally admitted that RAPP had been backward in reacting to these new demands under its present leadership. And the bloc of leftists calling itself the Literary Front, with clear support from powerful party figures, was announcing in every issue of the *Literary Gazette* its willingness to remedy this situation. It was a difficult moment for the leaders of RAPP.

One of the moves against the bloc was a public censure of Olkhovyi as editor of the *Literary Gazette*. *On Literary Guard* also reacted immediately and violently to Bezymenskii's play *The Shot*. The RAPP critical remarks on that drama are not confined to its faults as a work of art, but extend to the author's political past, with hints as to his political unreliability in the present. Their condemnation was so absolute that the RAPP secretariat felt called upon to admit some time later that its criticism of *The Shot* had been extreme. Averbakh and Panfërov belabored the Litfront leaders with the charge that they were "Trotskyites."[26]

Very early in the course of the controversy Averbakh seems to have been willing to beat a strategic retreat, to admit the correctness of many Litfront propositions by the simple device of asserting a prior claim on them for the RAPP leadership. An opportunity presented itself in the appearance of an *Almanakh* produced by the Smolensk APP. This was a collection of short stories and sketches on the progress of reconstruction in the Smolensk region, and in its writing the Smolensk APP had exhibited a tempo to which no one could object: they had turned it out in two weeks! Averbakh devoted a special article to praise of the content of the *Almanakh* and the methods of the Smolensk APP. He calls for the orientation of writers to the broad masses:

> Writers prefer to compose plays (for instance) for the great theaters. . . . They continue to write five-act tragedies, paying no attention to the lesser genres. . . . No one who does not turn out plays for the workers' clubs deserves to be called a proletarian dramatist.[27]

He cites the slogans "RAPP to the factories," "RAPP to shock-work," "RAPP in the struggle for the Promfinplan," and makes the rather brazen claim that these slogans have proved themselves in practice. However, he also reminds his readers that the RAPP doctrine of the "living man" is still a valid one.[28]

Bezymenskii lost no time in exposing this attempt at a "victorious retreat." He wrote:

Averbakh neglected to say that the slogans he speaks of are *not* the slogans of the *On Literary Guardists* but that they are the slogans of *our* group, and that they were presented by us at the Seventh Conference of RAPP in 1928, but in that year were characterized as the work of "intellectual worker-lovers." Instead of our program the Ermilov-Fadeev slogans of the "living man," and others, were adopted at that conference.[29]

And he emphasized that Averbakh is *forced* to talk in this way because of the pressure and criticism of the Litfront group:

Averbakh in bringing *our* slogans to the fore has shown to everyone's satisfaction whose literary program has "proved itself in practice."[30]

And indeed the pressure upon RAPP from the Party and other agencies of culture and enlightenment must have been considerable. The feeling that there were serious faults from the Party viewpoint in RAPP's leadership is vividly illustrated at the Sixteenth Party Congress (1930), where Bezymenskii, as we have already seen, was given the platform to make a scathing attack upon the RAPP leaders and theoreticians[31] as the chief factor in the backwardness of proletarian literature. He called for a more militant and active spirit in proletarian literature and for its participation in the tasks of the day. The stenographic report of the meeting indicates that a considerable section of the delegates was warmly sympathetic to his attack.

Immediately after the Sixteenth Party Congress there is observable a disposition on the part of the RAPP leadership to admit its "mistakes" and to try new methods of work. A letter of the RAPP secretariat addressed to all members of RAPP admitted that the leadership had made mistakes of a "rightist" nature. The same issue of the *Literary Gazette* which printed the RAPP document carried a bitter answer from Litfront, in which the RAPP leadership is ironically congratulated for its belated admission of errors. Yet it is suggested that RAPP is indulging in mere sham self-criticism and emphasized that the errors now admitted by RAPP were first pointed out by the Litfront itself, and that the RAPP leadership *had defended them as long as it could.* The implication is that only continued public criticism of RAPP had succeeded in forcing from its leaders this partial admission of "errors."[32]

After the Sixteenth Congress there was considerable activity on the part of all organizations to mobilize forces for the fulfillment of production plans and the liquidation of all backwardness.[33] The Congress and the Central Committee had issued definite directives to this effect. These were taken especially seriously by the literary organizations, whose backwardness was a cause for general concern. The organizations chiefly concerned in the new campaign to "liquidate backwardness" were the Federation and RAPP. In September of 1930 the Federation (which was in effect controlled by RAPP) was engaged in organizing groups of writers to take part in reconstruction in vital areas.[34] The RAPP secretariat announced that *within ten days* it had produced and published a collection of articles on themes of the day intended for workers' clubs, and useful to the masses in their present struggles.[35]

4. The Call for Shock-Workers

It is in the context of this effort to liquidate the backwardness of proletarian literature that the RAPP call for literary shock-workers was announced. The "call" was a powerful campaign to recruit into RAPP more writers from the working class and to increase their relative importance in the creation of proletarian literature. It was a final herculean effort to correct one of the basic anomalies of RAPP: its failure, namely, to develop writers of pure proletarian origin. This defect in the work of RAPP was a frequent source of complaint and "self-criticism," and the leaders had often waxed eloquent on the subject of "proletarianizing" and "bolshevizing" the ranks of RAPP.[36]

The first hint of such a call occurs soon after the Sixteenth Congress in a *Literary Gazette* article by Averbakh in which he tacitly admits many of the faults lately ascribed to the RAPP leadership, especially the backwardness of RAPP in comparison with the "gigantic strides" made by industry and agriculture. The failure to organize a genuine workers' movement in literature is his chief complaint:

RAPP has been unable to reform itself so as to organize in a practical way and really to lead the working-class movement in literature. RAPP has not yet dealt adequately with the task of bringing forward these new cadres. It has not overcome a certain distance which separates those cadres from the majority of professional proletarian writers.[37]

The article is of special importance for us in that it reveals beyond any doubt that the movement to recruit writers from the working class on a broad scale had already been in progress for some time, and that it had taken place independently of RAPP and outside the latter's jurisdiction. Averbakh emphasizes that the Central Office of Trade Unions has already developed many new working-class writers and has been publishing their work. He regrets that this movement has been going on largely *outside of RAPP.*[38]

The decision was soon taken by the secretariat of RAPP to bring about the mass movement of worker-writers into RAPP. This project was undertaken in collaboration with the Central Office of Trade Unions, and the first announcement of the call was subscribed to by both the RAPP secretariat and the Trade Union body:

The secretariat of RAPP and the secretariat of the Central Office of Trade Unions have made a decision to call worker-*udarniki* [shock-workers] into the proletarian literary movement.

The worker-*udarnik* must become in fact the central figure of the proletarian literary movement. "Face to the worker-*udarnik!*" must become both a creative and an organizational slogan of RAPP.

The RAPP secretariat considers that the call of the worker-*udarniki* must play a historical-revolutionary role in the proletarian literary movement. . . .[39]

The leadership of RAPP regarded this campaign as of the first importance for the future of proletarian literature; moreover, it regarded the worker-*udarnik* approach as the best means of eliminating the backward tendency of proletarian literature, and of bringing it into immediate and active contact with socialist construction and collectivization. This emphasis appears quite plainly in a definitive RAPP statement of policy which appeared during the Litfront dispute, and which we shall have to examine in more detail later:

The "call of the shock-workers" is of the first importance for the development of a literature capable of reflecting the contemporary stage of the revolution. . . . The literary production of the shock-workers, who describe their own experience in the day-to-day work of building socialism, is coming in a mighty stream into proletarian literature.[40]

A few months after issuance of the call, *On Literary Guard* made an effort at a critical assessment of its results. It was found that the number of beginning writers counted in the various organizations was indeed impressive: in Moscow there were fifteen hundred, in Leningrad five hundred, in the Ural districts four hundred, and so on. But it is admitted that these figures do not give a true picture of the situation, since workers actually attending courses and meetings were much fewer.[41]

The new worker-writers who had come into RAPP were, for the most part, young Communists. Most of them were factory correspondents who had already had some experience in that type of writing. The point is made, however, that they are quite undeveloped, and should be treated first as *readers*, and only later gradually trained to be writers.[42]

The most important task upon which they were working was the "literary formulation of their experience in socialist competition, shock work, and other aspects of industrial development. They have been working primarily on diaries, and these diaries constitute the raw material—the personal experiences of the authors—which will produce a whole series of books on industrialization." In a number of enterprises experiments in collective writing were being made. One factory boasted an "authors' collective" of forty men engaged in writing a book of sketches about that factory. One magazine, *Nastuplenie* (Advance), had already published a series of stories written by the worker-*udarniki*. The results so far achieved, though admittedly modest, gave promise that a new type of literary production would soon begin to find its way even into the literary journals.[43]

A resolution of the RAPP executive gives further details on the policy and methods to be pursued in the work with the *udarniki*. It is emphasized again that the shock-worker is now the central figure in the proletarian literary movement:

> The call to the shock-workers has radically changed the face of our organization. Shock-workers of socialist labor, fighters for the socialist Five-Year Plan, have become the most active participants in our organization, and literature has become a part of the general proletarian movement.[44]

Many faults were found in the movement, the chief of which was the failure of established professional writers to work with the *udarnik* study-circles and to make available to them their own experience. It was resolved to obligate every established writer to give individual consultations to beginning writers. Furthermore, the cadres of lecturers and study-circle leaders attached to the shock-worker movement should be both improved and increased.[45]

> Carrying out the basic slogan of RAPP for the combination of ever deeper creative work with militant participation in socialist construction, the literary circles in the factories should develop their work on wall-newspapers, description of shock brigades, keeping of diaries for such brigades, the creation of brigades for the struggle with production failures and for the fulfillment of the Industrial Financial Plan . . . for the fulfillment of the Five-Year plan in the shortest possible time.[46]

About a year after the issuance of the call, Kirshon, who was chiefly responsible for this aspect of RAPP's work, could announce that the make-up of RAPP had significantly changed. The working-class nucleus of the organization had increased by 80 percent, and many workers had been promoted to the leadership of the organization. Kirshon belies his own statements, however, by the admission that in many areas the figures of membership meant nothing, since as many as 80 percent of those "called" had soon drifted away from the movement.[47]

There is much high-flown eloquence on the importance of the call for moving Soviet society a long stride nearer the attainment of a true communist society, wherein the barrier between physical and mental labor would be abolished, and there would be, not writers, but "men who, among other things, write." The rapid transformation of workers into writers of belles-lettres was striking evidence, said the ineffable theorists of RAPP, of this gradual abolition of the distinction between mental and physical labor.[48]

Programs of study for the shock-workers were frequently and understandably criticized. The workers called to be writers were taught from such documents as Stalin's speeches, Averbakh's report at the First Congress of Proletarian Writers, The History of the On Guard Movement, and Lenin's articles on Tolstoy and Gorky. They took up such subjects as "literature of the class enemy," the "cultural heritage," and the "foundations of Marxist-Leninist criticism." In a program of study approved by the RAPP secretariat, only a few hours out of fifteen devoted to study are to be given to discussion of the technique of composition. For the rest of the time the half-literate workers would fill their heads with the pronouncements of Stalin and Averbakh, the details of "struggles on the literary fronts," and misunderstood fragments of Marx, Engels, and Lenin.[49]

By the end of 1932 it was generally admitted that the *udarnik* movement, though it produced a number of new worker-writers, had largely failed in its more grandiose purposes. It seems fairly evident that it represented an effort on the part of the RAPP leadership to come closer to the masses, and to produce the kind of literature demanded by the Party and by the critics in the Litfront. In that respect it had some measure of success, though it was later admitted that most of the literature was completely worthless.[50]

However, the facts relating to the call of shock-workers into literature should effectively dispel the notion that this was a project for which the RAPP people bear a peculiar or sole responsibility. It was indeed a culmination of their long fight for proletarian hegemony in literature. It cannot be denied that the efforts of RAPP and the Central Office of Trade Unions to promote the literary efforts of workers "from the bench" caused a debasement of literary values and gave much embarrassment to writers outside the RAPP milieu, who found the pressure of competition from the newcomers unfair and unreasonable. Complaints had already begun to reach the Party that the role of fellow-travelers in contemporary literature was being severely restricted.[51] For this deliberate cheapening of literary currency in the years 1929–31 the Soviet apparatus of control was fully responsible; and the leaders of RAPP were part of that apparatus.

The attitude of RAPP toward the literary fellow-travelers at this time paralleled in every respect the attitude of the Communist authorities toward the bourgeois technical intelligentsia. This was the period of the Shakhty affair and the Industrial Party trial,[52] which fostered distrust and suspicion of experts, intellectuals, and the educated element generally. It was the period during which the Party sought to develop its own "Red specialists," and in its decrees and pronouncements often stressed the importance of promoting simple proletarians from the ranks. It was during this period, according to no less an authority than Stalin, that "our attitude toward the old technical intelligentsia was mainly expressed by the policy of routing them."[53] The literary equivalent of the Shakhty and Industrial Party trials was the persecution in the *Literary Gazette* writers Boris Pil'niak and Evgenyi Zamiatin on the fabricated charge that they had collaborated with the foreign press.[54] The fellow-travelers in literature, as in many other fields,[55] lived in an atmosphere of suspicion and under constant pressure to demonstrate their loyalty; and as in many other departments of Soviet life they felt the pressure of "proletarianization."

The behavior of Averbakh and his comrades was certainly no more reprehensible and probably less so than that of other Party administrators. RAPP had been distinctly behindhand in the mass promotion of proletarian writers; RAPP did not insist on dictating themes and prescribing tempos to the writer; and the leaders of RAPP continued to support a literary policy which, amid a welter of ignorant and vulgar pseudo-Marxist pronouncements, stands out as relatively enlightened and humane.

5. The Statement of Literary Principles

Though it survived the mild insanity of the summer of 1930, the leadership of RAPP was obliged to issue to the whole membership and the public generally a comprehensive restatement of past activity and present aims in the literary field. This document takes up in detail the questions raised by Litfront and the Party, reviews the past history and struggles of RAPP "on the literary fronts," admits certain errors in its doctrine, and announces certain adjustments in its approach to the new problems of the reconstruction period. This incredibly long though certainly not dull statement of RAPP principles appeared serially in three successive numbers of the *Literary Gazette:* October 4, October 9, and October 14, 1930. It is a basic document in the history of RAPP, and an important one for the history of Soviet literature generally.

The statement came as a result of pressure, propaganda, and criticism of the RAPP leadership instigated and largely carried on by the Litfront. This criticism undoubtedly had support in high Party circles. The fact that the pages of the *Literary Gazette* feature it for several months during the editorship of Olkhovyi is proof of this; the fact that the On Literary Guard leaders definitely react to it with a clear, though grudging, admission of errors is another proof.

However, the statement of the RAPP leaders is not by any means a complete abandonment of their previously stated position on literary matters. Errors are not characterized as implicit in the literary approach and theory of RAPP, but as "accidental," almost inevitable lapses on the part of individuals. It is admitted that the leadership has been at fault for not criticizing these errors sooner and more sharply; but the general line is still defended as "basically correct." The old RAPP slogans are not specifically rejected, though they are de-emphasized. The terms "living man" and "psychological analysis" are used in the articles in a favorable context, though not emphasized as slogans.

The document is important enough to examine a little more closely. The following are its statements on the most important issues facing the proletarian writer:

Backwardness. This is reflected in a certain "petrifaction" and "immobility" in the forms of the proletarian literary movement, in the "weak and slow growth of new forms capable of satisfying the new demands," and also in the fact that "proletarian literature in a creative sense lags behind the new epoch of socialist building." The basic means for overcoming this backwardness is the fulfillment of the resolution of the secretariat of September 29, 1930, for the call of shock-workers into literature. The new slogan raised at this point was "proletarian literary movement, face to the shock-worker!"[56]

Reasons for this backwardness. "Humanism in relation to the class enemy," and exaggeration of the irrational and subconscious element—"such characteristics of Voronskyism have appeared in the proletarian literary movement."[57] Indeed, they had appeared prominently in the writings of its leaders.

History of the movement. There follows a history of the leadership of the On Literary Guardists during this period, relating in the jargon of the day the struggle against left and right deviation in the literary field. This is interesting for its account of the origin and function of the RAPP slogans which had been under attack from Litfront for some time. The historical statement is to a large extent a justification of the very psychological approach which had found such wide disfavor. The emphasis is on the correctness of these slogans for the period when they arose, and as an answer to the naïve tendentiousness of early proletarian literature.[58]

Errors of the On Literary Guard group. The leadership acknowledges certain serious mistakes. Some of these have lately been pointed out by the Litfront. The errors of Iurii Libedinskii are singled out for special treatment, especially his unfortunate doctrine of immediate impressions. It is explained that Libedinskii fell into this "Voronskyite" error as a result of overemphatic rejection of the rationalistic and mechanical approach to literature of the Left Front of Art and the RAPP left opposition:

In waging war on the one hand with the LEF-Proletcult–left-RAPP line, and on the other hand with Voronskyism, some of the workers of our movement, emphasizing the importance of art as a means of cognition and combating efforts to deny this cognitive role of art, have at times overemphasized the cognitive factor, and thus have run the risk of minimizing the significance of literature as a means of changing reality.[59]

Psychologism.

All of reality is the subject of the proletarian writer. . . . In treating the personality he must not limit himself to the rational character of man, but must enter more deeply into psychological facts, being careful to avoid the pitfalls of Voronskyism and "idealism."[60]

Themes of the reconstruction period.

The slogan "for themes of the reconstruction period" is at the same time the slogan for deepening of the dialectical-materialist method. . . .

One of the chief characteristics of the reconstruction period is the conscious, planning role of the proletariat in remaking the world. . . . It represents the victory of reason over the unconscious and the elemental. We should, therefore, strongly emphasize the active revolutionary function of art . . . that is, in the last analysis, its utilitarian role in the practical service of the class. . . . But to change the world does not mean to invent a new world. Art addressed to the feelings of man changes reality by relying on that reality itself, discovering in it new tendencies, processes. Thus we are against passive registering of facts, and we are also against romantic varnishing of reality (Litfront). In reproducing the whole . . . of social phenomena and artistically portraying the Bolshevik or the class enemy, the writer must not shrink from an objective revelation of reality. He must not be led by abstract ethical criteria.

. . . Equally incorrect and harmful is the urge to limit the themes of proletarian writers to those of the present day. The On Guardist realizes the necessity for themes which are of the greatest historical importance for the present day. And this means that such historically important subject matter can (and should) be found in themes of the civil war, of the underground, and other historical themes, if in treating them the author takes as his starting point the basic problems raised by the proletariat in the present time.

In this period we must especially stress themes of the reconstruction period, for the backwardness of literature is most strikingly revealed in the thematic estrangement of the proletarian writer from the epoch of socialist reconstruction.[61]

The problems of genres and tempo.

The attempt to limit proletarian literature only to certain genres is harmful. . . . Yet the proletarian writer must overcome his prejudice against the lower genres: the struggle with the "prejudices of gentility" must go hand in hand with the relentless criticism of potboilers; everyone who uses these lower genres (sketches, reports, etc.) must master the idea that to write much and rapidly does not necessarily mean to serve the proletariat.[62]

New slogans.

For a Great Art of Bolshevism!
Against the Varnishers of Reality!
For the Hegemony of Proletarian Literature!
Liquidate Backwardness![63]

The document from which we have quoted so liberally is admittedly a strange and not entirely clear one. The reason for this lack of clarity is, I believe, that the leadership of RAPP is attempting to steer a middle course between the cultivation of literature as "cognition of life"—the understanding of art given to them by Voronskii—and the Party demand that it be cultivated as a handmaiden of the "class," as a means for "changing the world"—in practical terms, as propaganda for the Five-Year Plan. Though in its day-to-day leadership of Soviet literature RAPP was of course obliged to give weight to enforcing such a literary program, and therefore was forced to modify its literary theory and devise new literary slogans of a utilitarian character, yet the subsequent history of the organization indicates that in steering its compromise course the leadership continued to lean in the direction of "Voronskyism," and to resist the intrusion of utilitarian ideas which it could not absolutely reject.

Chapter X

Further Pursuit of Proletarian Error, 1931

1. "Under the Banner of Marxism"

THE CENTRAL COMMITTEE RESOLUTION of January 25, 1931, which censured the editors of the philosophical journal *Pod znamenem marksizma* (Under the Banner of Marxism) and their leadership in the philosophical field and in effect raised to the leading position in philosophy a group of young men under the command of P. Iudin and I. Mitin, had serious implications for the program and policy adopted in literature by RAPP. For one of the most important sources of error detected by the new men in the writings of Deborin and those associated with him on the editorial board of the magazine *Under the Banner of Marxism*, was their overvaluation of Plekhanov as a theoretician of Marxism and their neglect of Lenin. Now the leading ideas of the RAPP theoreticians had been developed with explicit reference to the pioneer work of Plekhanov in applying the Marxist dialectic to literature.[1] In addition, it was felt that the leading group in philosophy had lagged behind in the development of theory, and that in Soviet philosophy theory had failed to "keep up with practice." One can hardly fail to notice the curious similarity of these charges to the frequent complaints that literature, under the guidance of RAPP, was "lagging behind" and was divorced from the "tasks of the day."[2] Philosophy as well as literature was required to adjust itself to the needs of the Five-Year Plan.

The leadership of RAPP apparently had no doubt that the outcome of the philosophical discussion had serious implications for itself. Shortly after the appearance of the Central Committee resolution on philosophy the Executive of RAPP met and expressed its complete solidarity with the "new leadership" in philosophy, calling for close and active contact between RAPP and this new leadership.[3]

The philosophers themselves drew important conclusions for literature from their recent victory. Mitin, in summing up the philosophical discussion, thus applied its results to the literary field:

> When we pass over to the literary front we must point out in the first place that for a number of reasons this sector of the theoretical front should be most intimately bound to the philosophical sector; for the basic questions which now arise in the work of literary experts . . . add up to the necessity for a decisive battle for the Marxist-Leninist world view, and for the dialectical method in literary science.[4]

Mitin goes on to point out that on the literary front all is not well. While RAPP has been carrying out a "basically correct line in literature," yet questions of a theoretical nature have not yet been raised to such a high level of discussion as would guarantee the penetration of the Marxist-Leninist method into literary science.[5] A number of theoretical "errors" have accumulated in the work of RAPP, for the ideas contributed by the Deborin school could not but have their effect on this sector of the ideological front also.[6] The basic error of RAPP has been that it has not "understood" the concept of Leninism "as a new and higher level in the development of the dialectical-materialist world view."[7]

> In their theoretical work certain leaders of RAPP have proceeded in fact, and in late years officially, under the banner "For Plekhanov orthodoxy," and thus they have underestimated the fact that the whole history of our Party is the struggle for the hegemony in the working-class movement of Leninism, not only against any and all openly Menshevik theories, but also against Plekhanov's theories, which are to a considerable extent used by Menshevism.[8]

Mitin feels that psychologism and such "inexact, abstract, and easily distorted" slogans as the "living man" and "for the tearing off of masks" have arisen as a result of the mistaken theoretical position of the RAPP leadership.

The contemplative attitude, objectivism, the failure to understand the Party spirit of science, philosophy, and literature, characteristic of the whole world outlook of Menshevism, were reflected in all the questions resolved by Plekhanov, and were reflected also in his aesthetic views.[9]

Such attitudes have also characterized the leading theoreticians of RAPP. Mitin continues his catalogue of RAPP errors: an inadequate understanding of the class viewpoint, "objectivist errors," extra-class criteria of the beautiful, etc. And he concludes that "the decisive condition for the current development of literary science is the task of mastering and working out Lenin's theoretical testament in this field. . . . We have in Lenin a *colossal theoretical wealth*. . . . "[10]

2. Colossal Wealth

What did the new leadership in philosophy really mean when they appealed to the authority of Lenin? The pontiffs of the "Leninist stage" do not of course treat the question of Lenin's primacy in "literary science" as one which is open to argument. For them it is a well-established fact vouched for by authorities. And their opponents were not free at this time to reveal that Lenin did not even pretend to have any special knowledge of literature, and that what he said and wrote about it is quite unimportant in the history of Marxist criticism.

Only a few years earlier it had been possible for the critic Polonskii, in spite of being an admirer of Lenin, to state quite objectively that his voluminous writings are almost devoid of literary studies:

> [Literature and art] stood on the fringes of his attention. . . . In our enormous literary heritage from Lenin only four small articles about L. N. Tolstoy are directly devoted to creative literature. Literature is touched upon obliquely in a note to Herzen, and in the article "Party Organization and Party Literature." Even in his extensive correspondence occasional remarks about art and literature are extremely scant. Lenin's consciousness was so occupied with the fundamental problems of the struggle that there remained neither time nor interest for these realms.[11]

The Leninist philosophers whose product we have been sampling succeeded eventually in raising an edifice of authority on these random and "scant" literary opinions. The recollections of Lenin's friends and co-workers were drawn upon for evidence as to his tastes and preferences in literature. It was found that he liked the established classics of Russian and European literature; that he read Pushkin, Tolstoy, Turgenev, Flaubert, and many others, while confessing himself frankly puzzled and even bored by new literary schools and movements such as futurism and acmeism. His tastes might be described as those of a conservative. He was attracted, moreover, chiefly to those Russian authors from whom something could be learned about the social and intellectual life of nineteenth-century Russia; among his favorites were Tolstoy, Saltykov-Shchedrin, Uspenskii, and Chernyshevskii.[12]

He wrote a number of articles on Tolstoy, but these are literary criticism only incidentally, for they deal chiefly with the teaching of Tolstoy in its social significance.[13] In short, Lenin, a political revolutionary, had an acquaintance with literature which was no more than average for a man of his background and education; and the range of his interest was limited.

The wealth bequeathed by Lenin to literary science was to be found neither in his occasional critical comments, nor in his articles on literary figures. That part of his "testament" to which the official philosophers felt themselves drawn in 1931 was contained in his statements concerning the authority of the Party in the literary field. For these statements reveal a preference for strong Party guidance in the area of belles-lettres, and for the Party viewpoint as obligatory at least upon Communist literary men. His most important single article on this subject is one published in *Novaia zhizn'* (New Life) in 1905 and entitled "Party Organization and Party Literature."[14] The importance of this article in the development of literary organization in Russia can hardly be exaggerated. Its basic idea is that literature cannot be free of the social milieu in which it arises, and it is an answer to those groups in the Party who maintained that belles-lettres should be free of direct Party control. The freedom which the bourgeois artist and writer believes in is an illusion, according to Lenin:

To live in a society and be free of it is impossible. The freedom of the bourgeois writer, artist, actress, is only a camouflaged dependence on the moneybag. We socialists expose this hypocrisy, we tear off the false masks, not so as to establish a classless literature and art, for that will be possible only in a classless, socialist society, but in order to substitute for a literature which is hypocritically free but in fact subservient to the *bourgeoisie,* a literature really free, and openly bound to the proletariat.[15]

This statement is of the first importance in understanding the development of the policy of the Central Committee toward the function of literature during the period under discussion. Not only are these words of Lenin referred to with regularity and insistence by literary critics and Party functionaries in their controversies on the role of literature in the reconstruction period, but they are quoted as basic doctrine in authoritative statements on the role of the Party in relation to belles-lettres:

The idea of *partiinost* [Party spirit], that is, an open, honest, direct, and consistent service to the Party as the vanguard and leader of the people—such is the basic proposition of Lenin's article, which lays down the guiding principles of the Bolshevik leadership of Soviet literature.[16]

It can be shown conclusively that not only in 1905 under the conditions of that time, but later, after the success of the 1917 revolution, Lenin's activity and statements indicate a preference for Party guidance in the field of belles-lettres. His statements and his activity were so interpreted as to justify a policy of increasing control on the part of Party organs. These statements do lend themselves easily to such interpretation.[17]

An important instance of Lenin's activity in the direction of establishing the principle of Party dominance in literature has already been mentioned in connection with the Proletcult controversy of 1920.[18] At that time he himself prepared a resolution which was to be passed by the congress of the Proletcult. This resolution, which, he said, "must be prepared with great speed, passed by the Central Committee, and brought before this session of the Proletcult," had the effect of cutting the ground out from under the basic organizational premise of the Proletcult: its independence of state and party organs of culture and enlightenment. The resolution, drafted by Lenin himself, was accepted by the Central Committee at his insistence. There would appear to have been no possibility of its rejection by the congress of the Proletcult. There is no evidence that the latter was consulted. Lunacharskii, the future Commissar of Education, who relates the incident in his memoirs, says that he was commissioned by Lenin to make a speech at the congress insisting on the subordination of the Proletcult to the People's Commissariat of Education, but that, "not wishing to irritate the workers," he had somewhat softened the speech. This would seem to indicate that the policy of the Central Committee was far from meeting the approval of the Proletcult congress.[19] Lenin, impatient with Lunacharskii's vacillation, promptly drafted himself the necessary resolution, which was submitted to the congress and as promptly passed.

A letter published in *Pravda* by the Central Committee shortly after the passage of the resolution explained and justified its action in the following terms:

> The Proletcult arose before the October Revolution. It was announced as an "independent" workers' organization, independent of the Ministry of Public Education of the days of Kerensky. The October Revolution changed all perspectives. The Proletcult continued to be "independent," but now that meant independence from the Soviet power. Because of this and for a number of other reasons, elements hostile to us, *petit-bourgeois* elements, have sometimes in fact seized the leadership of the Proletcult: futurists, decadents, partisans of an idealistic philosophy hostile to Marxism, and simply ne'er-do-wells from the ranks of bourgeois publicists and philosophers. . . . [20]

The letter goes on to make the following point:

> The creative work of the Proletcult should be one of the component parts of the work of the People's Commissariat of Education, as an organ which is building the dictatorship of the proletariat in the field of culture. . . .
>
> From the instructions worked out by the Narkompros [People's Commissariat of Education] and approved by the Central Committee, all comrades who are interested will see that full autonomy . . . in the field of artistic creation is guaranteed. The Central Committee has given exact directives on this point for the guidance of the Narkompros, and will follow up its instructions.[21]

It is perhaps important that in 1920 the Central Committee felt it necessary to mitigate its announced policy of subordination by giving the assurance that "full autonomy" in the field of artistic creation is to be preserved. The exact nature and limits of this area of autonomy are not defined, and it is not easy to reconcile the guarantee of autonomy with the general policy. The letter suggests that perhaps "full autonomy" need not be granted to futurists, "decadents" (does this mean formalists, symbolists, constructivists, imagists, acmeists, or all of these?), writers hostile to Marxism as Lenin interpreted it, and many others whose position was not clearly defined. Thus "full autonomy" is at a stroke of the pen denied to a rather large area of twentieth-century Russian letters. The rest, presumably, might enjoy it.

However, the following points emerge from the whole affair of the Proletcult: (1) It was Lenin's policy that no organization engaged in cultural activity be independent of Soviet power, that is, of the Central Committee. (2) There is no freedom of activity in a Soviet cultural organization for individuals or groups philosophically alien to the Central Committee and in opposition to its policy. (3) "Freedom of artistic creation" is guaranteed by the Central Committee; it (the "freedom") is defined in instructions laid down by the Commissariat of Education and approved by the Central Committee; compliance with these instructions on the part of government organs is to be secured by the Central Committee; the final guarantee of "full autonomy," such as it is, is the vigilance of the Central Committee.

The initiative of Lenin in the affair of the Proletcult set a precedent from which Soviet literature did not ultimately escape. It is important to emphasize it here because of the appeal to Lenin's authority by the Central Committee through its official philosophers, Iudin and Mitin, during the 1931 dispute in philosophy and literature.

In addition to conservatism in form and the "Party spirit" in literature, the idea is prominent in the reminiscences of Lenin left to us by his friends that literature and art should belong to the masses, serve them, and aid in raising their cultural level. Clara Zetkin records that Lenin once said:

> Art belongs to the people. It must send its deepest roots down into the broadest working masses. It must be understandable to them

and near them. It should unify the feelings, thought, and will of these masses, elevate them. It should awaken and develop artists among them.[22]

The Party and the Soviet state had by 1931, as we have already seen, given their full support to the idea of using literature as an educative force, though they wished to give all art a direction and a content not necessarily foreseen by Lenin.

The philosophical representatives of the Central Committee were quite conscious of the real meaning of their Leninist slogans on the need for the "Party spirit" in literature and philosophy. The following paragraph is from a resolution authored by P. Iudin and directed at bearers of false doctrine in philosophy and literature:

Moribund academism, an attempt at a metaphysical distinction between philosophy and politics . . . *failure to acknowledge the Central Committee of the Party as the theoretical center of Marxism-Leninism*—these are the things which characterize the Deborin school in its attitude toward the Party spirit in philosophy.[23]

We have described this discussion solely in terms of its political implications and have given very little space to the ideas contributed by the "new leadership" in philosophy. No doubt more attention could be given to the thinking of these new men. Such a study would, in the opinion of the present writer, be laborious and probably unprofitable. The following paragraph from the resolution cited above is a fair indication of the "philosophical" level of this whole discussion:

The Deborin group's menshevizing idealist propositions, which combined the shortcomings of Feuerbachian materialism, mechanism, and the Kantian dialectic with their own basic theoretical line, which was a Hegelian idealistic distortion of the materialist dialectic . . . also have had a harmful influence on literary science and criticism.

This "new leadership" maintained as we have seen, that their own advent marked a new stage in the development of Marxism-Leninism in the Soviet Union. That is undoubtedly true. Their writings are on a lower level than anything we have seen so far. Their stock in trade is the broad, sweeping, and essentially meaningless declaration, buttressed by citations from authority and defended by accusations of heresy against any and all opponents. They identify themselves with all manner of "positive" concepts: "a new and higher stage," "guarantee the penetration of a genuine Marxism," "the contributions of Lenin to literary science . . . "; their opponents are made to move only in the area of "negative" concepts: "academism," "idealistic distortions," "failure to grasp the significance of . . . ." They pompously affirm the trite, the meaningless, or the false. They never argue, because argument might require the consideration of other possible viewpoints, and this in turn might lead to pregnant thought and the weakening of conviction. The intrusion of the Leninist philosophers upon the literary scene in 1931 marks a further closing of the fist of Party control on Russian intellectual life. These men—the Eidnunens of modern Russia—are not philosophers, scientists, literary men, or critics. They are implacably anti-intellectual. They function simply as reliable instruments of the Party dictatorship.

3. Free Competition of Groups

We have seen that one of the criticisims leveled at the leadership of RAPP in 1930 by the Litfront group was that it had hindered the free development and free competition of various creative tendencies and styles within RAPP. The On Literary Guard leadership had, the Litfront maintained, propagated its own creative method and creative slogans as the "high road" of proletarian literature, while treating as harmful "deviations" from a correct literary "line" any tendency to oppose those slogans. The Litfront had sought to restore within RAPP that "free competition of styles" guaranteed by the 1925 Party resolution on belles-lettres, as well as by the resolutions of the First Congress of Proletarian Writers in 1928.[24]

However, after the "overturn" in philosophy the literary slogans of the RAPP leadership had fallen under a cloud. Psychological realism, it appeared, concealed certain dangers and pitfalls. Therefore in April, 1931, the demand was made once more that there be full and free discussion of questions of form, style, and content, but this time the demand was made by the Party itself through an editorial in *Pravda*. The article pays glowing tribute to proletarian literature as a form of activity which is becoming "a mighty factor . . . for the education and organization of the will of the masses, for raising the level of labor enthusiasm, of shock-work . . . for the struggle with breaks on the labor front . . . which is becoming a mighty factor in socialist construction."[25] It points out that the basic organization on the literary front, carrying out the line of the Party, is RAPP, and that, precisely because it is such an organization, RAPP has a heavy responsibilty to develop self-criticism within its own ranks.

However the leadership has itself made serious mistakes, says *Pravda.* Among these are noted their "erroneous" ideas on the primacy of Plekhanov as a literary theoretician, and the failure to criticize adequately Libedinskii's *Birth of a Hero.* The article then takes up another fault of the RAPP leadership: its tendency to think of its functions as administrative rather than ideological and educational, and the consequent stifling of free competition within RAPP.[26]

Indeed the accusation that the RAPP leadership had gotten a monopolistic position for itself within RAPP and that it ruthlessly discouraged the development of writers whose tastes and preferences in literature were out of harmony with the literary program of Averbakh, Libedinskii, Fadeev, Kirshon, Afinogenov, Chumandrin, and other members of the leading group, is a frequent complaint heard during the year 1931, the justice of which was later admitted by all involved. They tended to regard any deviation from psychological realism as a step backward and a threat to the future hegemony of proletarian literature.

It was certainly, in part, as a result of criticism directed at the leaders of RAPP by the philosophers that a "creative discussion" was opened in the summer of 1931 within RAPP. At this discussion the members of several groups were heard and allowed to contribute their ideas as to how proletarian literature might be enriched.

The discussion was participated in by seven "creative groups." In the course of the meetings a basic cleavage was revealed between those groups which supported or echoed the literary program of the leadership of RAPP and those which departed from it. The most important of the latter was the group led by Panfërov and Il'enkov and called "Panfërov's group." It is clear from the course of the discussion at this time, as well as from the later development of literary polemics within RAPP, that Panfërov and his group had parted company with the RAPP leadership and were attempting to develop a literary method and approach more in tune with the "demands of the reconstruction period." They were in fact devoting their main efforts to works on industrialization and collectivization.

The most important RAPP writers adhering to the Panfërov group were: Stavskii (the future leader of the post-1932 Union of Soviet Writers), Izbakh, Platoshkin, and Gorbatov.[27] The position of Panfërov's group was shared in all important particulars by a Leningrad worker-writer group called Zakal (Tempering). The Smithy occupied an independent position, though it tended to reject the RAPP emphasis on imitation of the classics in favor of working out new forms and, especially, reworking the rich verbal material at the disposal of the proletarians. Three groups supported the On Literary Guard leadership of RAPP: Novaia Kuznitsa (New Smithy), Napostovskaia Smena (On Guard Relief), and Napostovskyi Prizyv (On Guard Summons).[28]

The three last-named groups for the most part repeated the basic propositions of the On Literary Guard leadership as these were expressed in the famous document of the RAPP secretariat.[29] New Smithy declared itself in favor of "themes of the reconstruction period," but laid its emphasis on reflecting in literature "changing productive relations,"[30] and on the portrayal of the "living worker" who bears these changes in himself. It announced that "literature is cognition of life."[31] On Guard Relief, through its spokesman Mitrofanov, enunciated a literary approach which was hardly distinguishable from that of the On Literary Guard group. Mitrofanov spoke up for quality as against tempo, and against narrowing the themes of proletarian literature: "We consider those people vulgarizers who would narrow our subject matter only to themes of the factory and construction."[32] On Guard Summons went right down the line on all the current RAPP slogans.

A quite different note was struck by Tempering and by Panfërov's group, and in their quarrel with the On Literary Guard leadership of RAPP they went right to the heart of the basic disagreement on the nature of literature and of art which had split the ranks of Communist criticism since the days of Voronskii and the early On Guardists. The spokesmen of Tempering considered that proletarian literature consisted of two *distinct currents.* There was first an "older" current represented by such writers as Fadeev, Libedinskii, Chumandrin, and Sholokhov, whose work is characterized by "passive" registration of reality and a contemplative, neutral attitude toward the world. These qualities prevent the works of the authors concerned from developing the greatest possible *tendentiousness* in the spirit of the Party program. Tendentiousness, in the opinion of Tempering, was the basic characteristic needed by proletarian literature in the period of the socialist advance. The second current distinguished by Tempering in proletarian literature was that represented by such authors as Panfërov, Stavskii, Platoshkin, Il'enkov, and others. This group was favored because it laid emphasis on the *active* role of literature, on its proletarian tendentiousness and usefulness to the Party.[33]

Of these two streams the first—the "passive and contemplative" stream—represented the On Literary Guard leadership of RAPP, and the second an opposition to the creative program of that leadership. Moreover, their chief disagreement was on the question of "contemporaneity" of themes: for the second stream laid particular emphasis on "themes of the reconstruction period."[34]

Panfërov's group was represented at the discussion by the novelist Il'enkov, who stated frankly, directly, and simply that the main efforts of his group were being directed toward reflecting the reconstruction period in literature.[35] He stressed the importance of collective work on such subjects, and the importance for the writer of mastering thoroughly some aspect of industry. He recounts the trips to Stalingrad and other places made recently by himself and Panfërov. He concludes: "The way to create a great art of Bolshevism is in the fire of socialist reconstruction."[36]

The *Pravda* editorial which preceded this discussion had called upon the RAPP leadership to make sure that the best possible conditions were created for the work of Panfërov's group. To some extent this directive would seem to have been complied with, although the leading product of that group, *Driving Axle*, was attacked by the On Literary Guardists as soon as it appeared. The secretariat of RAPP soon took action, however, against the second opposition group, Tempering. The secretariat issued a resolution condemning the theory of the "two currents" as an attempt to belittle one section of proletarian literature to the advantage of another section of the same literary movement. Tempering abandoned the theory as erroneous.[37] Herein we see the advantage possessed by the On Literary Guardists in that they were at one and the same time a "creative group" and also the leadership of RAPP. This is what was meant by the "monopolistic position" of Averbakh and his group.

The "creative discussion" within RAPP had, however, clearly revealed the existence of a determined and important opposition to the literary theory and program of its leaders. This opposition to Averbakh believed that the proletarian literary movement should devote itself with greater energy to the reflection and inspiration of the reconstruction period. Party spokesmen were inclined to favor its program.

4. Literary Pronouncements of the Marxist "Youth"

Shortly after the opening of the "creative discussion" within RAPP, the organ of the Komsomol (Youth League), *Komsomol'skaia pravda* (Young Communist Truth), began to publish articles attacking the dominant group in RAPP. The questions at issue in this voluminous controversy may be briefly summarized. The leaders of the Youth League made the following points:

1. They criticized as harmful and misleading the RAPP slogan "Overtake and Surpass the Classics."[38] For the prole-

tarian writer, armed with the world view of Marxism, was, they said, already ideologically far in advance of the classics of bourgeois and landlord literature.

2. They were against the continued use of the "living man" slogan and the approach to working-class themes which it represented. Because of this slogan, they said, workers of the reconstruction period were being portrayed by the same methods used to portray "intellectual weaklings."

3. They objected to the manner in which the leadership had conducted the "creative discussion," characterizing its behavior as an attempt to evade issues.

4. They took exception to the speech of Fadeev at the last plenum of RAPP. In this speech Fadeev had referred to Tolstoy and quoted Stendhal, and he had recommended that the proletarian writer pay more attention to the *psychological changes* taking place in workers: their changed attitudes toward religion and death, among other things. He had urged the importance of mastering the "great ideas of Marxism-Leninism" and had quoted Stendhal on the decline of Italian literature: "Italian literature declined because it lacked a great idea." The spokesmen of the Youth League accused Fadeev of substituting the "eternal problems of life and death" for the burning present-day problems of socialism.[39]

5. The Youth League, in condemning the ideas of Fadeev, expressed its preference for the approach and method of Panfërov and his group.[40]

6. They objected to the use of the slogan "for the removal of masks."[41]

The criticisms of the Communist Youth organ were answered by Averbakh personally and were dealt with point by point in a special resolution of the RAPP secretariat. Averbakh expressed himself as opposed to attempts being made at the moment to convert RAPP into an administrative body, and to have it assume the functions of other government and Party organs. He calls this a "leftist program of monopoly" which is contrary to Party policy, and by implication he ascribes such a leftist program to the Youth League itself.[42] He scornfully rejects the criticism directed against Fadeev as an ignorant distortion of the latter's remarks at the RAPP plenum.[43] He dismisses as evidence of "Communist conceit" the idea that proletarian writers are already in a position to "surpass the classics." He says that the ideological and artistic level of the proletarians is still very low, and characterizes the Youth League position as an attempt at a theoretical justification of the low cultural level and refusal to study of those writers who have "transformed themselves into classics of proletarian literature." He regards the Youth League approach as another attempt of the "varnishers" to have proletarian literature evade "the torment and the troubles" which accompany forward movement.[44]

Many observers of this dispute felt when they looked back upon it from the vantage point of 1932 that the quarrel with the Youth League really marked the beginning of the end for the RAPP leadership.[45] And that is certainly the case. At this point it is already becoming quite clear that the days of Averbakh are numbered. We shall soon see that the Party itself intervened in this dispute and that it *supported the position of the Youth League.*

5. Defense of RAPP

The principal "error" of the RAPP theoreticians had been their failure to "grasp" the Leninist "Party spirit" of literature. That is why they had lagged behind and were, to some extent, not carrying out the "literary tasks of the day." A word used fairly frequently to characterize their position in literary theory and practice is "objectivism," and this attitude the philosophers and other opposition groups sharply contrast with the "partisanship" which is to be demanded of literature in its new, higher, Leninist phase. The idea of revealing in literature the "living man" and of "tearing the masks" from reality, of showing forth in art "immediate impressions of the real world," indeed the whole emphasis on realism as the leading people in RAPP understood it, is now characterized as a harmful heresy with its source in the writings of Plekhanov and Deborin.[46]

The criticism of the new leadership in philosophy and of the "youth," which enjoyed at this time the support of the Central

Committee, had its effect upon the activity of RAPP. There was, however, no wholesale admission of errors. Averbakh defended his colleagues Libedinskii, Fadeev, and Ermilov with spirit. He was still defending himself and them six months after the dissolution of RAPP, a type of behavior which brought down upon him accusations of "egotism" and "unwillingness to admit his errors."

In defending RAPP against the accusation of "Deborinism" Averbakh points out that the Deborin school had until recently been the most influential group in the philosophical field and that its influence had appeared not only in RAPP, but in many other sectors of the ideological front.[47] He admits that Libedinskii had been mistaken in his idea of "immediate·impressions." He grants that the movement had been mistaken in raising such a slogan as "for Plekhanov orthodoxy!" but points out that "we do not throw Plekhanov overboard completely," for there is much that is valuable in his teaching.[48] On the use of Deborin by RAPP theoreticians, he admits that they had occasionally quoted him, but "that is no crime."[49] And he declares that, after all, the influence of Deborin was not important in the movement, and that RAPP critics were among the first to attack certain adherents of the Deborin school.[50] He has no patience with the critical method employed by the philosophers, who searched the writings of their opponents in their pursuit of "erroneous" quotations.[51]

At this point Averbakh and some of the other leaders of RAPP took the viewpoint that literary problems were the province of literary specialists and that Party workers who had no special training in literature could add little to the discussion then in progress. The new leaders in philosophy complained of such arrogance. In a *Pravda* article they accused RAPP of having developed a "general line" in literature which it defended as the "RAPP line" as distinct from the *Party* line. They also complained that the efforts of Party workers to aid in the solution of RAPP's problems were not welcomed:

A number of workers in RAPP have tried to represent the field of literature and criticism as a matter exclusively for specialists. Thus Comrade Averbakh refers in a most haughty manner to those Party workers who, though not specialists in the field of literature, have tried on the basis of the Party understanding of the theory of Marxism-Leninism to help raise proletarian literature to a higher level.[52]

Averbakh's answer to those who thus proffered literature a helping hand was: "One must have at least an elementary knowledge of the business before he sticks his nose in it."[53]

But the new leaders in philosophy continued their work of ferreting out heresies in RAPP through 1931, and even after the dissolution of RAPP in 1932, Iudin and others continued to publish articles and write brochures in which the works of Averbakh were examined microscopically for quotations which, given out of context, could be used to convict him of theoretical unsoundness.[54] However, their basic charge, that Averbakh and the other theoreticians of RAPP had been influenced in their work by Plekhanov, was never denied and could not be.

6. Action of the Party

The disputes with the Youth League and the "new leadership" in philosophy had continued through most of the year 1931. Near the end of that year the Party itself intervened unmistakably on the side of those who had censured RAPP.

The Party criticism of RAPP was contained in two articles which appeared in *Pravda.* The first of these, authored by G. Vasilkovskii, offers the thesis that under RAPP's leadership proletarian literature has not answered the demand of the working class for literary productions "worthy of the socialist epoch."[55] It calls for the development of "genuine self-criticism" in RAPP, for freedom of literary "groupings" and genuine creative competition within the organization. It calls attention once more to RAPP theoretical errors and deplores the failure to accept wholeheartedly the criticism of the philosophers.[56]

This article was simply ignored by the RAPP leaders. It was neither reprinted nor commented on in any way in the magazine *On Literary Guard.* Of all the recent "mistakes" of the RAPP leadership this was regarded as one of the most serious. Another editorial statement on the work of RAPP appeared two weeks later in *Pravda*, this time under the signature of L. Mekhlis, secretary of the editorial board of *Pravda*, and there could be no doubt that the *Pravda* statement carried the weight of directive.

The Mekhlis article states that the RAPP leadership was mistaken in not reacting to the "correct" article of Vasilkovskii, and thus endorses all the criticism of RAPP which that article contained.[57] Mekhlis agrees with one of the main contentions of the Youth League: that RAPP had not properly conducted the "creative discussion," and had not provided for genuine freedom of competition among the RAPP groups. Under the circumstances, he complains, the work of such a creative group as that of Panfërov is extremely difficult. This, of course, has already been pointed out in *Pravda*. It thus becomes abundantly clear that when *Pravda* speaks of "freedom of groupings" in RAPP it has in mind first of all the interests of Panfërov's group, which has departed from the literary slogans of the leadership and is now bitterly at odds with it. In other words, the RAPP leadership is being called upon to refrain from doing anything which will interfere with the work of Panfërov and with the development of his literary method, a method designed to answer the demand of the Party for a literature devoted to topical themes.[58]

Mekhlis, too, gives a catalogue of "errors." He rejects the RAPP emphasis on "learning from the classics"; he censures their inordinate praise of Bednyi,[59] whose "Get off the Stove!" was, he says, a coarse attack on the Russian people; he deplores the sharp criticism of Panfërov; and he returns once again to Libedinskii's *Birth of a Hero* as an important symptom of the faults of RAPP:

> In it we have an emigration from the class battles of the proletariat in the direction of eternal problems and the eternal laws of human development. And this idealistic rubbish has been praised by some people (Ermilov has been "at his post" here, too) as a sign that the author has mastered the dialectical-materialist method.[60]

Mekhlis also feels that the work on the portrayal of heroes has been vitiated by the tendency to cultivate Libedinskii's type of psychological analysis, which only leads into a "philistine swamp."[61]

Mekhlis believes that what is required in the work of proletarian writers is "planning." "It is a question of living down the relics of bourgeois freebooting, as a result of which some of the most important problems of socialist construction have not found their reflection in proletarian literature."[62] He concludes:

> The burning problems of the day, which are moving the masses, should be raised to a high political level . . . and deserve to be clarified in every way. . . .
>
> The most important problems of the present day cannot be ignored by the proletarian writers.[63]

Apparently there was no answer which the leaders of RAPP could make to this editorial statement other than to take immediate action in the direction of correcting those faults which it pointed out. The same issue of the *Literary Gazette* which carried the Mekhlis article printed also a statement of the RAPP secretariat to the effect that it agreed completely with the article in question (!), and the announcement that a plenum of RAPP would soon be called to discuss the problems involved.[64]

7. Kaganovich and the "Literary *Magnitostroi*"

The deliberations of the Fifth and last Plenum of RAPP (December, 1931) proceeded under the inspiring banner of the slogan "for a *Magnitostroi* of literature." The meaning of this is not immediately clear, and will have to be explored. The general import is that Soviet literary works should be comparable somehow to giant industrial projects, such as *Magnitostroi* in the Ural mountains. The slogan is often ascribed to the RAPP leadership and offered as evidence of their oversimplification of literary problems, their exclusive emphasis on the need for portraying the Five-Year Plan in literature, and their regimentation of the literary world.

The fact is that this slogan together with the particular kind of emphasis which it represented was quite uncongenial to the On Literary Guard leadership and was not invented by Averbakh nor by any of his associates, but was given to them by the Party itself. The person to whom credit must be given for this slogan is a member of the Politburo of the Communist Party, L. D. Kaganovich. In the course of a meeting with literary men, Kaganovich had remarked: "What we need is a *Magnitostroi* of literature."[65] And there is no doubt that what he meant was not simply great literary works as monumental as the industrial giants being created in the Soviet Union, but literary works *dealing with* these industrial giants and describing the mighty developments of industrialization and collectivization. That is the way the slogan was understood by Panfërov, by Troitskii of the Youth League, and by the RAPP writer Stavskii, who quotes Kaganovich as complaining that "more is written abroad about the 'new Moscow' than is written by all the proletarian writers and journalists taken together."[66] And Stavskii, in an article written shortly after the Fifth Plenum, said:

> The slogan "for a *Magnitostroi* of literature," given to us by the secretary of the Central Committee Kaganovich, which deepens and further develops the basic creative slogans of the movement, places before us the task of strengthening our literary activity on themes of the period of socialism and the portrayal of the heroes of labor.[67]

It was under the inspiration of this personality that the Fifth Plenum of RAPP proceeded. There was now no room for doubt that it had been called because of Party dissatisfaction with the work of RAPP. Said *Pravda:*

> The calling of this Plenum was the result of the realization that a decisive reconstruction in the work of RAPP was necessary. This realization developed as a result of the discussion with the Youth League and of directives of the Party to the effect that RAPP lags behind the tasks of the contemporary stage of socialist construction.[68]

The realization that the Party's patience with the RAPP leadership was rapidly running out is clearly shown in the speeches of the writers and critics who participated in the sessions. In fact it would seem that all bars were down so far as criticism of Averbakh and his friends was concerned: both the old and recent enemies of *On Literary Guard* took the occasion to unburden themselves of a resentment which had long rankled in them. The bitterest antagonists of Averbakh were

Bezymenskii and Panfërov, both of whom had recently suffered for their advocacy of a literary method not to the liking of the On Literary Guardists. And for the first time in these discussions it is broadly hinted by both of these writers that the reason for RAPP's performance lies deeper than most people suppose, and that there is something "wrong" in the leadership which cannot be explained merely as the result of "errors" made in good faith. In the speeches of Panfërov and Bezymenskii at this meeting we find a vague suggestion of the later charges that Averbakh and some of his people were "enemies" and hostile "agents."[69]

The most important speeches at the Plenum were those of Troitskii, chairman of the Central Committee of the Youth League, of Panfërov, and of Averbakh. A brief consideration of these three speeches will serve to illustrate the points which were at issue on the eve of the dissolution of RAPP.

Troitskii once more points out that in its conduct of the literary discussion the RAPP leadership had behaved in a spirit of lamentable "clannishness," and had taken upon itself the role of one of the disputants instead of the leader of the dispute. The result of this was the tendency to treat purely literary disagreements as deviations from the Party line.[70] It is inexcusable that the leaders of RAPP, which is now a mass organization, should behave as they did in the days when they were only a small group fighting for recognition, concludes the Youth League leader. Moreover, the leaders of RAPP did not understand the great growth in the demands of the masses, and the fact that the youth and the Party had turned their attention to literature. They did not welcome the interest of these masses in the literary field; they said to them in effect: "Don't push your dirty faces into our exceptionally subtle and delicate area of activity."[71] They arrogantly advised the young Communists to "devote a little more time to study," and to be careful lest they smash "the delicate instrument of literature."[72] Such an attitude was indeed inadmissible in the mass organization of proletarian literature. Troitskii sums up the results of the whole discussion. RAPP, he says, had failed to take into consideration the new demands upon literature arising from its growth in significance as a Party weapon in the fight for socialism.[73]

Panfërov's speech is especially interesting as a statement from the leader of that group which Party spokesmen now demanded that the RAPP leaders treat with special tenderness. He now not only makes clear the attitude of that group toward the leadership of RAPP and its literary approach, but he contributes an exceptionally illuminating statement of the new ideas worked out by the members of his own creative group, especially by himself and Il'enkov.

The first part of his speech Panfërov devotes to what he regards now as an established fact: the leadership of RAPP had not properly carried out the directives of the Party.[74] He then describes at length his own experiences during the summer at Kuznetsstroi.[75] He describes his close contact with the workers there and their enthusiasm for the job; he sketches the man in charge of the construction and his creative enthusiasm for the whole project.[76] On the new slogan, "for a *Magnitostroi* of literature," he says:

I must say that to write about the present day is considerably more difficult than to write about yesterday. I must also say that a number of comrades, in attempting to equate the slogans "for a great art of Bolshevism" and "for a *Magnitostroi* of literature" are destroying the sharpness and the point of the latter slogan. For if the slogan "for a great art of Bolshevism" has reference not only to today but to yesterday also, the slogan "for a *Magnitostroi* of literature" places its emphasis mainly on the material of today. Using the current and timely material of the present day to show the great ideas of our time means to contribute productions of high artistic form; otherwise you will not express the great ideas of our epoch. Emphasis on *today*, that's what you must understand. No "*Magnitostroi* of literature" will you give us if you evade and avoid the material of the present day, using the material of yesterday.

At this point Averbakh interrupted Panfërov, remarking, very significantly: "We will give them. Without fail." Panfërov continued:

We will see how you give them. Don't dull the edge of the new slogan. We are finishing the Five-Year Plan and what is there in literature about the Five-Year Plan? You know that in a kind of way we did reflect the heroism of the civil war, but what do we have about the Bolshevik heroism on the front of economic construction? . . . Don't wait ten or fifteen years, but give us a literature about *Magnitostroi* along with the construction of Magnitogorsk.[77]

Recognizing that creation of such a literature at the tempos expected is extremely difficult, Panfërov believed the solution lay in the direction of *collective* literary labor within a "creative group."[78] On this point there were bitter exchanges between Panfërov and Libedinskii, who objected that working in a collective group would crush the individuality of writers. The extreme violence of the "literary" disagreements at this meeting is suddenly lighted up for us when Panfërov answers that Libedinskii's attitude is like that of the individualist peasants who refused to join the collective farms.[79]

Panfërov violently attacks those figures in the proletarian literary movement who are given to the writing of declarations and platforms. He refuses to submit a platform or statement of principles for his group, for, he says, their literary works will constitute their only platform.[80] He asks the question: "Who among us is against the groups?" and answers it himself:

Those of us who do not yet fully understand the significance of the rebuilding of RAPP, those for whom RAPP is only an actor's dressing room; those who still remain feeble individualists; those who have come into proletarian literature only by accident, who can write only hackneyed unnecessary resolutions and who know that when RAPP is reorganized and creative groups are formed they will be thrown out of the organization like rubbish, like chinch bugs; those who are not one with the great ideas of our age and who have a secret contempt for our socialist reality; those who only look upon literature as a job providing them with an income . . . and those who are timid in their thinking.[81]

In such strong language does the novelist Panfërov describe his erstwhile close associates, the leaders of RAPP; for there could be no doubt that the reference here is to the secretariat of that organization, and in particular its chief member, Leopol'd Averbakh.

The latter, according to his unbroken custom, made a spirited defense of the policies of RAPP and attacked the opposition with great vigor, irony, and vicious sarcasm.[82] The fact that the Central Committee of the Party itself had now joined that opposition did not cause him to soften or abate his attack.

As a text for his remarks Averbakh took a passage from the works of the late V. M. Friche, in which the latter had advanced the idea that in the stage of industrial development under capitalism and in the socialist order which grows out of it, man becomes primarily rational. Mathematics and science take the place of religion. Art, which is a form of intellectual life midway between science and religion, will die out, except as an adornment of life. Averbakh does not, of course, agree with this. He maintains that the ideas of Friche are the chief theoretical justification for the development of LEF and Litfront ideas about art; and these ideas, he claims, would liquidate art in favor of lower forms of agitation and propaganda.[83] Since he had already identified the current enemies of RAPP with LEF and the Litfront,[84] the reference here was perfectly clear: the literary "experts" of the Youth League and the new leadership in philosophy would liquidate genuine art in favor of agitation and propaganda.

Still not referring directly to the Youth League, the philosophers, or to Kaganovich, but concentrating his fire ostensibly on the already defunct LEF and Litfront groups, he compared their program for art with that of Adolf Hitler. He quotes Hitler as one supporter of the idea that "we don't need all kinds of psychological analysis. What we need is an 'art of the day,' an art of slogans, of agitation, an art of the daily newspaper." Once again, the initiate could not miss his point: he had already stated that the present attack on RAPP was a recrudescence of Litfront and LEF ideas.[85] What, then, is to be said of those personages who are *now* dissatisfied with the RAPP program?

Might it not be said with some justice that they knew nothing of literature and its special problems? Averbakh had already said just that in referring to the "youth" and the "philosophers": "Don't butt in on something of which you haven't even an elementary knowledge." And Mekhlis? Is such a person competent to pass judgment on literary problems? It was not possible for Averbakh to ask this question in so many words, but he managed to convey the idea very well through innuendo, indirection, and hints. In the first place, Mekhlis, said Averbakh, had made a "mistake" in calling for the inclusion of proletarian writers in the "Leninist stage"; for RAPP really began the criticism of Plekhanov and others who deviated from Lenin's ideas.[86] It is established, then, that Mekhlis, too, can make mistakes. In what field would such a man as Mekhlis—an administrator, publicist, and propagandist—be especially prone to error? In literature, very likely. Such is Averbakh's thought, and it is not hard to follow, though it is deviously expressed:

> In my criticism of Comrade Mekhlis on the question of empiricism there was no offense meant. I have taken and I still take the viewpoint that against Comrade Mekhlis I may cite the greater authority of Goethe, not because Goethe is a dialectical materialist—on the contrary, Comrade Mekhlis is a dialectical materialist and Goethe is not—but because Goethe is a great artist whose statements on questions of artistic method and artistic creation have greater weight than his.[87]

What is Averbakh's opinion on the direct intervention of the Central Committee in literary life as represented by the slogan contributed to Soviet literature by Kaganovich? Here, too, it is impossible for Averbakh to express his idea forthrightly and clearly. But express it he must. He does so—by indirection:

> We have a situation now in which slogans are given to us in the name of the Party. In the past it was said that the Party granted full freedom in creative questions. This creative slogan represents something quite different in comparison with what we used to say. But to answer this way is to give only a half-answer. With what aspects of our practical experience is that slogan connected? Who paved the way to such a slogan, whose practical experience prepared the material so that the Party might give such a slogan? That is how the question ought to be stated. We answer that our old creative slogans have turned out to be basically correct, and that they withstand examination in the light of the latest slogan of the Party. . . . [88]

This statement must be interpreted in the light of the effort now being made by Averbakh and others to equate the latest Party slogan with the old RAPP slogan "for a great art of Bolshevism!" Panfërov had objected to this procedure as destroying the point and blunting the meaning of the slogan given by Kaganovich. Averbakh says, in effect, that if the policy of freedom on literary questions as enunciated in the resolution of the Politburo of July, 1925, is to be abandoned and the Party is now giving directives on "questions of form and style," it is only because of the practical experience of the On Literary Guardists and their long struggle for a genuine literature that the Party slogan can have any meaning and any real value for proletarian literature. In this same context he disputes with those who deny the role of the On Literary Guardists in building RAPP into a mass organization and claim that credit should be given to the Party leadership. This is not so, says Averbakh. Such successes have been achieved in literature through the labor of the On Guard group.[89] Credit should be given to the *literary men* themselves, who have known how to carry on the fight.

Unless an attempt is made to interpret it in this way, the speech of Averbakh at this meeting is completely unintelligible gibberish. The following interpretation of his remarks is offered: "We do not welcome the direct interference of the Central Committee in literary work. Literary men, under the over-all guidance of the Party, should be the judges of literary questions and should formulate literary policies (don't stick your noses in!). But if the Party is now giving us slogans we must realize that it is only because of *our* previous work in this field that such a slogan can be given real meaning and be useful to literary men."

The fear is expressed at this last Plenum that the leaders of RAPP have no real intention of reforming. Troitskii believed that the leadership only wanted to talk about reforms and to admit "errors" formally without any real attempt to correct them. He cites a number of articles which had recently appeared characterizing the participants in the Youth League discussion as "varnishers" and Litfrontists.[90] In view of all this, he says, the speeches of the leaders sound rather insincere. And indeed they do.

Shortly after the close of the Fifth Plenum, Kirshon published an article in *Pravda* under the title "For a Great Art of Bolshevism." He said:

> The ideas of the "left vulgarizers" have arisen in proletarian literature before; the theory of the left opposition which would reduce all literature to propaganda and the contents of today's newspaper is, in essence, a theory for the liquidation of art.
>
> . . . .

We are in favor of material of the present day and for timeliness in artistic works. We consider that the basic tempos of our creation ought to be the tempos of socialist construction. We have fought for proletarian works about the revolution and against the avoidance of revolutionary themes. We have fought for the Party spirit in literature and against "classless creation." . . .

But we are against those who would oppose material of the present day and timeliness to ideological saturation, to the creation of generalized types, to philosophical depth. And we are against those who, vulgarly understanding the slogan of "activity" and political timeliness in a work of art, suppose that *all* our work should be reduced to the contents of today's newspaper, written on themes of the present day, and written not later than tomorrow. We consider that such people are liquidators of literature.[91]

On the manner of representing the workers Kirshon has the following to say:

The social map of the country is changing, and man is changing. For all is accomplished by him and through him. In rebuilding, he himself is rebuilt. His psychology is changing. Yet the accursed traditions, habits, and prejudices of the past are still not overcome in very many people who have already ideologically joined in the building of socialism. *Petit-bourgeois* influences make themselves felt even in some sections of the Party and the Young Communist League. . . . The proletarian comes from village to factory and he grows and develops; but anyone who thinks this growth is easy and peaceful and simple is badly mistaken. And the proletarian collective must carry on continuous war for the education of these cadres.

In answer to the Youth League charge that RAPP methods mean treating workers as though they were "intellectuals" he says:

We are fighting not to burden the worker with the intellectual's contradictions, but for the portrayal of the real psychology of the proletarian in all its complexity, many-sidedness, and individuality, for the fact that the working class is a "collective" does not at all signify that it is cast in one mold and may be reduced to a single type.[92]

A resolution was passed by the Fifth Plenum recommending, among other things, changes in the organizational structure of RAPP which would reduce the burden of administrative work on writers and give them more time for creative work. It recommended also that the development of Panfërov's group be encouraged, and that a concrete Marxist criticism be worked out. It admitted the correctness of the recent Party criticism of RAPP. It accepted the new slogan "given to us by the Party." It said: "The slogan 'for *Magnitostrois* of literature,' which has been given to us by the Party, correctly orients proletarian writers for a struggle with left and right capitulators, and for the creation of 'a great art of Bolshevism!' "[93]

But the Party was still far from satisfied with the situation on its literary front.

Chapter XI

The Party Liquidates Its Instrument

1. The Official Documents

On April 23, 1932, the Central Committee issued a resolution dissolving the proletarian organizations in literature and the arts. The resolution read as follows:

> The Central Committee ascertains that, as a result of the considerable successes of socialist construction, literature and art have, in the past few years, exhibited a considerable growth, both in quality and quantity.
>
> Some years ago, when literature was still under the strong influence of certain alien elements, which flourished particularly in the first years of NEP, and when the ranks of proletarian literature were still comparatively feeble, the Party helped, by every means in its power, in the creation of special proletarian organizations in the spheres of literature and art, with a view to strengthening the position of proletarian writers and art workers.
>
> Now that the cadres of proletarian literature have had time to grow, and new writers have come forward from factories, mills, and collective farms, the framework of the existing literary organizations (VOAPP, RAPP, RAPM, etc.) has become too narrow and holds back the serious growth of literary creation. This situation creates the danger that these organizations may be transformed from a means for the greater mobilization of Soviet writers and artists around the tasks of socialist construction into a means for the cultivation of group insulation, for isolation from the political tasks of the day, and from those significant groups of writers and artists who now sympathize with the aims of socialist construction.
>
> Hence the necessity for an appropriate reorganization of the literary-artistic associations and for the extension of the basis of their work.

Therefore the Central Committee resolves:

1) To liquidate the Association of Proletarian Writers (VOAPP, RAPP);

2) To unite all writers upholding the platform of the Soviet power and striving to participate in Socialist construction into a single Union of Soviet Writers with a Communist fraction therein;

3) To promote a similar change in the sphere of other forms of art;

4) To entrust the Organizing Bureau with the working out of practical measures for the application of this resolution.[1]

The fact that this decision was Stalin's personal contribution to the development of Russian literature was revealed two years later by Kaganovich, who said, at the Seventeenth Congress of the Communist Party:

A group of Communist writers, taking advantage of RAPP as an organizational instrument, incorrectly utilized the power of their Communist influence on the literary front, and instead of unifying and organizing around RAPP the broad masses of writers, held back and impeded the development of the writers' creative powers. . . .

It might have been possible to bring out a big resolution on the tasks of the Communists in literature; it might have been possible to suggest that the RAPP people alter their policy. But this might have remained merely a good intention. Comrade Stalin posed the question differently: it is necessary, he said, to alter the situation in an organizational way.[2]

A *Pravda* editorial published a short time after the decision to liquidate RAPP is at some pains to explain the motivation for this action. Let us examine this document also:

The decisive successes of socialist construction in the last few years have occasioned a decisive transition of the overwhelming majority of the old technical intelligentsia to the side of the Soviet power, a clear and consistent transition to this position of the greatest scholars of the land, who are giving their great knowledge to the cause of socialism, as shown in part by the fact that the All-Union Academy of Sciences has turned in the direction of working on the contemporary tasks of socialist construction.

In the field of literature this change has been evidenced by the active participation of the broad cadres of writers in socialist construction, and has found its expression in their artistic production (Leonov, Tikhonov, Shaginian, Malyshkin, and others). . . . [3]

The organizational structure of the literary and artistic organizations does not answer to the new conditions and new tasks of Soviet literature, especially since elements of clannishness, and administrative methods, in spite of directives from the Party itself, have not been overcome. . . .

Among the most glaring mistakes of a literary character is the insistence on individual psychology. On the basis of this was evolved the idealistic theory of the living man, more fully formulated in the thesis: "The world is man."[4] This conclusion was closely bound up with the following methodological formulation: "The analysis of individual psychology is the best road to the understanding of social psychology" (Averbakh, *O zadachakh proletarskoi literatury*). . . .

Gross political errors were also made with relation to the fellow-travelers. On the pages of *On Literary Guard* there was cultivated a clearly leftist slogan: "Not fellow-traveler, but ally or enemy!" . . .

Such an approach to the task of remaking and reeducating the fellow-travelers radically contradicts the line of the Party. . . . [5]

2. Averbakh's Polemic against the Liquidation

The reaction of the RAPP leaders to the Politburo decision dissolving their organization appears to have been one of consternation, sheer disbelief, and, finally, indignation. The issue of *On Literary Guard* which appeared on May 10, 1932, more than two weeks after the dissolution was announced in *Pravda*, did not even print the news. When the editors were taxed with this omission, they offered the excuse that that issue had been on the presses and could not be withdrawn. This was shown to be a falsehood, and the editors later printed a statement to the effect that their failure to publish the resolution had been a "mistake."[6]

The *Literary Gazette*, at this time edited by Selivanovskii, did not reprint the resolution in its issue of April 23, 1932. The resolution of the Politburo was not reprinted by Selivanovskii until the issue of May 11, and even then it was accompanied by an editorial which, it would seem quite deliberately, de-emphasized the *dissolution* of RAPP. This editorial statement explained the new policy as one which meant "broadening the framework of proletarian literary organizations so as to include all talented writers," and overlooked the crucial point that "proletarian" organizations as such had been completely done away with.[7] It also pointed out that RAPP had "contributed much" to Soviet literature, a position which was found to be quite inadmissible at this time. Selivanovskii submitted his resignation as editor of the *Literary Gazette* on May 23, 1932.[8]

It would seem that this strange behavior of the important RAPP publications was due in part to the failure of the leadership to understand that the resolution really meant what it said. Even when the word "liquidation" was finally admitted as a reality, they attempted to interpret it as meaning merely a broadening and strengthening of the activity of *their* organization.[9] When the real meaning of what had happened finally became clear, the anger and sense of wrong felt by the RAPP leaders was expressed in a polemic against the Politburo resolution.

We have seen that the issue of *On Literary Guard* which appeared on May 10 failed even to print the resolution. The next issue printed the resolution together with the explanatory article which appeared in *Pravda* on May 9, 1932, and which we have already examined.[10] Immediately following these there appeared an article by the editors of *On Literary Guard* entitled "Answer to the Critics." This article was ostensibly an answer to criticism of RAPP which had appeared earlier in *Pravda*, the work of a "brigade" from the Institute of Red Professors which had recently been seeking out "errors" in the critical literature of RAPP.[11] But the "Answer to the Critics" appears in Averbakh's magazine immediately after the official resolution calling for RAPP's liquidation, and thus occupies space which would normally be given to comment on so important a statement of the Party. There is little room for doubt, therefore, that it was printed as an answer, not to the Red Professors, but to the Politburo itself. The article in question was recognized as such and bitterly commented on some days later in the *Literary Gazette*.[12] Open debate with Stalin was not possible for the leaders of proletarian literature, but Averbakh seems to have used this rather transparent device in order to publicize indirectly a criticism of the Party's literary program. This is one more evidence of the opposition to Stalin which we have already seen operating beneath the surface in RAPP.

What is the answer to Stalin's liquidation of RAPP? The critics are accused of intolerable methods in argumentation: of basing their case on false conclusions reached by tearing quotations out of context.[13] This, of course, was a favorite method of the "philosopher" Iudin, and the *Pravda* article on the liquidation of RAPP also bases some conclusions on quotations given out of their original context. Thus the not uncommon method of argument by "citation" which had been used against RAPP for some time is roundly condemned by the editors of *On Literary Guard*, even when its practitioner is *Pravda*.[14]

The editors managed in their "Answer" to speak their final word on the question of "publicism" in art. The "brigade" of professors had found fault with RAPP cricitism as too much under the influence of the idealistic theories of Plekhanov. An example of such idealism the Red Professors had found in a criticism of the Smithy writer Zhiga published in *On Literary Guard*, where Zhiga's strength as a "publicist" was contrasted with his weakness as an artist. The editors of *On Literary Guard* answer:

> This defense of publicism in art is in essence a repetition of the LEF and Litfront refrain. It always occurs where the artist is powerless to portray in images the phenomena of reality. The theory of the publicistic function of art is essentially hostile to proletarian art and to proletarian literary science.[15]

This must be taken as the answer of the RAPP leaders to the Party demand for a literature reflecting and aiding the great work of reconstruction, and the formulation of that demand in the slogan "for a *Magnitostroi* of literature."

We have already seen that Averbakh took exception to the interference in the literary field of Party figures who knew nothing about literature and its special problems. Such had been his attitude at the time of the dispute with the Youth League and the philosophers; and he had gently hinted that the secretary of the *Pravda* editorial board, Mekhlis, was no competent authority on literature. The concluding paragraphs of his "Answer" to the Politburo resolution dissolving RAPP again emphasize this point:

> In answering our critics we have been forced not only to explain basic principles of literary theory and to expose peculiar methods

of citation and primitive argumentation, but also to analyze errors which result from ignorance by the critics of the most elementary propositions of Marxist-Leninist literary theory, and their insufficient acquaintance with the situation on the literary front.

This insufficient acquaintance of the authors with basic questions . . . can only be explained by their failure to master completely the experience of the theoretical struggle accumulated in the fight for Leninism, for the general line of the Party in the proletarian literary movement.[16]

This "Answer to the Critics" was soon recognized for what it really was, namely, an answer to the dissolution of RAPP.[17] It was not quite Averbakh's final word. At the meeting of the Organization Committee of the new Union of Soviet Writers in October, 1932, Averbakh was given the floor along with other former leaders of RAPP. It was clearly expected of him that he would admit his errors in "true Bolshevik fashion" and thereby aid in the reorganization of literature.[18] He did admit some errors, but the main burden of his speech is a defense of the past activity of RAPP, and particularly its understanding of the dialectical-materialist method.

3. Why Was RAPP Dissolved?

We have seen the documents which set forth and explain the action of the Central Committee in dissolving RAPP. Though we have already had occasion to observe that such statements are often but slight help as a guide to the meaning of policy, yet it must be admitted that the present documents do inadvertently throw light on the reasons for the dissolution of RAPP.

A. *"It was an impediment to the growth of literature."* The Central Committee resolution is extremely revealing in both what it does say and what it does not say. It confirms the evidence that the Party had given a special place to the proletarian literary organizations, that is, to RAPP. It declares that under the leadership of RAPP not only has the proletarian literary movement been very successful, but literature and art have in general "exhibited considerable growth, both in quality and quantity." But what practical conclusion does the Central Committee draw from this? That the activity of RAPP should be further supported and its leaders perhaps rewarded? Quite the contrary. It concludes that RAPP should be liquidated.

Why? Because the existing literary organizations hold back "the serious growth of literary creation." This is not necessarily a contradiction, for it might have been argued that without RAPP there would have been an even more luxuriant growth. And perhaps the authorities had reason to believe that the continued existence of separate proletarian organizations would hamper and impede the *future* "growth" of literature. The resolution points clearly to the danger that these organizations may not mobilize writers "around the tasks of socialist construction," and may isolate themselves from the "political tasks of the day." Here we see revealed once more the Party's overriding concern with the practical uses of literature.

That the danger indicated in the Politburo resolution was indeed a real one is now quite clear. RAPP had resisted and at times discouraged the "mobilization" of writers; because they did have some experience as writers the proletarian leaders felt that the intrusion of "political tasks" in the form of direct propaganda would cripple their literary product; many of them wanted to reveal the truth about life, no matter how dangerous that might seem from the Party's utilitarian point of view. Kaganovich, whose chief contribution to literature was the "*Magnitostroi*" slogan, maintained that RAPP "held back and impeded the writers' creative powers." But what kind of literary creation did the RAPP theory and practice "hold back and impede"? Was Kaganovich likely to have been really concerned about *literary* quality? It seems more likely that such a person would be concerned about the purely utilitarian side of literature: its usefulness to the Party in promoting current programs and ideas. We must conclude that this is the kind of development in literature which he felt the RAPP leaders were "holding back."

Fortunately we are left in no doubt about this, for the statements of L. Subotskii, spokesman of the Party on the Organization Committee of the new Union which replaced RAPP, describe the kind of literary activity which grew and flourished *after* the dissolution of RAPP:

We all know [he said] that last summer, the summer of 1932, was a time of great literary activity. Large groups of writers spent the summer at our new industrial enterprises, visiting the sovkhozes and kolkhozes, gathering such material as must in a very short time be realized in great artistic productions.[19]

Subotskii furnishes us with a list of titles of a large number of works already submitted to publishers, indicating a great increase in the activity of writers on topical themes. He emphasizes that one important political theme which has been thoroughly "grasped" and embodied in a number of literary productions is the theme of "capitalist encirclement." A number of eminent Soviet writers were working on this "political task of the day": Pil'niak, Iurii German, Lidin, and Tikhonov. Other practical matters occupied the attention and the talent of Soviet literary men: "Dybin is writing on the fishermen's trade, Bakhmet'ev on a large metallurgical factory and the people working there. . . . And many others have chosen similar themes."[20]

In such glowing terms does Subotskii describe the kinds of literary activity which "found no impediment to their growth" *after* the dissolution of RAPP. Lest there be a lingering doubt in anyone's mind as to the real meaning of the great "reorganization of literature," Subotskii says quite explicitly that the *first task* of his Organization Committee is to unify and guide the whole mass of Soviet writers in the mighty labors of socialist construction. It would seem that literature is now firmly harnessed to the Party program. This should finally dispose of the completely groundless notion that RAPP was the author of the utilitarian emphasis in Five-Year-Plan literature and that it was dissolved because of errors in that direction. On the contrary, it was dissolved partly because of its reluctance to accept such an emphasis.

Another spokesman of the Central Committee, the "philosopher" and discoverer of heresy P. Iudin, writing on the literary shortcomings of RAPP after its dissolution, had this to say of their "erroneous" slogans:

In our condition what does the RAPP slogan "tear off the masks" mean? First of all, from whom? From the proletarian state? But our proletarian state does not conceal its class character. . . . To bring out such a slogan without indicating from whom the masks are to be removed is inadmissible.[21]

Iudin's point here is that the bourgeois state, which claims to represent the whole people, but according to Lenin is simply an instrument for the oppression of the proletariat, can and should be "unmasked." But the proletarian state by its very nature *cannot* be unmasked since it wears no mask but is quite frankly a "class" state. Why, then, were the Party spokesmen so exercised about the slogan? What need was there to indicate "from whom" the masks were to be removed? Surely there was no reason to be concerned about the possibility of literary men's tearing the masks from the proletarian state and its infallible leaders. Or was there? The Party was surprisingly sensitive on this point.

A second RAPP slogan which particularly disturbed Iudin and other Party spokesmen was "for the living man." This slogan meant, said Iudin, that men have the "dialectic" lodged in their souls, and that the proletarian artist should therefore show forth the dialectic contradictions in the human psyche: "he should reveal the positive and the negative, for and against, 'yes' and 'no,' in man himself." Averbakh's insistence on the probing of individual psychology; Ermilov's firm belief in the importance of the subconscious; Libedinskii's "calumny" against the best Party workers in the character Eidnunen—all of these things Iudin characterizes, using his rich vocabulary of compromising epithets. Iudin objects to these slogans. For him they are "erroneous," and they have held back the development of a "Marxist-Leninist literature." The real meaning of his strictures on the RAPP "creative line" are no doubt to be found in the following statement regarding the kind of literature which should and would have developed had the leadership displayed the proper Leninist "Party spirit":

> We have such a vast material for literature today that it is possible through studying this material to foresee what will develop tomorrow. Imaginative literature should see through to that "tomorrow" which we are building today and illustrate the Marxist-Leninist teaching about socialism in all its flesh and blood.[22]

The real reason for Party disapproval of the RAPP literary program should now be somewhat clearer. The proletarian leaders, dogmatic and doctrinaire though they were, regarded literature as primarily a means for revealing what people are like and how they experience life. Obviously this was not at all the view of the Party leadership on the primary function of literature. The statements of both Subotskii and Iudin leave little room for doubt that Stalin and the practical men around him regarded literature as primarily an instrument of education and indoctrination which they intended to control and use for their own purposes. In all of these discussions of the RAPP "errors" we see, perhaps, the genesis of "socialist realism," and the real significance of the remark attributed to Stalin that writers should be "engineers of the human soul." The leaders of RAPP thought of literature as a light throwing the life around them into sharp focus, and revealing it as it really is. The leaders of the Party could not allow the powerful light of Russian literature to throw its beams freely over the surface of Russian life. They had observed that even their "trusted" Communist writers of RAPP had sometimes thrown light into corners of Soviet life that were better left in the dark. So the Party leaders were determined to control literature, to give it a program, a purpose, and "good" slogans. That was why they felt it necessary to dissolve and discredit RAPP and to gather all writers into a single Union under direct Party auspices.

B. "*RAPP was mistaken in its treatment of the fellow-travelers.*" Such was the second big reason given officially for the disappearance of RAPP. The documents which treat of its dissolution argue that the continued existence of separate proletarian organizations may cause the latter to "isolate themselves" from nonproletarian writers who sympathized equally with "the aims of socialist construction," and who were therefore equally useful to the Party. We have already seen evidence that the proletarian group had been given a place of special power and prestige as the "organization closest to the Party," and that its leaders, taking advantage of this position, had promoted their own literary interests to the detriment of writers outside the proletarian movement. Complaints that the rising proletarian tide threatened the fellow-travelers had begun to reach the authorities as early as 1930; and at the meeting of the Organization Committee of the new Union of Soviet Writers in

October, 1932, some months after the demise of RAPP, bitter complaints against the latter were heard.[23]

The October, 1932, meeting was in part an opportunity for those writers who felt they had been maltreated during the preceding period to speak out. It is extremely significant that although the tone of the meeting was distinctly anti-RAPP, many writers (e.g., Prishvin, Gronskii) admitted they were at a loss as to whom they should blame. Some (Belyi, Olesha) had a word of praise for the RAPP critics and even expressed a naïve bewilderment as to why everyone was attacking them. Many others, however, felt that they had been hampered in their work by RAPP's methods, particularly its sectarianism and its penchant for labeling writers who failed to measure up to its own dialectical-materialist standards. The proletarian exclusiveness of the most favored and most Marxist organizations in literature and in the arts was undoubtedly one important reason for their dissolution in 1932.[24]

But the Party's action in dissolving them had far more significance than appears on the surface. Some extremely pertinent evidence of the reasons for the liquidation of RAPP is contained in an article on the mistakes of Averbakh, published in *Pravda* on April 23, 1932, the very day on which the Central Committee reached the decision to abolish RAPP. This article was authored by the same P. Iudin whom we have quoted above, and who was at this time a spokesman of the Politboro in philosophical and literary discussions. It bears the characteristic title: "Against the Distortion of the Leninist Teaching on the Cultural Revolution."[25] Its thesis is that Averbakh denied the socialist nature of Soviet culture. Averbakh maintained, said Iudin, that it is *proletarian*, and not yet *socialist*.

It is impossible to take Iudin's argumentation seriously, for he employs a method which depends entirely upon the use of quotations carefully culled from Averbakh's works and given out of context. Yet the fact that so much time and effort was given to proving that Averbakh held heretical views on the subject of the "cultural revolution" seems to indicate that an accusation of major importance was intended in the labored and pontifical prose of this Leninist philosopher. Both in the

Pravda article which has been mentioned and in an article which appeared two months later in *Bolshevik*, Iudin contends that Averbakh did not "see" that the culture of the class building socialism is, in its essence, *socialist culture*. Iudin has no need to argue this hair-thin point, for he is able to find quotations in the works of Lenin and Stalin which seem to support it. These, too, are given out of context.[26] Averbakh's view, however, as given in a number of isolated quotations, is that in the USSR there exists a proletarian culture of the transition period, which will dialectically be transformed into a classless, socialist culture.

Other quotations from Averbakh's early works are used to show that he favored a policy of gradual elimination of classes rather than their forcible destruction. He is therefore indicted as a partisan of the theory of civil peace, of gradual development into socialism, and as a disciple of Bukharin![27]

Even without the aid of Iudin's exhaustive research in the works of Averbakh it might have been possible to conclude that some such attitude would have been characteristic of the RAPP leadership. Their ideas were formulated as early as 1926 and were based on the Party program for literature as expressed in the Politburo resolution of 1925. That resolution was in large part the product of Bukharin and it is explicit regarding the prospect of a rather long period during which the task of the proletariat will be confined to "peaceful organizing work."[28] It was the view of Bukharin that during this prolonged transition period a proletarian literature would gradually develop and earn the right to "hegemony." Such a view was characteristic of the NEP period not only in literature but in other sectors of Soviet life. Iudin's quotations from Averbakh date mostly from that period, and at least in one case involve a passage in which Averbakh is defending the policy of the 1925 Party resolution against the left opposition![29] With the beginning of the first Five-Year Plan this tolerant policy had been abandoned, classes were being forcibly eliminated and socialism constructed at an unheard-of tempo, and Averbakh is now convicted of error ex post facto.

One of the cardinal points of the 1925 resolution on literature is that the creation of a proletarian literature is not only possible but certain, and that at some time in the future the hegemony of proletarian writers will surely be won. The RAPP policy regarding hegemony was based explicitly on the 1925 statement of the Party program. One of the basic aims of the RAPP movement was to develop proletarian literature to the point where it could "claim the historical right" to hegemony.

What is the point, then, of Iudin's characterizing as foul heresy Averbakh's routine statements regarding "proletarian" literature and "proletarian" culture? The sense of his argument would seem to be that the policy of Averbakh and RAPP in emphasizing the importance of *proletarian* literature was a "mistake"; for the culture and literature being produced in the USSR in 1931, whether by proletarians or fellow-travelers, was, according to Iudin's authorities, socialist "in its essence." In this "socialist" society it was therefore very wrong to cultivate a *separate proletarian* literature. In an article written after RAPP's liquidation he makes his meaning quite clear: "They [RAPP] said that our literature was a proletarian class literature. But if a writer truthfully portrays our socialist productive relations, he is producing a literature which is socialist in its essence."[30]

Close attention should be given to Iudin's thoughts on the subject of "proletarian" culture and "socialist" culture, because they suggest the real meaning of Stalin's decision to abolish RAPP and other proletarian artistic organizations. For it should be emphasized that not only RAPP but *all* proletarian organizations in the arts, including the proletarian musicians' association (RAPM), were abolished at this time. Hereafter there is to be no special organizational means for supporting and subsidizing the proletarian artist. His place in literature, it would seem, is to be determined by his usefulness to the Party in promoting the "aims of socialist construction," rather than by his membership in a favored organization. Efforts to build proletarian culture and the talk about "proletarian hegemony" are now suspect, if we have correctly interpreted Iudin's *Pravda* article on Averbakh. There is no longer to be any special importance attached to a literary work because of the "class" it supposedly represents.

Both the resolution liquidating RAPP and the editorial in *Pravda* which elucidated it mention with peculiar emphasis those "significant groups" of writers who now do support the aims of socialist construction. These "significant" groups were, of course, nonproletarian, fellow-traveler writers. Such writers are now no longer to be considered "bourgeois" or "fellow-traveler," but "socialist," provided, as Iudin put it, they "truthfully portray our socialist productive relations," and provided also they "uphold the platform of the Soviet power and strive to participate in socialist construction."

To continue the struggle for proletarian hegemony when a rather large number of talented nonproletarian writers were producing literature which seemed both "loyal" and useful to the Party no longer made sense to the practical mind of Stalin. Besides, proletarian literature had been slow to react to the "new demands" and had not contributed significantly to the stream of "reconstruction" literature.[31] By 1932 it had become quite clear that special treatment of the proletarians could not be justified on any sound calculation of profit and loss to the Party.

Therefore the distinction between "proletarian" and "fellow-traveler" was officially abandoned. All writers supporting the program of the Party were now to be designated as "socialist," or "Soviet," writers. The culture of the USSR was declared upon the highest authority to be a "socialist" phenomenon. All writers were to belong to a single organization, membership in which was conditioned only upon their support of the "aims of socialist construction," that is, the policy of the Party.

Almost a year before the dissolution of RAPP Stalin had made a speech in which he foreshadowed the new policy of the Party toward "classes" in the Soviet Union. He announced in unambiguous language that the unfriendliness of Party organizations toward nonproletarian experts in many fields had not yielded good results, and that a change in policy toward the "old technical intelligentsia" was called for. Of course he did not at all admit that the former policy had been a tragic mistake and that the Party was now forced to revise its attitudes. On the contrary, exhibiting considerable skill in the use of the slippery "dialectic," he maintained that the policy had been justified *at the time* by the "wrecking" activities of the old experts, but that now, "when the intelligentsia are turning to the side of the Soviet power," a new policy must be devised. The old intelligentsia and the specialists in all fields are to be shown "greater attention and solicitude."[32]

The leaders of RAPP should not have missed the significance of Stalin's speech for their own area of activity. But they signally failed to react to it. As a matter of fact they rejected it as a directive for their dealings with the fellow-traveler wing of literature. A resolution of the RAPP secretariat issued immediately after the speech does not even mention that it may have implications for the RAPP policy toward the fellow-travelers.[33] A second resolution states that one cannot "mechanically" equate the changes taking place among the technical intelligentsia with the problem of the fellow-travelers.[34] And a new slogan devised early in 1931, though not particularly emphasized at that time, was brought forth as a statement of the RAPP attitude toward the nonproletarian wing of literature. By this slogan, "ally or enemy,"[35] the proletarians meant that the old term "fellow-traveler" was now out of date. In the period of the advance of socialist elements and the liquidation of classes the nonproletarian writer was either an ally of the proletariat or an enemy. There could be no middle ground for fellow-travelers. The list of those who according to RAPP standards were unsuccessful in their efforts to qualify as allies was indeed a long and impressive one. It included some of the best talent in twentieth-century Russian literature: Pil'niak, Zamiatin, Alexey Tolstoy, Budantsev, Zoshchenko, Fedin, Platonov, Shishkov, Kaverin, and a number of others.

The leadership of RAPP, even after Stalin's speech on the new approach to "fellow-travelers" in all fields and the need to utilize them fully, continued to distinguish between fellow-travelers of the right and of the left, and even sharpened their struggle against the former variety. For instance, not long before the dissolution of RAPP an article by Ermilov in the *Literary Gazette* bitterly attacked Alexey Tolstoy as nothing less than an enemy in the Soviet literary world, and characterized Kaverin's book on collectivization, *Prolog*, as "deeply reactionary." The real meaning of the dissolution of RAPP begins to grow clearer when it is realized that under the dispensation decreed by Stalin in April, 1932, such writers as Tolstoy and Kaverin were among the most successful and the most honored. And the use of the term "proletarian literature" was gradually abandoned.[36]

The new departure in Soviet policy announced by Stalin in his speech on new conditions and new tasks was either not understood or was rejected consciously by the RAPP leaders. It seems more likely that the latter was the case, for individuals as close to the Party as Averbakh, Kirshon, and Libedinskii could hardly have misunderstood the significance of the new policy.

It was said that the chief reason for the dissolution of RAPP was this failure to apply correctly the new policy in literature. It should be pointed out that the dissolution of RAPP is one of several events which indicate that the Party was moving away from the policy of relying on the development of proletarian specialists and that it was prepared to treat on a basis of equality *all* those who sympathized with the aims of socialist construction, regardless of "class" background.[37]

The significance of the dissolution of RAPP and of the "new conditions and new tasks" posed for Soviet literature by that step is evident from the changes which occurred soon after it was dissolved. An Organization Committee charged with paving the way to setting up the new Union of Soviet Writers was soon appointed. It consisted of twenty-four members, of whom only four represented the former leadership of RAPP. It included two "literary administrators," Gronskii, editor of *Izvestiia*, and Kirpotin, vice-director of the Leningrad section of the Communist Academy. Nine of its members were fellow-travelers, and nine were former members of RAPP who had never been associated with its leadership and some of whom had violently opposed the latter. None of the leading critics and administrators of RAPP were to be found in the Committee, which included only writers of belles-lettres.[38] Thus the fellow-traveler wing of Soviet literature was represented in the leading organ of the new Union on almost equal terms with the proletarians, and it far out-weighed that of the former leadership of the proletarians.

Notice was soon published that the make-up of editorial boards both in the journals and in the publishing houses had been changed, and again it is significant that only a few of the former leaders of RAPP reappear on the new boards.[39]

Soon after the dissolution we find that the pages of the *Literary Gazette* are to a considerable extent given over to the favorable discussion of nonproletarian writers whose works had either been totally neglected or characterized as "counterrevolutionary" during the preceding period: Tolstoy, Babel, Ehrenburg, Il'f and Petrov, Fedin, and many others. Very often these articles are accompanied by large pictures of the authors discussed, together with sympathetic biographical information.[40] The sudden transformation of the *Literary Gazette* after the dissolution of RAPP called forth bitter comment from Fadeev, who complained that writers whose works were "genuinely counterrevolutionary," even though they might be concerned with themes of the Five-Year-Plan period, were being indiscriminately praised to the skies, while many proletarian writers were unjustly criticized.[41]

Two incidents, it seems to me, epitomize the "revolution" which had occurred on the literary front. At a creative discussion sponsored by RAPP shortly before its dissolution the poet Saianov described the work of a "brigade" of poets to which he belonged. This "brigade" was made up of three RAPP writers and one "left-wing fellow-traveler," a certain Comrade Braun. The assembled proletarians broke into derisive laughter when they heard of this mixture of classes. Saianov, becoming quite indignant, read them a lecture on the correctness of working with fellow-travelers and bringing them over to the side of the proletariat. He defended Comrade Braun as a poet whose ideological development was progressing smoothly.[42]

One year later, in 1933, another conference of poets was

held under the auspices of the new Union of Writers which replaced RAPP. At that conference the main report was given by—Comrade Braun.

It was the new policy of the Party, in literature and in other departments of intellectual and social life, to break down the preferred position and splendid isolation of the proletarian organizations. Their members were now to mingle on more or less equal terms with their nonproletarian counterparts. They were no longer to regard the latter as beyond the pale, or as objects of their missionary zeal: for all were now "socialists" together. Such was the authoritative doctrine.

Here, then, we have a second reason for the liquidation of RAPP, and it is closely bound up with the first. The end of RAPP meant that the Party under Stalin's leadership had finally scrapped the idea of "proletarian hegemony," and looked now for support to the "best" writers, those "most valued in a literary sense," whether proletarian or bourgeois, as long as they were ready to support "the aims of socialist construction."[43] And many former fellow-travelers later became the recipients of Stalin prizes and other literary honors.[44]

But by that time RAPP was only an unpleasant memory.

4. The Party Giveth . . .

Issues of the *Literary Gazette* published immediately after the liquidation of RAPP feature the joyful and thankful reaction of the Soviet literary world to the wise decision of the Politburo. Though it is fairly certain that no other public reaction was possible after the decision had been taken, and though we should question the complete sincerity of many of the statements, yet there is no reason to doubt that many Soviet literary men, particularly the former fellow-travelers, experienced a tremendous relief of spirit when they read on the front page of *Pravda* the Party resolution which meant the end of the proletarian organization and the formation of a new Union for all writers. Indeed the VSP, predominantly a fellow-traveler organization, had many years earlier recommended the formation of a single Union of Writers, but their idea was contemptuously rejected by VAPP in 1926 on the ground that there could be no single, homogeneous body of writers[45] as long as the class struggle in literature continued. But now the class struggle had ended, and the equal rights of the former fellow-travelers would be guaranteed.

But equal rights does not necessarily mean freedom. The tone of Stalin's resolution of April, 1932, with its emphasis on "political tasks" and "support of the Soviet power"; the speeches in October, 1932, of the Organization Committee leaders Kirpotin and Subotskii; the ominous authoritarianism of P. Iudin; the insistence on a single, though vaguely defined, "style" for all Soviet literature: socialist realism;[46] the evidence of increased concern on the part of the state for the material welfare of writers—[47] all of these things argue that though the fellow-travelers would be equal to the proletarians they would be far less free than they had been during the NEP period, and even more closely tied to the Party and its program than during the days of RAPP. And occasionally, above the chorus of gleeful approval which came from the fellow-travelers, there was sounded a sober note, as when Leonov reminded his friends of their added responsibilities under the new dispensation.[48] Though the demands upon literary men might not now be couched in such rigid "Marxist" terminology, nevertheless there were still to be demands, and they would indeed inhibit the functioning of the artist.

For the Party had reorganized literature on its own terms. There would no longer be any separate literary groups. The end of RAPP meant also the end of Pereval, the Smithy, and any other semiautonomous literary group which had continued to exist from the liberal period of the twenties. Now all writers would belong to a single organization under the direct auspices of the Party. The condition against which Bukharin had warned in 1924 was accomplished in 1932: the fist had closed on Soviet literature.

Conclusion

THE HISTORY of the proletarian literary movement has been traced from its origins in the Proletcult to its final development in RAPP and its disappearance with RAPP in 1932. The effort to develop a separate class literature of the proletariat occupying a special and favored place characterizes all the proletarian literary organizations: the Proletcult, the Smithy, On Guard, RAPP. The belief in the possibility and the need for a class literature of the proletariat, and faith in the proposition that "hegemony" belongs to that literature as a historic right, are tenets held in common by all these groups at each stage of development.

Upon this general proposition all branches of the proletarian literary movement would agree. They disagreed on almost all other points touching literature and literary organization. They disagreed on the relationship of their movement to the Party. The Proletcult, until its statutes were modified by the direct intervention of Lenin, maintained that proletarian literary development should proceed independently of the Party and of the state organs of education and enlightenment. The young Communist writers and critics of On Guard, on the other hand, proposed that their organization should, under strict Party guidance, become the administrative center of literary life. The attitude of RAPP was ambiguous. While it claimed to be working under the direct guidance of the Party, the policies it developed late in its career showed a preference for independence from direct Party guidance, at least in matters of literary style and content. Later critics said that this substitution of its own general line for the line of the Party was one of the reasons for its dissolution.

At each new stage in its development the proletarian literary movement possessed a theory of literature and art, and on the basis of its theory explained the class nature and function of proletarian literature. The Proletcult, under the influence of Bogdanov, understood art and literature as an expression of collective labor and as a means for the organization of the powers of a given class. The early resolutions of On Guard do not depart essentially from this analysis: their emphasis is upon the nature of literature and art as an expression of class ideology and their function as a weapon in the class struggle.

The theory of proletarian literature dominant in RAPP was its most distinctive and characteristic contribution to the movement. This theory was worked out in the heat of controversy with Proletcult and On Guard ideas on the left, and the views of Voronskii and the Pereval critics on the right. In its final form it included elements of both. The theory described the nature of proletarian literature as cognition of life from the viewpoint of dialectical materialism, and its function as aiding the proletariat in its advance along the road to communism. It maintained that literature is an important instrument in the hands of the working class, and can be an effective means of changing reality, but only insofar as it deals directly with that reality itself. When it is unfaithful to reality—when it fails as "cognition of life"—then it is not literature and it is not an effective instrument. Proletarian literature must be realistic. It must continue the tradition of nineteenth-century Russian realism and accept as its cultural heritage the great masters of that school, particularly Tolstoy.

During the period of the first Five-Year Plan, this theory of literature and the practice based upon it came into conflict with the tremendous effort to rebuild the country which had been undertaken by the Party. In this effort the Party endeavored to enlist all forces, and its campaign affected every department of life. The psychology cultivated among the builders was essentially a military one, and the plan itself resembled a military campaign in its scale, its tempo, its slogans, and in the feeling of imminent war nourished by the Party. The urgent demand was to expend all energies so as to aid in fulfilling the goals of the plan. No exception was made for literature and the arts. Writers, too, had a function to perform, and literature was regarded as a means for mobilizing the masses. Thus under the pressure of its own program, the Party had adopted in its simplest form the traditional viewpoint of the "left" in Soviet literary theory. It proposed to use literature as an instrument of its policy.

This development led to a curiously anomalous situation in which the organization supported by the Party and commissioned to mobilize proletarian forces on the literary front was out of harmony with the Party program for literature, both disapproving and resisting the effort to make literature an instrument of publicistic aims. Because of its leadership's lack of enthusiasm for carrying out Party directives, the organization was constantly torn by inner dissension, and heavily criticized from without by the Party press and Party spokesmen.

When RAPP was liquidated in April, 1932, many reasons were officially advanced for that step. The resolution of the Central Committee claims that a great growth in literature had taken place during the years of its activity, but concludes that RAPP should be liquidated. Kaganovich explained that liquidation was necessary because a few selfish Communists in RAPP had been "holding back the writers' creative powers." Party spokesmen in the years immediately following its dissolution gave a number of additional reasons for this step: the clannishness and isolation of the leading group, their administrative excesses, their theoretical deviations and "idealistic" alienation from the "Party spirit" of literature. All of these things may have been factors in the final decision.

The investigation undertaken here has produced evidence that there were two basic reasons for the dissolution of RAPP: its resistance to the Party's use of literature as an instrument of direct propaganda for the Five-Year Plan, and its hostility to a talented group of writers—the majority of them outside the Communist and proletarian milieu—of whose value to the Party as literary allies there was little doubt. It is suggested further that the dissolution of the proletarian literary organization was one indication of a decisive change in policy regarding the relative position and importance of the proletariat and other social groups. Thus ended the struggle for "proletarian hegemony," and all the discussions and disputes carried out in its name.

The period of the first Five-Year Plan was indeed a devastating one in the history of Russian literature. It marked the ruthless extension by the Communist Party of its political power into the field of belles-lettres. Russian literature has never recovered from that experience. RAPP was designed as an agency for the extension of Party power and as such it has occupied an unenviable place in literary history. Yet it must be remembered, to its credit, that at some time during this period Averbakh and the literary men associated with him discovered in themselves at least a modicum of care for the literature which others wished to use as an "instrument." Within the narrow limits of their class ideology—and they allowed themselves no other—they tried to save it.

Epilogue: the Fifth Anniversary

DURING THE FIVE YEARS immediately following the dissolution of RAPP a definite version of its role and an estimate of its activity were worked out in the Soviet Union. According to this version RAPP had performed well for the Party in the days of its ascendancy by combatting Trotskyism and other harmful deviations in the literary field. Yet it had accumulated many false values and had itself disseminated some unsound ideas, and its methods had tended to alienate and discourage the fellow-traveler wing of literature. By 1932 it had outlived its usefulness, and so the Party, under Stalin's wise inspiration, had decided to liquidate it.[1]

This version of the activity of RAPP was radically altered just five years after its dissolution, when the RAPP leaders Averbakh, Kirshon, Makar'ev, Chumandrin, Libedinskii, and some others were, shortly after the Moscow trial of 1937, accused of having been themselves Trotskyites, and in some cases traitors and spies.

The involvement of literary men in the alleged plots against the Soviet government had already begun during the 1936 (Kamenev-Zinoviev) trial, among the principals of which had been the drama critic Pikel.[2] The name of only one of the leading figures in the RAPP apparatus appears in the accusations made during the 1936 trial: Selivanovskii, a young poet and literary administrator who had been editor of the *Literary*

Gazette in the last months of RAPP's existence. In addition to Selivanovskii, the writers Serebriakov, Grudskaia, Troshchenko, and Tarasov-Rodionov were branded as Trotskyites and expelled from the Union of Writers. Also implicated in the alleged Trotskyite conspiracy were Ivan Kataev, a writer of high talent and a member of the Pereval group, Semën Rodov, a leader of the left wing in RAPP, and the literary critic and theorist Voronskii.[3]

The chief author of these revelations in 1936 was Stavskii, whom we last met in 1931 as a member of the Panfërov group, and who, after the dissolution of RAPP, was one of the most violent critics of Averbakh.[4] By 1936 he had become an important figure in the Union of Soviet Writers. His articles in the *Literary Gazette* at this time place the brand of Trotskyist and traitor on a dozen or so writers. He wrote, "It was only during the trial that a whole nest of Trotskyites was expelled from the ranks of the Union," and gave a list of names, some of which are mentioned above. Of Voronskii's close friend Ivan Kataev he had this to say: "Ivan Kataev, with a group of his literary companions-in-arms from Pereval, visited Voronskii in exile to get directives from him, and he collected money to send to the exiled Trotskyites."[5]

The results of the revelations on the literary front were summed up in the following *Literary Gazette* editorial:

> In these years there have been exposed the contemptible enemies of the people, the Zinoviev-Kamenev and Trotskyite bandits, agents of fascism and right-wing renegades, who had their own agents in literature, entrenched in various sectors of the literary front, in writers' organizations, magazines, and publishing houses: those poisonous snakes Pikel, Serebriakov, Ter-Vaganian, Voronskii, and others who strove to disorientate Soviet literature. . . . [6]

The issue of the *Literary Gazette* for February 1, 1937, published soon after the close of the second great trial (Radek-Piatakov) contains speeches by Kirshon, Fadeev, Bezymenskii, and other literary men commenting on and approving the verdict in that trial.[7] There is a suggestion that additional literary men may be involved. Fadeev's speech is especially interesting in that it calls attention to the fact that there are still "enemies" active in the literary field who have not yet been "unmasked." He stresses the need for increased vigilance, and the close examination of all doubts and hesitations with a view to determining who spreads them and to whom they are useful.[8]

At a meeting of the Plenum of the Executive of the Union of Soviet Writers, Ermilov, a former RAPP leader and now editor of *Red Virgin Soil*, was accused of insufficient vigilance in his editorial work for having printed several articles by the now unmasked "enemy of the people" Ter-Vaganian. At the same meeting Gronskii, now editor of *New World*, was sharply criticized for having allowed counterrevolutionary agents to use its pages. The latter is described as being extremely nervous under these accusations and of making the rather poor defense that the "counterrevolutionary content of the material printed was not obvious, but masked."[9]

The same issue of the *Literary Gazette* which carried the above item contained an article by Stavskii branding the former leaders of the RAPP "left," Gorbachëv and Lelevich, as "enemies of the people" who had great influence and did much harm in Leningrad.[10]

Early in April, 1937, a general meeting of the Moscow writers heard accusations leveled at Gronskii, Kirshon, and Dmitrii Mirsky, the literary historian and former *émigré* who had chosen to return to the Soviet Union. Those attacked attempted to defend themselves; but the fact that the leaders of the opposition at the trials had confessed, not merely to opposition, but to sabotage, spying, and treason—and the charges brought by Stavskii tended to implicate others in such activity—seems to have unnerved the victims. Gronskii, who was again attacked for opening the pages of *New World* to "enemies," made what is described as a very weak defense, and the *Literary Gazette* reports that the meeting was quite unsympathetic to him.[11] Kirshon, whose plays were attacked for having introduced alien and harmful ideas, is described as reacting in an extremely nervous manner to this "criticism."[12] Mirsky, according to the same account, confined himself to "vague and incoherent statements."[13]

Up to the middle of April, 1937, there had been no mention

of Averbakh in these accusations. It is true that some of his close collaborators had been labeled as "enemies," and Kirshon had been subjected to the most serious criticism. But until April 20, 1937, there is no mention in the Soviet press of the possibility that Averbakh himself and the activity of RAPP under his leadership were "treasonable" and "Trotskyite." The first mention of Averbakh as an enemy of the people occurs in the *Literary Gazette* for April 20, 1937. This date may have some significance, for it is shortly after the date given for the arrest of Averbakh's brother-in-law, Iagoda, the former head of the G.P.U., who was executed after a trial in 1938.[14]

On April 20 the *Literary Gazette* carried an editorial which listed the many mistakes of RAPP under Averbakh's leadership. The mistakes listed are the usual ones, those which had become the stock in trade of RAPP's critics even before its dissolution. But now it is pointed out that these vile distortions of the Party line were "Trotskyite" in nature. "Covering his activity with two-faced vows of loyalty to the line of the Party, Averbakh in his scribbling constantly dragged in Trotskyite and Bukharinite ideas."[15]

The RAPP ideas which are now discovered to have been Trotskyite or Bukharinite are listed as the "living man" slogan, the slogans "for Plekhanov orthodoxy" and "ally or enemy."

The Trotskyite group identified as having made its way into the leadership of RAPP included at this point: Averbakh, Makar'ev, Maznin, Grudskoi, and Karev.[16]

By April 26 it was already possible for the *Literary Gazette* to print an editorial in which this statement appeared:

> It is now known to everyone that Averbakh and his paltry school were an agency of Trotskyism in our literature. . . .
>
> RAPP, which in its time played a significant role in the consolidation of the forces of proletarian literature, had by the year 1932 been transformed into a brake on the development of Soviet literature, especially as a result of that heinous role played in it by the Averbakh school, which happened to be in the leadership.[17]

A relatively new interpretation of the "living man" slogan is here offered:

> At the very time when the remains of the defeated class enemies within the Soviet Union were becoming ever more fierce and blood-

thirsty in their opposition to victorious socialist construction, at such a time Averbakh and his Trotskyite school brought forward the "living man" slogan calling upon writers to show the "good" in "evil," and so on. And in the popularization of that slogan, that rotten and harmful theory, Kirshon and Afinogenov showed no little zeal.[18]

And indeed the editors of the *Literary Gazette* would have had to add other eminent names to their list of "Trotskyites" if they had been entirely consistent in their claim that the "living man" slogan was a counterrevolutionary one. For its chief theoreticians were Libedinskii, Fadeev, and Ermilov.

It should be emphasized that no new information touching the activity of Averbakh during his six-year leadership of RAPP was brought forth at this time. All of the old "errors" of the RAPP leadership were resurrected and rehashed. Now, however, these "distortions" were explained as the result of the leadership in RAPP of a group of "Trotskyites" with Averbakh at their head. No convincing evidence was ever offered that Averbakh or any of his associates actually were members of an organized opposition directly connected with Trotsky. The "harmful" literary theories of RAPP, which had so often been criticized before 1932, were now described as "Trotskyite" ideas by individuals such as Iudin and Stavskii, who did not feel called upon to argue the point or offer proof of their statements. All possible objections were answered by the formula: "It is well known to everyone. . . . " Examples of "Trotskyism" brought forth by Iudin are the "living man" slogan, which Iudin says was invented in order to disorientate and weaken Soviet writers at the very height of the struggle against hostile classes, and the slogan "tear off the masks!" which Iudin said meant to Averbakh "unmasking" all of Soviet reality, including the proletarian state and its leaders.[19] Iudin, it will be remembered, had always maintained that these institutions should not be unmasked. The idea of the "dialectical-materialist method" was developed, according to Iudin, in order to confuse and inhibit Soviet writers.[20] In addition, Iudin reveals some unpleasant features of Averbakh's character and personality: his egotism and arrogance, and his use of the literary organizations in order to make a career for himself.[21]

Some new information does come to light, however, regarding Averbakh's activity after 1932. The most serious offense charged to him is that even after the RAPP organization was dissolved he maintained intact a faithful clique of followers with the idea of eventually reinstating himself in the leadership of Soviet literature.[22] Stavskii maintained that in his work on the editorial boards of *God XVI* (Year XVI), a collection, and *Isotoriia fabrik i zavodov* (History of Factories and Plants), Averbakh, by means of offering higher honorariums than was customary, grouped around himself a corps of faithful supporters, in an effort to regain his former position in literature.[23] This type of post-dissolution activity was summed up in the following terms by the *Literary Gazette:*

It is now clear to everyone that after the resolution of the Central Committee of April 23, 1932, Averbakh carried on a struggle against this resolution, and against the Organization Committee created by the Party, striving to make his way at any cost into the leadership of literature, from which he had been removed, in order to continue his Trotskyite work.

Averbakh proceeded to the creation of his own parallel center in literature. He began to place in various sectors his own Averbakhite cadres, and to undermine the work of the Organization Committee. He strove to discredit the Organization Committee, and to upset it, in the hope that, if successful, he might, with the help of his own people, return to the leadership in the capacity of benefactor, savior, and victor.[24]

The full significance of Averbakh's connection with Iagoda, who had recently been arrested, is never fully explained. Yet there is a hint that this aspect of his activity was important:

With the help and support of Iagoda, Averbakh attached himself to the publication of a collective work on the Belomor canal, gathered together a group of writers, and, throwing dust in their eyes, spending state funds without giving any account of them, sought to secure for himself the glory of a brilliant organizer and "skilled craftsman of literary affairs."[25]

Iudin, in an article on the occasion of the fifth anniversary of the dissolution of RAPP, pointed out that Averbakh, immediately before the Congress of Writers which took place in 1934, attempted to work his way into the leadership of the Union of

Writers. In this enterprise he supposedly had the active assistance of Kirshon, Bruno Iasenskii, and the critic Korabel'nikov.[26]

According to Iudin, Averbakh also had the support of Dmitrii Mirsky, the famous literary *émigré* who had recently returned to the Soviet Union. The aid given by Mirsky to Averbakh, apparently, was connected with the latter's efforts to reestablish himself in literature. Iudin wrote:

> With the help of Mirsky, that filthy Wrangelist and White Guard officer, they made an attempt to discredit Fadeev for the simple reason that he had broken finally with Averbakh.[27]

Such was the main burden of the charges brought against Averbakh in April, 1937. There is no record that he was ever tried for his offenses. He has disappeared, and it has not been possible to learn anything of his present whereabouts, if, indeed, he is still alive.[28]

The fire of accusation was directed not only at Averbakh but also at those closest to him in the leadership of RAPP, of whom one of the most prominent was Kirshon. An article by the playwright Vishnevskii, who had been a leading member of the Litfront and was a longstanding enemy and rival of Kirshon, called upon the latter to explain his fourteen-year association with the "enemy of the people," Averbakh. Vishnevskii also demanded an explanation of Kirshon's defense of the RAPP organization after the Party decision to liquidate it. Vishnevskii called upon his playwright enemy Kirshon to explain the fact that during the latter's editorship of *Rost* (Growth), one of the minor RAPP journals, such "Trotskyites" as Pikel and Makar'ev were to be found on its editorial board, or contributing articles to its pages.[29]

The attack on Kirshon grew more fierce as time went on. At a meeting of the dramatists in Moscow it was again brought out that for fourteen years he had been one of Averbakh's closest collaborators, that between him and Averbakh there had never been any disagreements, and that he faithfully carried out the literary line of an "enemy of the people." It was brought out, further, that even after the Central Committee decision to liquidate RAPP, Kirshon had opposed the resolution, and had even attempted to bring Averbakh into the leading organs of the new Union of Soviet Writers so as to preserve the latter's influence in literature.[30] It was revealed that one of his closest friends had been a certain Solskii-Panskii, a former leader of RAPP who had fled to Germany in 1928 and afterward "occupied an official position in the Polish Intelligence Service."[31] Kirshon had secured a place for him, they said, in the Soviet film industry.[32] In addition to all these heinous crimes he had used his influence to promote his own plays and had often hindered the development of rival dramatists.[33]

An editorial in the *Literary Gazette* for May 15, 1937, announced that Kirshon had been expelled from the Party. He has since disappeared, and there is no information as to his whereabouts.

Almost all the close collaborators of Averbakh came under fire at this time. Chumandrin, a Leningrad novelist, editor, and one of the principal leaders of RAPP, was accused of having maintained a RAPP fraction along with Averbakh even after the dissolution in 1932.[34] He had, moreover, publicly defended the activity of RAPP after it had been dissolved.[35] At a meeting of the executive board of the Leningrad Union of Writers in May, 1937, one Tsilshtein complained that although Chumandrin's books had preached Trotskyite ideas, they had not yet been removed from the libraries.[36] Chumandrin, in his defense of himself at this meeting, admitted that in some of his novels there had indeed been dangerous ideas, but he absolved himself of any connection with Averbakh after 1932. He seems to have attempted to divert suspicion from himself by suggesting that the person who was really guilty of opposition activity was Libedinskii, who had also been a leader of RAPP in Leningrad. Said Chumandrin: "There are many dark places in the personal and political biography of that man."[37]

Libedinskii did not escape suspicion. He was heavily attacked, and at one point his expulsion from the Party was considered.[38] At the May meeting in Leningrad, mentioned above, Libedinskii was not present, but several speakers implicated him in the "machinations" of Averbakh. There was a feeling that he was concealing something, and that he had retired from

Leningrad in order to avoid having to answer his accusers. Kozakov declared that "Libedinskii is just as guilty as Chumandrin." And he related how Libedinskii, after the decision of the Central Committee to dissolve RAPP, came to him with the suggestion that a separate group of writers be formed, offering as payment to recommend his acceptance into the Party. "Libedinskii hasn't yet told us all he knows," concludes Kozakov.[39]

We have looked into the charges against the most important RAPP workers who were at this time accused of being Trotskyites or of being implicated in the activity of Trotskyites. The list does not include two of the closest collaborators of Averbakh during the great days of RAPP: Fadeev and Ermilov. The part played by Fadeev in the 1937 "revelations" is obscure and will probably remain so. He himself was never accused of "Trotskyism," and he is today one of the important spokesmen of Soviet literature. Ermilov, against whom the only accusation ever brought was that he had lacked sufficient "vigilance," was until 1950 an important figure as editor of the *Literary Gazette*. In that year he was removed from his post on account of recent "errors."

Thus the Soviet interpretation of RAPP as an organization which "in its time" did good work for the Party in the fight against Trotskyism was abandoned as a result of the 1937 "disclosure" that the leadership of RAPP had always been in the hands of "Trotskyites" and "wreckers."

The latest Soviet statements on the RAPP period indicate that the 1937 doctrine has not been substantially altered. At the Eighteenth Congress of the Communist Party in 1939, the novelist Sholokhov referred to the RAPP leaders as "enemies" who had rightly been driven from the midst of Soviet writers.[40]

Alexey Tolstoy, in a brief survey of Soviet literature written in 1943, gives a similar estimate of the RAPP period:

> In the activity of RAPP there was (in addition to ignorance and Russian nihilism) the direct work of fascist agents who had crept into literature.[41]

The recent Soviet *History of Contemporary Literature* for use in the secondary schools gives the following description of the period of the twenties in Soviet literature:

During the twenties "neo-bourgeois" moods were felt in certain sections of society. . . . Those moods were the cause of the penetration into certain literary groups of elements hostile to Soviet reality, which developed harmful and erroneous theories. Counterrevolutionary Trotskyites made their way into the leadership of Pereval, the constructivists developed grossly erroneous theories, reflected in their literary creation. . . . Finally, in the leadership of RAPP, an influential organization with branches throughout the country, there turned out to be a group of carefully masked enemies of the people. In the field of literature . . . the class struggle was going on. Enemies of the people strove to make useless the most important weapon of the cultural revolution.[42]

An authoritative survey of documents on the relationship of the Bolshevik Party to literature, published in 1947, has this to say of RAPP: "Enemies of the people found their way into the midst of Soviet writers. They wormed their way into the leadership of RAPP; they entrenched themselves in a number of publishing houses and editorial boards. . . . "[43]

No later statements have been found which indicate that the Soviet estimate of RAPP has undergone any change since the period of the trials in 1937. There is no reason to expect that it will in the forseeable future.

We might pose the question, "Can the charges against Averbakh, Kirshon, and the others be believed?" The question itself may appear to be somewhat naïve, for there were no formal "charges" publicized. We have to deal only with accusations authoritatively pronounced but unsupported by evidence and untested by serious examination. The requirement that definite charges be brought against an accused person, that they be supported by objective evidence and open to public examination by the friends of the accused is not just a device of certain legal systems but a requirement of the human intellect in its pursuit of justice and truth. The failure of such simple ideas to gain approval in official Soviet circles makes it impossible to accept at face value indictments and accusations issuing from those circles. And indeed these accusations refute themselves by their violent absurdity.

What, then, was the meaning of the events of 1937? The history of RAPP as it has been set forth here provides a part of the answer. The leaders of RAPP had never been at peace with the leaders of the Party, and during the critical period of the first Five-Year Plan they had supported a literary doctrine out of tune with expressed Party demands. They had often been criticized as heretics and deviationists; their organization was cruelly liquidated in 1932 and vilified thereafter. Some of them were inclined to defend their ideas and maintain their dissident group even after the dissolution of RAPP. It may be that they were members of a much broader underground opposition to Stalin. In the middle thirties the Party decided to destroy such opposition wherever it could be found, and there followed a widespread purge of its membership in all departments. It would seem that many of the former leaders of RAPP were believed to be involved in this opposition. They were therefore eliminated physically, after having first been denigrated as "Trotskyites" and "traitors." They were never brought to a public trial, either because they refused to confess to any crimes or because they were not considered important enough for such treatment.

This hypothesis has the virtue of fitting all the facts set forth here about the history of RAPP and its leaders. With this admittedly tentative effort to make sense of the events described we must for the present leave the investigation of RAPP. Material which will throw more light on this period will, we must hope, become available in the future.

Appendix A

ON THE POLICY OF THE PARTY IN THE FIELD OF BELLES-LETTRES: RESOLUTION OF THE TSK· RKP(b), JULY 1, 1925

1. The rise in the material welfare of the masses in recent times, together with the changes in their outlook which have been brought about by the revolution, the intensification of mass activity, the significant broadening of horizons, and so forth, is causing a great growth of cultural needs and demands. We have entered upon a phase of the cultural revolution which is establishing the necessary condition for further development toward a communist society.

2. A part of this mass cultural growth is the appearance of a new literature—proletarian and peasant in the first instance—beginning in embryonic forms, but at the same time unusually broad in its scope (worker correspondents, village correspondents), and ending ultimately in consciously ideological literary and artistic production.

3. On the other hand, the complexity of the economic process; the simultaneous growth of contradictory and even inimical forms of economic life, the consequent growth and strengthening of a new *bourgeoisie;* the inevitable, though at first unconscious, attraction to it of a part of the old and new intellegentsia; the constant secretion from the depths of social life of new ideological agents of this *bourgeoisie*—all of this must inevitably be reflected also on the literary surface of our social life.

4. Thus, as the class war in general has not ended, neither

has it ended on the literary front. In a class society there is not, nor can there be, a neutral art, though the class nature of art generally and of literature in particular is expressed in forms which are infinitely more various than, for instance, in politics.

5. However, it would be quite wrong to leave out of consideration the basic fact of our social life, namely, the fact of the conquest of power by the working class, and the existence in the country of a proletarian dictatorship. Prior to the seizure of power the proletarian party provoked the class war for the disintegration of the society as a whole; during the period of the proletarian dictatorship the Party is faced with the task of getting along with the peasantry while slowly changing it; it is faced with the problem of allowing a certain collaboration with the *bourgeoisie* while slowly driving it out. It must also solve the problem of securing the services of technicians and of all kinds of intellectuals for the revolution, and of taking them away from the *bourgeoisie.*

Thus though the class war has not yet ended, it has changed its form, for the proletariat before the seizure of power strives for the destruction of a given society, but in the period of its dictatorship gives first importance to "peaceful organizing work."

6. Always preserving, broadening, and strengthening its leadership, the proletariat should occupy a forward position in a number of new sectors of the ideological front. The process of penetration of the dialectical-materialist outlook into altogether new fields has already begun (biology, psychology, the natural sciences, etc.). The conquest of positions in the field of belles-lettres must in the same way sooner or later become a fact.

7. It must be remembered, however, that this problem is infinitely more complicated than other problems being solved by the proletariat. Even within the limitations of a capitalist society the working class could prepare itself for a victorious revolution, build cadres of fighters and leaders and produce a magnificent ideological weapon for the political struggle. But it could work out neither the problems of natural science nor the tasks of technical development; and by the same token the pro-

letariat, the class which was culturally deprived, was unable to develop its own literature, its own characteristic artistic forms, its own style. Although the proletariat has ready infallible criteria regarding the socio-political content of any literary work, it does not have such definite answers to all questions of artistic form.

8. What has been said above should determine the policy of the ruling party in the field of belles-lettres. In this field we must consider the following problems: relationships among proletarian writers, peasant writers, and the so-called "fellow-travelers," and others; questions of criticism; questions of the style and form of artistic works and methods of developing new artistic forms; and, finally, questions of an organizational character.

9. The relationships among various groups of writers are determined by our general policy. However, it must be borne in mind that leadership in the field of literature belongs to the working class as a whole, with all its material and ideological resources. The hegemony of proletarian literature does not yet exist, and the Party should help these writers to earn for themselves the historical right to that hegemony. Peasant writers should receive our full support. Our task consists in guiding their growing cadres onto the rails of proletarian ideology, *by no means, however, discouraging in their works peasant literary images, which are the necessary prerequisites for their influence upon the peasantry.*

10. With relation to the "fellow-travelers" we must bear in mind: (1) their differentiation, (2) the importance of many of them as qualified specialists of literary technique; and (3) the presence of vacillation in this group of writers. The general directive should be for tactful and careful relations with them, and for such an approach as will guarantee all the conditions for their earliest possible movement in the direction of communist ideology. While discouraging anti-proletarian and antirevolutionary elements (now quite insignificant), and while fighting to expose the ideology of the new *bourgeoisie* which is taking form among a part of the fellow-travelers—those of the "change-of-landmarks" stripe—the Party should

have a patient attitude toward intermediate ideological formations, patiently aiding those inevitably numerous formations to develop in the process of ever closer comradely cooperation with the cultural forces of communism.

11. In relation to the proletarian writers, the Party should take the following position: while aiding their development and in every way supporting their organizations, the Party should prevent by all means the appearance among them of Communist conceit as a most harmful phenomenon. The Party, just because it sees in them the future ideological leaders of Soviet literature, must oppose a light-minded and indifferent attitude toward the cultural heritage, as also toward specialists of literary expression. Equally deserving of condemnation is the position which underestimates the great importance of the struggle for the ideological hegemony of the proletarian writers. Against capitulationism, on the one hand, and against Communist conceit on the other, such should be the slogan of the Party. The Party should also fight against attempts to create a purely hot-house proletarian literature. A broad grasp of phenomena in all their complexity; a literature not shut up within the confines of the factory only; a literature, not of the factory, but of a great, struggling class, leading millions of peasants—such should be the scope of proletarian literature.

12. What has been said above determines the tasks of criticism, which is one of the chief educational weapons in the hands of the Party. While it should not for one moment retreat from the positions of communism, nor from proletarian ideology, and while it must reveal the objective class meaning of certain works, Communist criticism should fight mercilessly against counterrevolutionary phenomena in literature; it should expose the "change-of-landmarks" liberalism, and the like, and yet at the same time show the greatest tact, attention, and patience toward all those groups which can and will join the proletariat. Communist criticism must drive out the tone of literary command. Such criticism can have deep educational significance only when it relies on its own ideological superiority. Marxist criticism should once and for all drive out of its midst all pretentious, half-literate, and self-satisfied Communist conceit.

Marxist criticism should have as its slogan "to learn," and should resist every appearance of cheap judgment and ignorant arrogance in its own milieu.

13. While it has infallible criteria of judgment regarding the class content of literary tendencies, the Party as a whole must not bind itself to any one tendency in the field of literary form. Giving general leadership to literature, the Party cannot support any one faction in literature (classifying these factions according to their different views on form and style), just as it cannot by resolutions settle questions of the form of the family, though in general it does and should lead in the development of new ways of life. Everything indicates that a style proper to the epoch will be created, but it will be created by different methods, and the solution of this problem has not yet been begun. In the present phase of cultural development any attempt to bind the Party in this direction must be repulsed.

14. Therefore the Party should declare itself in favor of the free competition of various groups and tendencies in this province. Any other solution of the problem would be an official, bureaucratic pseudo-solution. In the same way it is inadmissible to legalize by a decree the monopoly of the literary printing business by any one group or literary organization. While morally and materially supporting proletarian and proletarian-peasant literature, and aiding the fellow-travelers, the Party cannot offer a monopoly to any of these groups, even the one most proletarian in its ideology. For this would be to destroy proletarian literature itself.

15. The Party must in every way root out all attempts at officious and incompetent administrative interference in literary matters; the Party should see to it that there is careful selection of persons for those institutions which have authority in matters of publishing, so as to guarantee a really correct, tactful, and helpful leadership of our literature.

16. The Party should indicate to all workers in belles-lettres the necessity of a correct limitation of functions as between critics and writers. For the latter it is necessary to transfer the center of gravity of their work to literary production in the narrow sense, taking advantage in this of the material of the present

day. It is necessary also to give increased attention to the development of national literature in the many republics and *oblasts* of our Union. The Party should emphasize the necessity for the creation of literature intended for the mass reader, both worker and peasant. It is necessary to break more decisively and boldly with the prejudices of gentility in literature, and, taking advantage of all the achievements of the old masters, to work out a proper form understandable to the millions. Only when it has solved this problem will Soviet literature and its proletarian vanguard fulfill its cultural mission.

Appendix B

ON THE SERVING OF THE MASS READER WITH LITERATURE: RESOLUTION OF THE CENTRAL COMMITTEE, DECEMBER 28, 1928

1. The current period of socialist construction greatly increases the significance of the mass book as an instrument for the organization of the masses and of Communist education, and for the raising of their cultural level. At the same time the publication and distribution of the mass book is greatly lagging, especially in quality, behind the demands of socialist construction and the demands of the wide masses. It is necessary to strengthen decisively the work of all organizations, not only the publishing houses, but all state, social, cooperative, and especially Party organizations in the field of serving the mass reader.

2. Realizing that the subject matter of the mass book is not satisfactory in this respect, it is necessary: (a) to give special attention to the publication of books popularizing the Marxist-Leninist history of the Communist Party and the revolutionary movement; (b) to strengthen the publication of mass literature on production, raising the level of technical knowledge of the workers and peasants; (c) to develop the publication of the popular scientific book, linking it up with the socialist reconstruction and adapting it to the demands of self-education; (d) to broaden the publication of belles-lettres, especially those works which develop present-day political themes and which are directed against bourgeois influences, philistinism, decadence, etc.; (e) to guarantee the greatest possible accessibility of the mass book (in its form and expression) for a wide reading audience.

The Central Committee considers it necessary to a greater extent that heretofore to see to it that mass literature be an instrument for the mobilization of the masses around the basic political and economic tasks (in the first instance, the industrialization of the country and the rationalization of production, the raising of the productiveness of agriculture and of its socialist rebuilding); for the active class education of the workers and of the wide masses of the toilers in the fight against bourgeois and *petit-bourgeois* influences and survivals; for aiding the masses in conquering the achievements of science and technique; for the propaganda of Leninism and the struggle against its distortions.

3. With the aim of this common task, it is resolved: (a) To oblige the publishing houses to increase the percentage of the mass book in their general publishing plans for the year 1929, and during January to offer their editorial plans for the mass book to consideration in the press and in Party and social organizations. (b) To oblige the publishing houses to draw into this work in the capacity of authors the most qualified Communists (in the form of tasks imposed by Party organizations), and also specialists in science, technique, and art (through the ITS and the SNR and the writers' organizations); to employ competitions in the writing of brochures by authors from the working class and the peasantry, giving the most promising of them methodological and editorial aid; to empower the APPO NK to include in the form of an experiment in the plan of work of certain institutions of higher learning for the year 1929, seminars for the training of popularizers. (c) To propose to the cultural sections of the unions that they set up through a library network systematic study of reader demand and interest, and that they organize in libraries circles of worker and peasant critics.

To propose to the publishing houses that they use preliminary reports on the themes of books, and preliminary reading of manuscripts to worker and peasant audiences; and that they organize the study and use by authors of readers' letters, notes presented at mass meetings, and the letters of workers and peasants to the newspapers.

(Points 4, 5, and 6 concern the reduction in the cost of the mass book, and the improvement of the library network.)

Notes

Chapter I: Proletarian Literature

1. Karl Marx and Friedrich Engels, *The German Ideology*, pp. 39–40.

2. "Bogdanov, A. A.," *Literaturnaia entsiklopediia*, I (1929), 527. This idea is implicit in Bogdanov's statement that "the struggle for the cultural liberation of the proletariat is indeed the struggle for its complete liberation as a class," quoted in V. Polonskii, "Literaturnoe dvizhenie oktiabrskogo desiatiletiia" *Pechat' i revoliutsiia*, No. 7, July, 1927, p. 33.

3. This was the pseudonym of A. A. Malinovskii (1873–1928) who, together with Gorky, Lunacharskii, and Pokrovskii, founded a Party school at Capri in 1909. It was against the philosophical "errors" of this group that Lenin's *Materialism and Empirio-Criticism* was directed. See V. I. Lenin, *Collected Works*, Vol. XIII: *Materialism and Empirio-Criticism.*

4. A. V. Lunacharskii, who had been associated with Malinovskii in the activity of the Social Democratic *émigrés*, became the first Commissar of Education in the government set up by Lenin in November, 1917. He held that post until 1929. In 1933 he was appointed ambassador to Spain, but died before taking up his duties there. On the relationship of Lunacharskii to Malinovskii, Lenin, and other Social Democratic refugees see Bertram Wolfe, *Three Who Made a Revolution.*

5. "Proletkult," *Literaturnaia entsiklopediia*, IX, 309–10.

6. Plekhanov, *Sochineniia* (Collected Works), XIV, 183.

7. "Bogdanov, A. A.," *Literaturnaia entsiklopediia*, p. 526.

8. Quoted in N. L. Brodskii, V. L. L'vov-Rogachevskii, and N. P. Sidorov, *Literaturnye manifesty* (Literary Manifestoes) (Moscow: Federatsiia, 1929), pp. 130, 131.

9. Quoted in "Bogdanov, A. A.," *Literaturnaia entsiklopediia*, p. 528.

10. *Ibid.* See also Polonskii, *Pechat' i revoliutsiia*, p. 34, and Brodskii, *Literaturnye manifesty*, p. 131.

11. Quoted in Polonskii, *Pechat' i revoliutsiia*, p. 35.

12. There would appear to have been some uncertainty among the theoreticians of proletarian literature on this important point, and the question whether a person of "bourgeois" origin was capable of creating "proletarian" characters and describing life from the viewpoint of the proletariat continued to agitate Soviet literary circles during the twenties. Bogdanov's statements leave the door open for "proletarians by orientation": "The class character . . . [of poetry] means that the poet takes the viewpoint of a particular class, thinks and feels in the manner that is characteristic of that class."—*Iskusstvo i rabochii klass* (Moscow: Proletarskaia Kul'tura, 1918), pp. 10–11.

On the other hand Bogdanov's close associate F. Kalinin appears to have disagreed on this point: "In the work of creating its own culture the proletariat cannot expect help from the old intelligentsia, for artistic creation is principally subconscious, and the subconscious has as its foundation *Byt;* therefore an intellectual can never be a proletarian in his subconscious mind." Quoted in P. S. Kogan, *Literatura velikogo desiatiletiia*, p. 53. The Russian word *byt* in this quotation means "the general manner of life peculiar to a particular social group."

13. Quoted in "Khronika sovetskoi literatury za dvadtsat'let," *Literaturnyi kritik*, No. 7, July, 1937, p. 132.

14. "Proletkult," *Literaturnaia entsiklopediia*, IX (1935), 309, 310.

15. *Ibid.*

16. *Ibid.* See also "Khronika," *Literaturnyi kritik*, No. 7, 1937, p. 158.

17. Polonskii, *Pechat' i revoliutsiia*, p. 34.

18. "Proletkult," *Literaturnaia entsiklopediia*, p. 310. "Bogdanov, A. A.," *Literaturnaia entsiklopediia*, p. 528.

19. L. D. Trotsky, *Literature and Revolution*, trans. Rose Strunsky, pp. 184–215.

20. Polonskii, *Pecrat' i revoliutsiia*, p. 34.

21. As has been pointed out in n. 3, Lenin had long been at odds with Bogdanov, the theoretical leader of the movement.

22. "Khronika," *Literaturnyi kritik*, No. 8, p. 103.

23. In this brief introductory chapter only the barest outline of the Proletcult, its ideas, and the voluminous discussions to which it gave rise can be given. There is an enormous literature on the subject, hardly any of it translated. A treatment of the movement in English is to be found in Eden and Cedar Paul, *The Proletcult.* See also Alexander Kaun, *Soviet Poets and Poetry*, pp. 98–126. For additional information on the Proletcult see the following works:

Bogdanov, *O proletarskoi kul'ture* (Moscow: Kniga, 1924); N.

Vasilevskii, "K sozyvu konferentsii proletarskikh kul'turno-prosvetitelnykh organizatsii," *Proletarskaia kul'tura*, No. 4, 1918, pp. 28–29; A. Lezhnëv, "Proletkult i proletarskaia kul'tura," *Krasnaia nov'*, No. 2, 1921, pp. 272–87; P. M. Kerzhentsev, "Kommunizm i kul'tura," *Tvorchestvo*, No. 2, 1920, pp. 46–50; V. Polianskii, "Pod znamenem proletkul'ta," *Proletarskaia kul'tura*, No. 1, 1918, pp. 3–7.

24. Semën Rodov, "O kruzhkovshchine, platformakh, i otryve ot mass," *Proletariat i literatura* (*sbornik statei*) (Leningrad: Gosizdat, 1925), p. 99.

25. *Pravda*, February 5, 1920, quoted in "Khronika," *Literaturnyi kritik*, No. 8, 1937, p. 84.

26. "Kuznitsa," *Literaturnaia entsiklopediia*, V (1931), 704–6.

27. "Deklaratsiia proletarskikh pisatelei Kuznitsy," *Pravda*, No. 186, 1923. Quoted in Brodskii, *Literaturnye manifesty*, p. 158.

28. "Osnovnye otlichitelnye priznaki proletarskoi literatury," quoted in Brodskii, *Literaturnye manifesty*, p. 152.

29. *Ibid.*

30. *Ibid.*

31. Quoted in Kogan, *op. cit.*, p. 63.

32. Liashko, *loc. cit.*

33. Kogan, *Literatura velikogo*, p. 65; also Trotsky, *op. cit.*, pp. 210–11.

34. Kogan *op. cit.*, p. 63.

35. Voronsky saw in this "other-worldliness" the influence of Gorky and Bogdanov. Their "monistic" philosophical views involved a breakdown of the distinction between subject and object, "self" and "not-self," and suggested the merging of the ego in something greater: the collective or even the cosmos. "Literaturnye otkliki," *Krasnaia nov'*, No. 3, May, 1923, p. 311.

36. The NEP provided for the revival of a limited amount of private trade under government supervision.

37. "Kuznitsa," *Literaturnaia entsiklopediia*, p. 705.

38. *Ibid.*

39. Kogan, *Proletarskaia literatura* (Ivanovo-Vosnesensk: Osnova, 1926), p. 44.

40. Rodov, "O kruzhkovshchine," p. 101.

41. "Kuznitsa," *Literaturnaia entsiklopediia*, p. 705.

42. Rodov, *op. cit.*, pp. 101–2.

43. *Ibid.*

44. Kogan, *Literatura velikogo*, p. 56.

45. Quoted in V. L. L'vov-Rogachevskii, *Ocherki proletarskoi literatury*, p. 178.

46. "Rodov, Semën," *Literaturnaia entsiklopediia*, IX (1935), 727.

47. Libedinskii's first novel and the best thing in early proletarian literature, *Nedelia* (A Week), appeared in 1922. It deals with the work of the Communist Party organizations in a hostile peasant environment, and its peculiar merit is that it avoids stereotyped characters and even presents the Red leaders as men with problems, doubts, and hesitations, though completely selfless in their readiness to sacrifice for the cause. It was published by Voronskii in *Nashi Dni* (Moscow: Krug, 1922).

48. G. Lelevich was the pseudonym of Laborii Gilelevich Kalmanson.

49. Leopol'd Leonidovich Averbakh (1905–?), the young critic and organizer who was the leader of RAPP during the years of its ascendancy, is a personality extremely difficult to assess. The whole history of his career has been covered by successive layers of hostile criticism, calumny, and official lies. Historians of all shades join in the chorus of abuse, and the Trotskyist writers are just as virulent as are the spokesmen of Stalin. One of the main tasks of a study such as this must be to remove, if possible, the successive deposits of partisan falsehood, and reestablish the man in his true nature. It is hoped that the whole story of RAPP as told here will succeed in this. A few facts about his life are in order now.

He was born in Saratov in 1905, the son of a wealthy Jewish merchant who contributed heavily to the Bolshevik movement. His mother was the sister of Iakov Sverdlov, one of Lenin's close associates. He was related also to another prominent Bolshevik, E. Iaroslavskii, and his sister was married to Iagoda, who became head of the G.P.U.

His secondary education was interrupted by the First World War and the revolution, and he became active very early in the youth movement. In 1919 he went to Germany as a delegate to an international conference of the Red Youth. He was a member of the editorial board of the Youth League magazine. His first published work appeared in 1923 and bore the title *Lenin and the Youth Movement*. Trotsky wrote an introduction for it. He was active at a very early age in the proletarian literary movement.

It must be admitted that Averbakh as a writer was a thing of poor quality. Seldom, indeed, has a man with so little knowledge of the writer's craft published so much, for if his works should be collected and published in book form they would fill several large volumes. His knowledge of literature was limited. His ability to express himself in terms of Marxist theory leaves much to be desired. His writings, especially in the early period, display little except ignorance, arrogance, and incomplete education. His chief claim to recognition was as an orator—even his enemies admitted that he was great, sometimes comparing him to Cicero and sometimes to Demosthenes —and as an energetic literary organizer. No doubt his excellent political connections were the chief reason for his prominence in literature. His frequent and violent attacks upon writers and critics who disagreed with him were a source of difficulty and discouragement to many literary figures.

Yet there is much to be said for Averbakh on the positive side. As he grew older in years and experience the arrogance and crudity of his early ideas on "proletarian literature" tended to abate, and at the time of RAPP's liquidation in 1932 he was supporting a literary program which was enlightened and liberal compared with his own early period, or with the demands being made officially upon literary men at that time. He was willing to, and he did, learn. One of his teachers, oddly enough, was the right-wing critic Voronskii, in whose presence he is said to have spent considerable time—not making speeches himself, but listening carefully.

He always displayed rare courage in defending his own ideas, and never failed to support his friends when they were embarrassed by the attacks of Party spokesmen. He is one of the few literary figures who never crawled at the feet of Stalin. He is one of the few who never beat his breast and "admitted his errors." Under his leadership RAPP became a formidable obstacle to the direct utilization of literature by the Central Committee of the Party in the years 1928–32.

In 1937 his enemies discovered that he was a "Trotskyite," "traitor," "fascist," and "spy." He disappeared at that time and is probably dead.

50. L'vov-Rogachevskii, *Ocherki*, p. 179.

51. "Ideologicheskaia i khudozhestvennaia platforma Oktiabria," quoted in Brodskii, *Literaturnye manifesty*, p. 183.

52. A. Bezymenskii, *Izbrannye stikhi*, pp. 16–17.

53. Lelevich, "Puti proletarskoi literatury," *Oktiabr'*, No. 1, June, 1924.

54. Demian Bednyi was a versifier with a flair for expressing the Party line of the day in lively popular language. For an extremely sympathetic and illuminating account of his literary activity see Trotsky, *op. cit.*, pp. 212–14.

55. I. Libedinskii, "Temy kotorye zhdut svoikh avtorov," *Na postu*, Nos. 2–3, August, 1923, pp. 117–26.

56. Quoted in A. K. Voronskii, "Iskusstvo kak poznanie zhizni i sovremennost';" *Krasnaia nov'*, No. 5 (15), August, 1923, p. 380.

57. As we shall soon see, one of the most important activities of VAPP was the organization of literary "circles," in which working-class writers could receive elementary literary education.

58. Kogan, *Proletarskaia literatura,* p. 50.

59. Rodov, "O kruzhkovshchine," *op. cit.,* p. 107.

60. The Moscow and Leningrad Associations of Proletarian Writers, respectively.

61. "Agreement between the Moscow and Leningrad Associations of Proletarian Writers," Brodskii, *op. cit.,* pp. 199–200.

62. Rodov, *op. cit.,* p. 108.

63. *Ibid.*

64. Ivan Maiskii, the editor and publicist who later became Ambassador to England, was very much interested at this time in the problems of proletarian literature. He complained that the October leaders of VAPP were actually "remote from the masses," and that their work with the "literary circles" was never at the high level which they claimed. See I. Maiskii, "O kul'ture, literature, i kommunisticheskoi partii," *Zvezda,* No. 3, 1924; reprinted in *Proletariat i literatura.* Other observers pointed out that VAPP had had little success in awakening interest among the workers (G. Seryi, "Blizhaishaia zadacha," *Proletariat i literatura,* pp. 130–31).

65. I. Polosikhin, "Chetyre goda," *Na literaturnom postu,* No. 8, April, 1927, p. 80.

66. M. Luzgin, "Zakal," *Na literaturnom postu,* No. 8, April, 1927, p. 92.

67. *Ibid.*

68. *Ibid.*

69. "Rabochaia Vesna," *Na literaturnom postu,* No. 8, April, 1927, p. 86.

70. *Ibid.*

71. Rodov, "O kruzhkovshchine," p. 107. See also "Antenna," *Na literaturnom postu,* No. 8, April, 1927, p. 94.

72. Furmanov, "Organizatsionnaia sistema VAPPa," *Na literaturnom postu,* No. 5, 1928, p. 20 (from a report given at the First All-Union Conference of Proletarian Writers on January 11, 1925).

73. *Ibid.,* p. 24.

74. LEF (The Left Front of Art) was the organization of the futurists under the leadership of Maiakovskii, Brik, and Aseev.

75. Speech of Voronskii, in *K voprosu o politike RKP(b) v khudozhestvennoi literature* (Moscow, 1924), p. 12.

76. Furmanov's diaries are published in part in "Khronika," *Literaturnyi kritik,* No. 12, December, 1937, p. 172.

77. These names are listed among the "collaborators" of the magazine *Na postu.* "Sotrudniki," *Na postu,* Nos. 2–3, August, 1923, p. 1.

78. Manilov is the landowner in Gogol's *Dead Souls* who re-

mained gently complacent and quiescent while his estate went to ruin.

79. "Editorial Manifesto of the On Guard Group," translated in George Reavey and Marc Slonim, *Soviet Literature; an Anthology,* p. 405.

Chapter II: The Fellow-travelers and the Orthodox

1. It was during this period that many young writers now established in Soviet literature began their careers.
2. Quoted from an article of Meshcheriakov in Rodov, "Originalnaia poeziia Gosizdata," *Na postu,* Nos. 2–3, 1923, p. 141.
3. Rodov, "Originalnaia poeziia," p. 142.
4. Voronskii, "O tekushchem momente i zadachakh RKP(b) v khudozhestvennoi literature," *Proletariat i literature,* p. 52.
5. William Edgerton, "The Serapion Brothers: an Early Soviet Controversy," *American Slavic and East European Review,* VIII, No. 1 (February, 1949), 51–52.
6. *Ibid.,* p. 48.
7. Trotsky, *Literature and Revolution,* pp. 56–115.
8. *Ibid.,* p. 57.
9. Quoted in Edgerton, "The Serapion Brothers," p. 56.
10. *Ibid.*
11. Voronskii, "Iskusstvo kak poznanie zhizni i sovremennost'," *Krasnaia nov',* No. 5 (15), August, 1923, p. 377; also *K voprosu,* p. 12.
12. For this brief outline of Voronskii's views and activities I am in part indebted to two studies of the man written in English: Morris Halle, "Early Literary Disputes in the USSR" (master's essay, University of Chicago, 1946), and Hugh McLean, Jr., "Voronsky and VAPP," *American Slavic and East European Review,* VIII, No. 3 (October, 1949), 185–200. Unfortunately, neither work adequately shows the derivation of Voronskii's ideas.
13. Voronskii, "Iskusstvo kak poznanie," pp. 349–52.
14. See below, chap. x, pp. 174 ff.
15. It should be pointed out that Voronskii's ideas on "intuition" and "immediate impressions" were not original, but reflected the influence of the philosopher Henri Bergson. See Raïssa Messer, "Estetika Bergsona i shkola Voronskogo," *Literatura i iskusstvo,* No. 1, January, 1930.
16. Quoted in McLean, "Voronsky and VAPP," p. 191.
17. *Ibid.*
18. *Ibid.*

19. Voronskii, "Iskusstvo kak poznanie," pp. 362–65.

20. *Ibid.*, p. 362.

21. *Ibid.*, p. 365.

22. Based on Voronskii, *Literaturnye zapisi,* pp. 36–55.

23. Voronskii, *Iskusstvo i zhizn'* (Moscow, 1924), quoted in Kogan, *Proletarskaia,* pp. 92 ff. At one time Voronskii agreed completely with Trotsky's idea that "there was not and could not be" a proletarian culture; later he modified his ideas, and at the time of the Press Section (Central Committtee) meeting of May, 1924, he was of the opinion that a proletarian literature was "possible" but that it did not yet exist and could only be created over a long period. On this subject see Kogan, *Literatura velikogo,* pp. 59–60.

24. Voronskii, "Iskusstvo kak poznanie," *Krasnaia nov'*, p. 379.

25. Zhdanov, now deceased, was the Party figure who took the lead in the criticism of Akhmatova, Zoshchenko, and other Soviet writers in 1946 for "ideological" failures. For a discussion of this criticism see *Bol'shevik,* Nos. 17–18, September, 1946, pp. 4–19.

26. See speech of Vardin, in *K voprosu o politike RKP(b) v khudozhestvennoi literature,* pp. 14–21 *passim.*

27. Kogan, *Literatura velikogo,* p. 58.

28. Speech of Vardin, *K voprosu,* p. 21.

29. The October group, which was the leadership of VAPP, came to be known, from the title of its theoretical and critical journal, as the "On Guardists." We shall therefore refer to them in that way.

30. This is an abridged version of a resolution passed by VAPP in 1925 on the motion of Vardin, and given by Polonskii in "Literaturnoe dvizhenie," *Pechat' i revoliutsiia,* pp. 60–61.

31. Rodov, "Pod obstrelom," *Na postu,* Nos. 2–3, 1923, p. 28.

32. "Literaturnoe dvizhenie," *loc. cit.*, p. 60.

33. The literary poverty and political presumption of the group is a frequent theme of its opponents.

34. Of course the Party had not been slow to act when a large-scale literary movement, the Proletcult, began to enunciate doctrine with which it could not agree. See above, chap. i.

35. Authority for this statement is the biographies of these figures given in the *Literaturnaia entsiklopediia.*

36. Demian Bednyi had been decorated for his agitational poems in 1922. See "Demian Bednyi," *Literaturnaia entsiklopediia,* I (1929), 378–87.

37. Ivan Maiskii, ed., *Proletariat i literatura,* p. 68.

38. Rodov, "Pod obstrelom," p. 15.

39. Speech of Trotsky, in *K voprosu,* p. 64.

40. Polonskii, *Pechat' i revoliutsiia,* p. 57.

41. Evgenii Zamiatin (1884–1937) was one of the inspirers and teachers of the Serapion group. Though he had been a Bolshevik in

his early days he reported himself as "not one" shortly after the revolution. In many of his short stories and plays a note of criticism of the new regime is clearly heard. His one long novel, *We,* the description of a beautifully organized state of the far-distant future in which all human activities are supervised and organized and even sex life is regulated by a card system, could never be published in the USSR. He left Russia in 1932 and died in Paris in 1937. Boris Pil'niak (the pseudonym of Boris Andreevich Vogau, 1884–?), a writer of rare talent, was undoubtedly one of the greatest names in twentieth-century Russian literature. His novel *A Bare Year* offers one of the most immediate and moving literary pictures of the civil war period. The Marxists and proletarians found fault with him for his tendency to understand the revolution as a return to pre-Petrine Russia and as, in the main, a great peasant revolt. He seems to have disappeared under a cloud in 1938, and is probably dead.

42. Rodov, "Pod obstrelom," p. 18.

43. The kulaks (fists) were relatively successful individual farmers, upon whom the cities became dependent for deliveries of essential grain.

44. G. Seryi, *op. cit.*, p. 129. Lydia Seifullina was a successful writer of the fellow-traveler persuasion.

45. "Soglashenie MAPPa s LEFom," in Brodskii, *op. cit.*, pp. 244–47.

46. See Voronskii, "Iskusstvo kak poznanie," pp. 372–73.

47. Quoted in Paul Milyukov, *Outlines of Russian Culture,* Part II, p. 91.

Chapter III: The Compromise

1. An excellent summary of this dispute is given in P. S. Kogan, *Proletarskaia literatura* (Ivanovo-Vosnesensk: Osnova, 1926), pp. 92–110. The collection *Proletariat i literatura,* I. Maiskii, ed. (Leningrad, 1925), contains reprints of articles by the leading figures on both sides, which originally appeared in the magazine *Zvezda.*

2. Quotations from Lenin are fairly frequent on both sides of the controversy. The most striking example of the use of Lenin by the supporters *and* opponents of the On Guardists occurred at a meeting of the Press Section of the Central Committee in 1924. Trotsky called upon the authority of Lenin to support his idea that a specifically proletarian culture was impossible. He was answered by Lunacharskii and Demian Bednyi with quotations of an opposite tenor. See *K voprosu,* remarks of Trotsky, pp. 60–61, and of Lunacharskii, p. 78.

3. The Proletkult under the leadership of Bogdanov had raised

no such problems, for they insisted on independence from state and Party organs.

4. *K voprosu,* remarks of Trotsky, p. 69.
5. *Ibid.,* p. 67.
6. Trotsky, *Literature and Revolution,* p. 202.
7. A leader of the proletarian literary movement. He was an editor of *On Literary Guard,* and later replaced Voronskii as editor of *Red Virgin Soil.*
8. *K voprosu,* remarks of Trotsky, pp. 56–57.
9. *Ibid.,* p. 65.
10. Trotsky, *Literature and Revolution,* p. 14.
11. *K voprosu,* remarks of Lunacharskii, p. 80.
12. *Ibid.,* pp. 76–78.
13. *Ibid.,* p. 78.
14. "Nikolai Bukharin," *Literaturnaia entsiklopediia,* I (1929), 631–35.
15. Bukharin, N., "Proletariat i voprosy khudozhestvennoi politiki," *Krasnaia nov',* No. 4, May, 1925, pp. 264 ff.
16. *Ibid.*
17. *K voprosu,* remarks of Bukharin, p. 36.
18. *Ibid.,* p. 37.
19. *Ibid.*
20. *Ibid.*
21. *Ibid.*
22. Bukharin, "Proletariat i voprosy," p. 272.
23. Of those who took a direct part in the public discussion, the majority favored some kind of compromise between the views of Trotsky and Voronskii and the demands of the On Guardists. Among those favoring a compromise were the critic P. S. Kogan, Karl Radek, Ivan Maiskii, and of course Bukharin and Lunacharskii.
24. *Izvestiia,* July 1, 1925.
25. *K voprosu o politike RKP(b) v khudozhestvennoi literature* (Moscow: Krasnaia nov', 1924), is a complete stenographic report of this meeting.
26. *K voprosu,* "Rezoliutsiia po dokladu Iakovleva."
27. *Ibid.*
28. *Ibid.*
29. "O pechati (iz rezolyutsii XIII s"ezda RKP(b) 23–31 maia, 1924)," *Resheniia Partii o Pechati* (Moscow: Gosizdat, 1941), p. 72.
30. *Ibid.*
31. "Otkliki Russkikh pisatelei na rezoliutsiiu XIII s"ezda RKP(b)," *Versty,* No. 1 (Paris), 1926, pp. 200–1.
32. A circumstantial though prejudiced account of this political struggle is to be found in N. N. Popov, *Outline History of the Com-*

munist Party of the Soviet Union, Part I. A more objective account is given in Isaac Deutscher, *Stalin.*

33. For a complete translation of this document, see Appendix A.
34. Appendix A, point 10.
35. *Ibid.*
36. *Ibid.*
37. *Ibid.*, point 14.
38. *Ibid.*, point 12.
39. *Ibid.*, point 13.
40. *Ibid.*, point 4.
41. *Ibid.*
42. *Ibid.*, point 2.
43. *Ibid.*, point 11.
44. *Ibid.*
45. *Ibid.*

Chapter IV: On Literary Guard, 1925–1928

1. This was apparently underlined in a number of authoritative statements which appeared in the Party press of the time. For instance Vareikis, an important personage in the Press Section of the Central Committee, attacked the program and policies of On Guard, especially as they affected fellow-traveler literature (*Pravda*, February 18, 1925); quoted in "Khronika," *Literaturnyi kritik*, No. 9, 1937, p. 59. See also P. Ionov, "O proletarskoi kulture, napostovskoi putanitse, i panike," *Bol'shevik*, No. 3, 1926.

2. Leopol'd Averbakh, *Nashi literaturnye raznoglasiia* (Leningrad, 1927), p. 89.

3. That Furmanov disagreed with the leadership is evident from his diaries, already referred to. Libedinskii's own description of these events places him in the group led by Averbakh. See Iurii Libedinskii, *General'nye zadachi proletarskoi literatury* (Leningrad, 1931), pp. 7–8. Kirshon together with Averbakh signed a statement called the "April Theses" which, even before the publication of the 1925 Party resolution, took exception to the policy of the VAPP leadership. Averbakh, *Nashi literaturnye raznoglasiia*, Appendix, pp. 246–48.

4. *Ibid.*, p. 88.

5. *Ibid.*, p. 85.

6. *History of the Communist Party of the Soviet Union*, p. 276.

7. *Ibid.*

8. Libedinskii, *General'nye zadachi*, pp. 7–8. "One group (Vardin, Lelevich) did not wish to acknowledge the mistakes pointed out by the resolution of the Party, and insisted that they

must continue to propagate the views condemned by the Party. . . . The discussion transcended literature and went over into politics, and at that time Lelevich and Vardin joined the opposition, which was then forming in Leningrad."

9. I. N. Rozanov, *Putevoditel' po sovremennoi russkoi literature* (Moscow, 1929), p. 334.

10. Of the Party men whose names have been mentioned here as participants in the discussions and disputes of the time, Furmanov, Lunacharskii, Polonskii, and Frunze died before the period of the great purge in the middle thirties. The following have "disappeared," been executed or, in the case of Trotsky, been murdered, and are now referred to as "enemies of the people": Trotsky, Bukharin, Radek, Voronskii, Averbakh, Kirshon, Vardin, Lelevich, Rodov, and Gorbachëv. It is possible that others mentioned here have had a similar fate, but the information is not yet complete. Libedinskii, Bezymenskii, and Demian Bednyi remained active in Soviet literature after the purges.

11. Quoted in Kogan, *Literatura velikogo desiatiletiia,* p. 61.

12. Averbakh, *Nashi literaturnye raznoglasiia,* p. 90.

13. *Ibid.,* p. 93. See also "RAPP," *Literaturnaia entsiklopediia.*

14. "Federatsiia," *Literaturnaia entsiklopediia,* IX (1935), 673–74.

15. Max Eastman in his *Artists in Uniform; a Study of Literature and Bureaucratism* has contributed an interesting and highly polemical history of the RAPP period in literature which, in my opinion, gives a rather misleading picture of RAPP itself. The reason for this is his indiscriminate use of the *Literary Gazette, On Literary Guard, Pravda,* etc., on the assumption that all of these represented the RAPP leadership. That assumption is not warranted.

16. "Literaturnaia gazeta," *Literaturnaia entsiklopediia,* VI (1932), 438–45.

17. "Kul'turnaia revoliutsiia i sovremennaia literatura (rezoliutsiia pervogo s"ezda po dokladu Averbakha)," *Na literaturnom postu,* Nos. 13–14, July, 1928, p. 8.

18. Since one of the "signs" of hegemony recognized by the On Literary Guardists was the predominant influence of proletarian writers among working-class and peasant readers, the study of reader interest became an important phase of their activity. A regular department of the magazine *Na literaturnom postu* was devoted to this investigation of reader demand. It was called "Chto chitaiut" (*Na literaturnom postu,* No. 2, January, 1928, pp. 36–38).

19. See below, p. 53. For the dispute regarding the Federation and VAPP see A. K. Voronskii, "O Federatsii sovetskikh pisatelei,"

Krasnaia nov', No. 4, April, 1927, pp. 214–21, and Averbakh's attempted answer in "Literaturye diskussii tekushchego goda," *Na literaturnom postu,* No. 13, June, 1927, p. 7. *Pravda* took issue sharply with Voronskii in this dispute: S. I. Gusev, "Kakaia federatsiia pisatelei nam nuzhna," *Pravda,* April 30, 1927. Voronskii's answer to this attack is to be found in A. K. Voronskii, "Ob uzhasnom krokodile, o Federatsii pisatelei, i o falshivykh frazakh," *Krasnaia nov'*, No. 6, June, 1927, pp. 238–49. Voronskii's activity was interrupted soon after the publication of his articles on VAPP and the Federation by his exile to the Urals. Shortly after the liquidation of the 1927 Trotsky-Zinoviev "opposition bloc," he was expelled from the Party and exiled with other members of that group. He returned to Moscow in 1930, where he resumed literary work but was never again prominent. He "disappeared" in 1937 at the time of the Radek-Piatakov trial and has not been heard from since. See "Voronskii," *Literaturnaia entsiklopediia,* II, 313–18; also Trotsky, *My Life,* p. 564. An interesting treatment of the relations of Voronskii with the VAPP literary school is to be found in Hugh McLean, Jr., "Voronskij and VAPP," *American Slavic and East European Review,* VII, No. 3 (October, 1949), 185–200.

20. V. Polonskii, "Literaturnoe dvizhenie oktiabrskogo desiatiletiia," *Pechat' i revoliutsiia,* No. 7, July, 1927, p. 77.

21. See Appendix A, point 11. The earliest issues of *Na literaturnom postu* were not available for this study. It has been necessary, therefore, to rely on P. S. Kogan, V. Polonskii, and articles in the *Literaturnaia entsiklopediia* for a description of their contents.

22. "Svoë no ne koriavoe," *Na literaturnom postu,* Nos. 5–6, 1926. Quoted in Kogan, *Literatura velikoga desiatiletiia,* p. 62.

23. His early articles on this subject are collected in Libedinskii, *Uchëba, tvorchestvo i samokritika* (Moscow, 1927).

24. Polonskii, *Ocherki literaturnogo,* p. 286.

25. Peredovaia, *Na literaturnom postu,* No. 8, April, 1928, pp. 2–6.

26. "RAPP," *Literaturnaia entsiklopediia.*

27. Gladkov and Panskii soon after left the executive of VAPP. Gladkov, until shortly before a member of the Smithy, had joined VAPP in 1925. He soon became dissatisfied with the leadership and resigned from the organization. Though at one time a tremendously popular proletarian writer and one of the personal favorites of Stalin, his work was severely criticised by VAPP (RAPP) critics after his abandonment of their organization. See speech of Gladkov in *Sovetskaia literatura na novom etape. Stenogramma I ogo plenuma orgkomiteta Soiuza sovetskikh pisatelei,* pp. 143–45.

Panskii (also called Solskii-Panskii), an official in the Soviet film industry, was given permission to visit Germany in 1928, but never returned to the Soviet Union. See *Na literaturnom postu,* Nos. 22–23, November, 1929, p. 95. He is at present a resident of New York City. He figured prominently in the accusations made against Kirshon and Averbakh at the time of the 1937 treason trial that they had associated with *émigrés* and "Polish spies." He is indeed an *émigré*. The charge that he was a "spy" is a vicious fantasy.

28. Peredovaia, *Na literaturnom postu,* No. 10, May, 1928, pp. 1–5.

29. *Ibid.,* p. 4.

30. "S"ezd VAPPa," *Na literaturnom postu,* No. 9, May, 1928, pp. 2–3.

31. "Dnevnik s"ezda VAPPa," *Na literaturnom postu,* No. 10, May, 1928, pp. 74–75.

32. *Ibid.,* p. 75.

33. *Ibid.,* p. 76.

34. See, for instance, Peredovaia, *Na literaturnom postu,* No. 10, May, 1928, pp. 1–5; Leopol'd Averbakh, "O sovremennoi literature," *Na literaturnom postu,* Nos. 11–12, June, 1928, p. 18.

35. Peredovaia, *Na literaturnom postu,* No. 10, May, 1928, p. 5.

Chapter V: The Theory of Literature, 1928

1. See above, chap. iv, p. 50.

2. See the reaction to RAPP ideas of a Left Front of Art critic, S. Tretiakov, "Chto proizoshlo v proletarskoi literature?" *Novyi LEF,* No. 6, June, 1928, pp. 1–3. Tretiakov gives special attention to the influence of Voronskii in proletarian literature.

3. See below, chap. x, pp. 172 ff.

4. L. Averbakh, *Nashi literaturnye raznoglasiia,* p. 24. L. N. Tolstoy is clearly one of Averbakh's sources for phrases and ideas.

5. Averbakh, "Doloi Plekhanova," *Na literaturnom postu,* Nos. 20–21, October–November, 1928, p. 21.

6. Averbakh, *Na putiakh kul'turnoi revoliutsii.*

7. *Ibid.,* pp. 1–10.

8. *Ibid.,* pp. 46–50.

9. *Ibid.,* p. 68.

10. *Ibid.*

11. *Ibid.,* p. 64.

12. *Ibid.,* p. 65.

13. *Ibid.* While the little brochure from which I have been quoting does not prove that Averbakh was at this time part of or even sympathetic to the Party opposition headed by Bukharin and Rykov and known as the "right" opposition, it does give some basis for the

speculation that he may have been so disposed even as early as 1928. To quote liberally from Rykov and Bukharin at a time when the right opposition was "gathering its forces" (*History of the Communist Party of the Soviet Union*, pp. 293–94) and in a context suggesting that industrialization at increased tempos cannot be carried out unless the working force is given better conditions of life, more education, medical care, etc., is enough to indicate that Averbakh was at least inclined toward the position of the right opposition. As far as I know there is no possibility of proving this, for in all his public statements after 1928 he supports Stalin and the program of the Party. Yet there are indications of a tendency to oppose the Central Committee in his activity as head of RAPP, and even in some of his published works on literature. These will be treated in the proper place. Other indications of a definite orientation toward the right opposition are: (1) the fact that he was accused as an "enemy of the people" in April, 1937, shortly after Iagoda, a member of the right, was arrested; (2) the fact that he disappeared completely after that and is now referred to as an "enemy of the people," a term usually applied to oppositionists convicted of crimes against the Soviet state; (3) the fact that Rykov in his final plea at the trial of the Bloc of Rights and Trotskyites refers to him as one who was part of the opposition (*The Case of the Anti-Soviet Bloc of Rights and Trotskyites* [Moscow: People's Commissariat of Justice of the USSR, 1938], p. 738); (4) his close family relationship with a leader of the "rights," Iagoda, who was married to Averbakh's sister. It should be borne in mind that these are indications only, and not conclusive proof. It should also be borne in mind that the dividing line between left and right opposition largely disappeared beginning with the thirties.

14. "Rezoliutsiia plenuma VAPPa po dokladu Averbakha," *Na literaturnom postu*, No. 4, March, 1927, pp. 63–67.

15. "Kulturnaia revolyutsiia i sovremennaia literatura (rezoliutsiia pervogo s"ezda po dokladu Averbakha)," *Na literaturnom postu*, Nos. 13–14, July, 1928, p. 5.

16. Averbakh, "Nekotorye momenty kul'turnoi revoliutsii i iskusstvo," *Na literaturnom postu*, No. 8, April, 1927, pp. 4–5.

17. "Kul'turnaia revoliutsiia i sovremennaia literatura," p. 4. Notice here the curious mixture of ideas from three separate sources: Bogdanov ("organize the feelings . . . ," etc.), Plekhanov ("thinking in images"), and Bukharin and Tolstoy ("art emotionally 'infects' the reader"). The young RAPP theorists of proletarian literature had no easy time applying the Marxian dialectic to this new and not yet authoritatively analyzed sphere of activity. They did their best with what was available.

18. "Kulturnaia revoliutsiia i sovremennaia literatura," pp. 5–6.

19. Averbakh, *Kulturnaia revoliutsiia i voprosy sovremennoi literatury*, p. 65. Notice again that Averbakh's language frequently recalls the phrasing of these ideas by Bogdanov and other Proletcult leaders. Yet his analysis includes the Voronskii thesis that art is primarily "cognition of life."

20. A. Fadeev, "Na kogo my orientiruemsia?" (speech at Biuro pravleniia VAPPa), *Na literaturnom postu*, No. 14, July, 1927, p. 14.

21. A discussion of the concept of social demand was initiated by V. Polonskii, and printed in *Pechat' i revoliutsiia*, No. 1, January, 1929, pp. 19–82. For a discussion of the literary views of LEF, the leaders of which were Maiakovskii, Aseev, and O. Brik, see "LEF," *Literaturnaia entsiklopediia*, VI (1932), 341–48. For the LEF attitude toward social demand, see O. Brik, "Ne teoriia a lozung," *Pechat' i revoliutsiia*, No. 1, January, 1929, p. 25.

22. For an account of the RAPP dispute with LEF, see Averbakh, "Literaturnye diskussii tekushchego goda," *Na literaturnom postu*, No. 14, July, 1927, pp. 5 ff.

23. Averbakh, *Kulturnaia revoliutsiia i voprosy sovremennoi literatury*, pp. 62–64.

24. For such a viewpoint see Harriet Borland, *Soviet Literary Theory and Practice during the First Five-Year Plan 1928–1932* (New York, 1950).

25. Libedinskii, "Temy kotorye zhdut svoikh avtorov," quoted in Brodskii, *Literaturnye manifesty*, p. 188.

26. Libedinskii, "Problemy tematiki," *Na literaturnom postu*, No. 13, July, 1927, p. 19.

27. Libedinskii, "Khudozhestvennaia platforma RAPP," *Na literaturnom postu*, No. 19, September, 1928, pp. 9–19.

An understanding though very brief account of this period is given in Part II, "Literature," of P. N. Milyukov's *Outlines of Russian Culture*, pp. 98–116, especially pp. 98 and 99, where the attacks of the minority upon the leadership of RAPP are described. "The opposition [to the RAPP leadership] demanded that the novels in which the living man was depicted against the background of a non-class family life be replaced by literary reports from various sectors of the Communist front."

Mate Zalka, a proletarian writer of some talent who dealt largely with civil war subjects, had no sympathy with the growing tendency to present the writer with a social demand. In an article in the RAPP literary magazine *Oktiabr'* (No. 4, April, 1929, p. 182) entitled, "O tvorchestve i sotsial'nom zakaze," he said: "Here I am working seriously to transform the raw material of the civil war into a novel, and along comes the social demander buzzing in my ear: 'Don't write about the civil war. Write about construction, about collective farming, about the new man. . . . ' " Zalka stated in the following terms the only possible meaning he could conceive for the term "social demand": "The writer feels the real social demand through that umbilical cord which binds him firmly and constantly, which nourishes him through maintaining him in close contact with his class."

28. "Kul'turnaia revoliutsiia i sovremennaia literatura," p. 4. See also "RAPP," *Literaturnaia entsiklopediia,* IX, 524.

29. *Ibid.*

30. Libedinskii, "Khudozhestvennaia platforma," *passim.*

31. Averbakh, "Tvorcheskie puti proletarskoi literatury, Doklad na Konferentsii MAPPa," *Na literaturnom postu,* No. 10, May, 1927, p. 16.

32. *Ibid.,* p. 15.

33. Fadeev, "Doloi Shillera!" *Na literaturnom postu,* Nos. 21–22, November, 1929, pp. 4–9.

For an interesting treatment of Fadeev's novel *The Rout* from the viewpoint of its direct imitation of the "classics," see O. Brik, "Razgrom Fadeeva," *Novyi LEF,* No. 5, May, 1928, pp. 1–5.

34. Fadeev, "No kakom etape my nakhodimsia," *Na literaturnom postu,* Nos. 11–12, June, 1927, p. 4.

35. Libedinskii, "Realisticheskii pokaz lichnosti," *Na literaturnom postu,* No. 1, January, 1927, p. 27.

36. *Ibid.,* p. 28.

37. A. Selivanovskii, "Tikhii Don," *Na literaturnom postu,* No. 10, May, 1929, pp. 46–57.

38. In an informal discussion with Leningrad worker-writers, Libedinskii stated that in *The Birth of a Hero* he thought he had been more successful than in any of his other works in expressing an idea dialectically in a work of fiction. See Libedinskii, *Generalnye zadachi proletarskoi literatury,* p. 148. This novel soon after its publication became the center of a storm of criticism, both official and unofficial.

39. G. Gorbachëv, "O samozvannikh dusheprikazchikakh kulturnogo nasledstva," *Polemika,* p. 138.

40. Often enough the "study of the classics" amounted to no more than mechanical imitation of scenes from a classical author, but with proletarian characters. In the case of unskillful writers it sometimes reached absurd lengths. Averbakh mentions ("Doklad na Konferentsii MAPPa," pp. 12–13) a poem in the style and meter of Pushkin's *Evgenii Onegin* which told the sad story of a proletarian Tatiana's adventures in a factory.

For Lenin's articles on Tolstoy, in whom he was deeply interested, see chap. x, p. 174 ff.

41. Gorbachëv, *Polemika,* p. 137.

42. Quoted in M. Serebrianskii, "Kritika khudozhestvennoi platformy RAPP," *Na literaturnom postu,* No. 17, September, 1930, p. 17.

43. Based on J. Stalin, *Dialectical and Historical Materialism.* I am indebted for this summary to the excellent article: Herbert Rubenstein, "Recent Conflict in Soviet Linguistics," *Language,* July–September, 1951.

44. Libedinskii, "Khudozhestvennaia platforma RAPP," *Na literaturnom postu,* No. 19, October, 1928, p. 9.

45. For a treatment of these ideas see above, chap. ii.

46. M. Luzgin, "K tvorcheskoi programme RAPP," *Na literaturnom postu,* No. 2, January, 1927, pp. 8–12.

47. M. Serebrianskii, "Kritika," *Na literaturnom postu,* No. 17, September, 1930, p. 9.

48. "Otvet kritikam," *Na literaturnom postu,* No. 12, April, 1932, pp. 6–9.

49. Letter to Margaret Harkness (April, 1888), quoted in F. P. Schiller and M. A. Lifshitz, *Marks i Engel's ob iskusstve i literature,* pp. 41–42.

50. Quoted in *Literature and Art* (New York: International Publishers, 1947), pp. 46–49.

51. Fadeyev, "Doloi Shillera!" p. 8.

52. Averbakh, "Doklad na Konferentsii MAPPa," pp. 10 and 12.

53. Fadeev, *op. cit.,* p. 9.

54. Libedinskii, "Khudozhestvennaia platforma RAPP," *Na literaturnom postu,* No. 19, October, 1928, pp. 9–19, and Nos. 20–21, October–November, 1928, pp. 6–14.

55. "Iurii Libedinskii," *Literaturnaia entsiklopediia,* VI (1932), 363–64.

56. "The Idea of Art," in V. G. Belinskii, *Selected Philosophical Works,* pp. 168–87.

57. *Ibid.*

58. Libedinskii, "Khudozhestvennaia platforma RAPP," *Na literaturnom postu,* Nos. 20–21, p. 11.

59. Libedinskii, *op. cit.,* No. 19, p. 12.

60. *Ibid.*

61. *Ibid.*

62. *War and Peace,* trans. Constance Garnett (New York: Modern Library, 1931), p. 775.

63. Libedinskii, "Khudozhestvennaia platforma RAPP," *Na literaturnom postu,* No. 19, p. 18.

64. Fadeev, "Stolbovaia doroga proletarskoi literatury," *Oktiabr',* No. 11, November, 1928, p. 171.

65. *Ibid.,* p. 182.

66. See Averbakh, "O Furmanove i proletarskoi literature,"

Oktiabr', No. 3, March, 1929, pp. 147–58. Here he emphasizes the need for constant self-analysis and self-understanding in order to develop clarity and certainty in one's "world view." The same idea is developed by Libedinskii in "Eshchë o khudozhestvennoi platforme RAPP," *Na literaturnom postu*, No. 1, January, 1929, pp. 26–28.

67. "Rechi Rappovtsev na XVI s"ezde Partii," *Na literaturnom postu*, Nos. 13–14, July, 1930, p. 14.

68. See above, chap. i.

69. "Kul'turnaia revolyutsiia i sovremennaia literatura," p. 8.

70. For a description of this phenomenon, see V. Friche, "V zashchitu ratsionalisticheskogo izobrazheniia cheloveka," *Krasnaia nov'*, No. 1, January, 1928, pp. 236–40.

71. Fadeev, "Stolbovaia doroga," *Oktiabr'*, No. 11, November, 1928, p. 171.

72. *Ibid.*

73. See the remarks of Voronskii and of Lunacharskii in *K voprosu.*

74. For a description of the typical proletarian product of the early period, see V. F. Pereverzev, "Na frontakh tekushchei belletristiki," *Pechat' i revoliutsiia*, No. 4, April, 1923, pp. 127–31. This is an estimate of their product by a Communist critic generally friendly to the proletarians.

75. Libedinskii, "Za chto boretsia napostovstvo (rech' na sobranii litkruzhkov LAPPa, April 25, 1930)," reprinted in *General'nye zadachi proletarskoi literatury*, p. 9.

76. Libedinskii, "Za chto," p. 10.

77. *Ibid.*, p. 44.

78. *Ibid.*, p. 56.

79. *Ibid.*

80. *Ibid.*, p. 58.

81. Averbakh, Libedinskii, and Fadeev were aware of the survivals of the "old" psychology in Communists and their allies, and always claimed to be concerned about the struggle with these survivals.

82. Libedinskii, "Za chto," pp. 15–16. Toom's views are quoted here.

83. *Ibid.*, p. 21.

84. *Ibid.*

85. Voronskii, "O Federatsii," p. 220.

86. A. Selivanovskii, "Korni tvorcheskikh raznoglasii," *Oktiabr'*, No. 5, May, 1929, p. 187.

87. Voronskii, *Literaturnye zapisi* (Moscow: Krug, 1926), p. 18.

88. E. Dobin, "Sryvanie masok," *Na literaturnom postu*, Nos. 31–32, November, 1931, p. 13.

89. "Rech' t. Stalina i zadachi RAPP (rezoliutsiia sekretariata

RAPP 12/VIII 1931)," *Na literaturnom postu,* No. 24, August, 1931, p. 4.

Chapter VI: The Party and Its Instrument

1. Quoted in "Bolshevistskaia partiia i sovetskaia literatura," *Novyi mir,* May, 1947, p. 133.

2. "Ob obsluzhivanii knigoi massovogo chitatelia (postanovlenie Tsentral'nogo komiteta, 28 dek. 1928)," *Resheniia partii o pechati,* p. 119. See Appendix.

3. "Bolshevistskaia partiia," *Novyi mir,* No. 5, 1947, p. 133. See also Edward J. Brown, *The Russian Association of Proletarian Writers (1928–1932)* (microfilm; Columbia University, 1950), pp. 195–200.

4. The clearest statement of the Party's support of RAPP and its expectations from the latter appeared in a statement accepted as a directive by the literary world: K. Tomas, "Za konsolidatsiiu kommunisticheskikh sil proletarskoi literatury," *Pravda,* Dec. 4, 1929. After the appearance of this statement a number of literary figures previously opposed to RAPP entered that organization. The statement called for a "consolidation of forces" within RAPP, which was following a line in literature "closest to the line of the Party."

5. "Novye zadachi," *Pravda,* February 17, 1930.

6. "Za proletarskuiu literaturu" (peredovaia), *Pravda,* April 19, 1931. Reprinted in *Na literaturnom postu,* No. 13, May, 1931, pp. 1–4.

7. The Brigade of Writers which visited Turkmenistan included Leonov, Ivanov, Tikhonov, Lugovskii, Sannikov, and Zozulia. Leonov says in his report: "We left for Turkmenistan at the invitation of the Turkmen Commissariat of Education. We had also received a 'mission' from *Izvestiia.* In addition, A. B. Khalatov, one of the initiators of those writers' trips, had proposed that we write a book about Turkmenistan." See *Literaturnaia gazeta,* No. 20, May 19, 1930, p. 1.

8. The most notable of these is his verse play *Vystrel* (The Shot), which deals in rather simple journalese fashion with the problems of management, shock-workers, the youth, wreckers, etc., in the work of a factory. His poems were regularly printed in *Pravda* during this period. *Tragediinaia noch',* which compares the attitude and technical capacity of an American (Zhak) worker with the collective methods of work of the Russian worker, first appeared in *Pravda,* November 7, 1931. Both were sharply criticized by RAPP leaders.

9. A. Bezymenskii, "Rech'na plenume," *Na literaturnom postu,* Nos. 35–36, December, 1931, p. 21.

10. Eastman, *Artists in Uniform*, p. 122. B. Pil'niak, *Tadzhikistan; sed'maia Sovetskaia.*

11. *Sovetskaia literatura na novom etape. Stenogramma I-go plenuma orgkomiteta Soiuza sovetskikh pisatelei,* speech of P. Romanov, p. 135.

12. *Literaturnaia gazeta,* December 3, 1931, p. 1. In his speech to this gathering Mekhlis took occasion to point out that in RAPP there were certain "theoretical shortcomings" which must be "liquidated."

13. "Ob izdatel'skoi rabote (postanovleniia TSK VKP[b], 15 avgusta 1931)," *Resheniia partii o pechati,* pp. 144–45.

14. *Gosizdat khudozhestvennoi literatury* (State Publishing House for Belles-Lettres).

15. "Ob izdatel'skoi rabote," p. 147.

16. *Ibid.,* p. 148. Italics mine.

17. For an account of the type of literary activity characteristic of this period, see Struve, *Twenty-five Years of Soviet Russian Literature,* pp. 114–27; Slonim, *Soviet Literature,* pp. 42–46; A. Tolstoy, "Trends in Soviet Literature," *Science and Society,* VII, No. 3 (1943), 233–50; Harriet Borland, *Soviet Literary Theory and Practice during the First Five-Year Plan 1928–1932* (New York, 1950).

18. "Postanovleniia TSK VKP(b) o rabote pechati Molodoi gvardii," December 29, 1931, *Resheniia partii,* p. 150.

19. P. Chagin, "Novyi etap izdatelskoi raboty i khudozhestvennaia literatura," *Na literaturnom postu,* No. 20, October, 1931, pp. 11–12.

20. *Ibid.*

21. "Khronika sovetskoi literatury za 20 let," *Literaturnyi kritik,* No. 1, January, 1938, p. 123.

22. "Ob izdanii Istoriia zavodov" (Postanovleniia TSK VKP[b], October 10, 1931), *Na literaturnom postu,* No. 30, October, 1931, p. 1.

23. "Za bol'shoe iskusstvo Bol'shevizma" (peredovaia), *Na literaturnom postu,* No. 14, May, 1931, p. 1.

24. *Pravda,* May 18, 1931.

25. The evidence that the Party gave special support and encouragement to RAPP in 1929, 1930, and 1931 is contained in a *Pravda* article (K. Tomas, "Za konsolidatsiiu kommunisticheskikh sil v literature," Dec. 4, 1929), in *Pravda* editorials, in the decree of the Central Committee dissolving RAPP (see below, chap. xi, p. 200), in Fadeev's article "Staroe i novoe" (*Literaturnaia gazeta,* October 23, 1932), and especially in the attitude toward RAPP taken by other organizations during those years. See, particularly, "Fraktsiia VKP(b) sekretariata RAPPa," *Na literaturnom postu,* No. 23, December, 1929, p. 3.

26. The evidence for this is circumstantial, but fairly con-

vincing; see chap. v, n. 10, and the whole of the Epilogue, which relates the ultimate fate of Averbakh and his friends in 1937.

27. "RAPP," *Literaturnaia entsiklopediia,* IX (1935), 520.

28. Fadeev, "Khudozhestvennaia literatura i voprosy kul'turnoi revoliutsii," *Literaturnaia gazeta,* No. 48, October 23, 1932, p. 3. Confusion need not arise from the designation of Trotsky and Voronskii as a "left" opposition. While this policy in literature was called a "right" policy, the Party opposition associated with them was always known as "left." In what follows it is not necessarily suggested that *all* the schools and tendencies were associated with the opposition.

29. A bibliography of these various schools and tendencies is perhaps in order here. Reference has already been made to the views of Trotsky, Voronskii, and the early On Guard leaders.

On the Pereval group, the following material should be consulted: "Ob"iavleniia Perevala" (1925), Brodskii, *Literaturnye manifesty ot simvolizma k Oktiabriu.* "Pereval i iskusstvo nashikh dnei," *Literaturnaia gazeta,* April 14, 1930. I. Zonin, "Novoe vystuplenie kapituliantov," *Na literaturnom postu,* No. 4, February, 1927, pp. 16–20. "Reshenie Kommunisticheskoi akademii o Perevale," *Literaturnaia gazeta,* May 19, 1930. M. Bochacher, "Galvanizirovannaia voronshchina," *Pechat' i revoliutsiia,* March, 1930, p. 13.

On the New LEF group, see articles, sketches, and stories published in their magazine *Novyi LEF* during 1927 and 1928. For their theoretical approach, see especially the following: N. Chuzhak, "Literatura zhiznestroeniia," *Novyi LEF,* No. 11, November, 1928. O. Brik, "Za novatorstvo," *Novyi LEF,* No. 1, January, 1927. S. Tretiakov, "Novyi Lev Tolstoy," *Novyi LEF,* No. 1, January, 1928. "Peredovaia," *Na literaturnom postu,* No. 7, 1927. L. Averbakh, "Literaturnye diskussii," *Na literaturnom postu,* No. 14, 1927, pp. 5–9. S. Tretiakov, "Chto proizoshlo v proletarskoi literature," *Novyi LEF,* No. 6, 1928.

On the Pereverzev group, see the following books and articles: V. S. Pereverzev, "Problemy marksistskogo literaturovedeniia," *Literatura i Marksizm,* No. 2, 1929, pp. 2 ff. A. Mikhailov, "K kritike metodologiia Pereverzeva," *Na literaturnom postu,* No. 5, 1929. V. S. Pereverzev, "O teorii sotsial'nogo zakaza," *Pechat' i revolyutsiia,* No. 1, January, 1929, pp. 60–61. "Rezoliutsiia Kommunisticheskoi akademii o Pereverzeve," *Literaturnaia gazeta,* April 2, 1930, p. 2. V. F. Pereverzev, ed., *Literaturovedenie* (*sbornik statei*) (Moscow, 1928).

30. For a more complete discussion of these schools and tendencies see Brown, *The Russian Association of Proletarian Writers* (*1928–1932*), pp. 222–36.

31. In the *Knizhnaia letopis'*, a chronicle of all books published

for the given period, the classification "belles-lettres" is broken down into several sections: agitational belles-lettres, agricultural belles-lettres, etc.

32. Typical of this kind of activity was the report of a "Writers' Shock Brigade," published in the *Literary Gazette* for March 17, 1930, p. 1:

> We, members of the Writers' Shock Brigade who have gone into the region of complete collectivization of the Central Black Soil Area, challenge to a socialist competition writers who have gone into other regions. We promise: (1) to set up not less than ten collective-farm village correspondent circles; (2) to edit not less than eight numbers of model wall-newspapers in the collective farms; (3) to instruct . . . not less than five hundred men in the work of village correspondence; (4) to aid the work of the country dramatic circles, presenting not less than four plays connected with the completion of the spring sowing. We challenge the writers who are active to set up another brigade for work in the village so as not to lose the time that is left before the completion of the spring sowing.

33. *Literary Gazette*, August 19, 1929, prints a "Report of the First Cultural Brigade of Writers." The brigade had spent two and a half months in the Urals. They had investigated twenty factories and five mines "in a detailed and attentive manner, becoming acquainted with the technique of production, new construction, socialist competition, social and economic position of the working class in the Urals."

34. An editorial in the *Literary Gazette*, May 27, 1929, announcing that its pages would be opened to a series of sketches on socialist competition, says: "To work, comrades! Down with delay! All our country and everything that is best in the world wish to know how the great experiment of socialist competition is going, and Soviet writers must tell about this."

35. "Za bol'shoe iskusstvo bol'shevizma," *Na literaturnom postu*, No. 14, May, 1931, p. 1.

36. *Na literaturnom postu*, No. 17, June, 1931, p. 21.

37. *Ibid.*

38. Stavskii was the secretary of the Union of Writers in April, 1937, at the time Averbakh, Kirshon, Mirsky, and many others were accused of vague crimes and removed from the scene. He is the chief accuser of Averbakh at that time in the pages of the *Literary Gazette* and at many meetings of the Union of Writers. His accusations will be dealt with later. He died on the Tallinn front in 1943. See L. I. Timofeev, *Sovremennaia literatura*, p. 256.

39. "Rezoliutsiia po organizatsionnym voprosam (po dokladu V. Stavskogo)," *Na literaturnom postu*, No. 19, 1929, pp. 8–11.

40. *Ibid.*, p. 11.

41. Averbakh, "Predrassudki barstva," *Na literaturnom postu,* No. 7, April, 1930, p. 3.

42. Averbakh, "Doklad na plenume," *Literaturnaia gazeta,* September 23, 1929.

43. Averbakh, "Zadachi RAPP'a v rekonstruktivnyi period," *Na literaturnom postu,* Nos. 21–22, October, 1929, p. 103.

44. *Ibid.*

45. *Ibid.*

46. *Ibid.*

47. Averbakh, "Predrassudki," p. 4.

48. "Khronika," *Na literaturnom postu,* No. 17, September, 1929, p. 78.

49. *Ibid.*

50. A. Surkov, "Za proletarskie kadry," *Na literaturnom postu,* No. 12, June, 1930.

51. "Pis'mo sekretariata RAPP mestnym organizatsiiam," *Na literaturnom postu,* No. 3, February, 1930, pp. 75–76.

52. "Khronika," *Na literaturnom postu,* No. 9, May, 1930, pp. 99–100.

53. "Rechi rappovtsev v XVI s"ezde," *Na literaturnom postu,* Nos. 13–14, July, 1930, pp. 21–22.

54. "Za perestroiku RAPP," *Na literaturnom postu,* No. 17, September, 1930, pp. 58–59.

55. Averbakh, "Za pisatelia soiuznika—rech' na plenume pravleniia VSSP, 16 maia, 1931," *Na literaturnom postu,* No. 15, May, 1931, pp. 1–6.

Chapter VII: October: the Proletarian Writers

1. Iurii Olesha, *Zagovor chuvstv,* published in *Oktiabr',* No. 1, January, 1929, pp. 33–51.

2. Valentin Kataev, *Avangard,* published in *Oktiabr',* No. 3, March, 1930, pp. 53–93.

3. L. Ovalov, "Boltovnia," *Oktiabr',* No. 4, April, 1929, pp. 23–40; No. 5, May, 1929, pp. 53–90.

4. Ovalov, "Lovtsy somnenii," *Oktiabr',* No. 6, June, 1930, pp. 89–152; No. 7, July, 1930, pp. 8–59.

5. A. Mitrofanov, "Iiun'-iiul'," *Oktiabr',* No. 7, July, 1930, pp. 96–160.

6. B. Levin, "Zhili dva tovarishcha," *Oktiabr',* No. 1, January, 1931, pp. 78–114; February, 1931, pp. 83–119.

7. For a discussion of the Sten incident, see M. Ezhov, L. Mekhlis, and P. Pospelov, "Pravyi uklon v prakticheskoi rabote i partiinnoe boloto," *Bol'shevik,* No. 16, August, 1929, pp. 34–63. Sten's appeal to the youth to think for themselves and shun "ideo-

logical cowardice" appeared in *Komsomol'skaia pravda*, No. 169, April, 1929.

8. I have been unable to find a copy of Averbakh's original resolution nor any complete description of its contents. The second resolution on Sten was published in *Na literaturnom postu*, No. 19, October, 1929, pp. 15–16. B. Olkhovyi, "Za chotkuiu partiinnuiu liniiu v rukovodstve proletarskoi literatury," *Pravda*, October 20, 1929.

9. L. Kopylova, "Sad ottsa Arseniia," *Oktiabr'*, No. 2, February, 1929, pp. 59–64.

10. I. Makarov, "Smert'," *Oktiabr'*, No. 1, January, 1929, pp. 86–96.

11. M. Kolosov, "Individual'noe Vospitanie," *Oktiabr'*, No. 3, March, 1929, pp. 4–12.

12. V. Gerasimova, "Sëstry," *Oktiabr'*, No. 7, July, 1929, pp. 41–62.

13. *Rozhdenie geroia*, published serially in *Oktiabr'*, No. 1, January, 1930, pp. 4–53; No. 2, February, 1930, pp. 41–62.

Chapter VIII: On Literary Guard: the Proletarian Critics

1. "Rezoliutsiia po dokladu Makar'eva," *Literaturnaia gazeta*, September 15, 1931.

2. A. Fadeev, "Za bolshuiu literaturu proletariata," *Literaturnaia gazeta*, January 28, 1932.

3. *Strana dolzhna znat' svoikh geroev.*

4. B. Mikhailov, "Za kachestvo pokaza geroev truda," *Na literaturnom postu*, Nos. 31–32, November, 1931, p. 53.

5. I. Makar'ev, "Pokaz geroev truda- general'naia tema proletarskoi literatury," *Na literaturnom postu*, Nos. 31–32, November, 1931, p. 30.

6. *Ibid.*, p. 27.

7. *Ibid.*, No. 33, November, 1931, p. 13.

8. M. Bekker, "Protiv obezlichki," *Na literaturnom postu*, No. 22, August, 1931, p. 33.

9. "Vsë, chto nuzhno znat' khalturshchiku dlia pokaza geroev," *Na literaturnom postu*, No. 30, October, 1931, pp. 32–33.

10. See above, chap. vi, p. 102.

11. L. Averbakh, "Zadachi RAPP'a v rekonstruktivnyi period," *Na literaturnom postu*, Nos. 21–22, October, 1929, p. 100.

12. *Ibid.*, p. 99.

13. *Ibid.*

14. Speech of Gladkov, *Sovetskaia literatura na novom etape*, p. 143.

15. The hero of the novel *Cement*.

16. A. Fadeev, "Na kakom etape my nakhodimsia," *Na literaturnom postu,* Nos. 11–12, June, 1927, p. 6.

17. Speech of Gladkov, *Sovetskaia literatura na novom etape,* p. 143.

18. *Krutaia stupen'; rasskazy kontrol'nika.*

19. I. Kublanov, "O 'Krutoi stupeni' A. Karavaevoi," *Na literaturnom postu,* No. 25, September, 1931, pp. 32–33.

20. I. Ermakov, " 'Samstroi' G. Medinskogo," *Na literaturnom postu,* No. 2, January, 1931, pp. 24–28.

21. F. Sashkov, "Obsuzhdali 'Nashgorod' B. Gorbatova," *Na literaturnom postu,* No. 2, January, 1931, pp. 23–30.

22. V. Zalesskii, "V Chëm oshibka Pogodina v 'Poema o topore,' " *Na literaturnom postu,* No. 29, October, 1931, pp. 29–31.

23. V. Kuzmin i V. Virginskii, " 'Poema o topore' i 'Temp' Pogodina," *Na literaturnom postu,* No. 22 (August), 1931, pp. 16–20.

24. Averbakh, "O razvërtyvanii tvorcheskoi diskussii," *Na literaturnom postu,* No. 25, September, 1931, p. 4.

25. Iurii Olesha, the author of the novel *Zavist'* (Envy), one of the best products of Soviet literature of the twenties, was as a rule on good terms with the RAPP leaders, who had many points of contact and sympathy with him. He is usually described as a fellow-traveler "close" to the proletarian literary movement. In this connection it is interesting to note that at the meeting of the Organization Committee of the Union of Soviet Writers in October, 1932, after the liquidation and disgrace of RAPP, Olesha spoke up in defense of the RAPP critics: speech of Olesha, *Sovetskaia literatura na novom etape,* p. 239.

26. A. Prozorov, "O 'Spiske blagodeianii' Iu. Olesha," *Na literaturnom postu,* No. 28, October, 1931, pp. 33–45.

27. *Ibid.*

28. G. Korabel'nikov, "Za partiinost' literatury," *Na literaturnom postu,* No. 6, February, 1931, pp. 14–18.

29. G. Morichnichenko, "Liniia naibolshego soprotivleniia," *Na literaturnom postu,* No. 19, July, 1931, p. 37.

I offer it as an interesting fact worthy of notice that perhaps the most frequent single RAPP criticism of reconstruction literature is that the "wreckers" who regularly appeared in it were portrayed mechanically and unconvincingly.

30. V. Pertsov, *O chëm i kak pisat' rabochemu pisateliu.*

31. "Bibliografiia," *Literaturnaia gazeta,* January 17, 1932.

32. S. Kirsanov, *Piatiletka.*

33. L. Levin, "Stroika stroiki S. Kirsanova," *Na literaturnom postu,* No. 8, March, 1931, pp. 44–45.

34. A. Bezymenskii, *Tragediinaia noch'.*

35. Averbakh, "Za khudozhestvennoe kachestvo," *Na literaturnom postu,* No. 6, February, 1931, p. 4.

36. *Ibid.,* p. 8.

37. Bezymenskii, "Sotsializm," *Pravda,* January 17, 1931.

38. Ef. Dobin, "Sryvanie masok," *Na literaturnom postu,* Nos. 31–32, November, 1931, pp. 21–22.

39. See below, chap. ix, p. 157.

40. A. Makedonov, "Tragediinaia noch," *Na literaturnom postu,* No. 22, August, 1931, pp. 21–27.

41. B. Minikh, *Litso professii.*

42. A. Surkov, "Ogon' po prisposoblencheskoi poshlosti," *Literaturnaia gazeta,* February 17, 1932.

43. D. Bednyi, "Slezai s pechi!" *Pravda,* September 7, 1930.

44. Libedinskii, "Doklad v ZOAPP," *Na literaturnom postu,* No. 1, January, 1931, p. 23.

45. *Ibid.*

46. *Ibid.*

47. *Komsomol'skaia pravda,* No. 64, 1931.

48. "Peredovaia," *Na literaturnom postu,* No. 7, March, 1931, p. 3. According to this account, his error had consisted in characterizing laziness as a national characteristic of the Russians.

49. Libedinskii, "O moei oshibke," *Na literaturnom postu,* No. 10, April, 1931, p. 33.

50. The criticism of Demian Bednyi came from the highest Party circles. The direct and vigorous involvement of Stalin in this affair was revealed only recently when, in the thirteenth volume of his collected works, the letter to Bednyi was published for the first time. I. V. Stalin, *Sochineniia,* XIII (Moscow, 1951), 23–27.

51. Averbakh, "Za khudozhestvennoe kachestvo," *Na literaturnom postu,* No. 6, February, 1931, p. 2.

52. *Ibid.*

53. "Ob itogakh soveshchaniia ocherkistov (rezoliutsiia sekretariata RAPPa)," *Na literaturnom postu,* No. 10, March, 1931, pp. 38–39.

54. See below, chap. x.

55. Libedinskii, "Problema rabochei tematiki," *Na literaturnom postu,* No. 16, August, 1929, pp. 14–15.

56. Averbakh, "O razvërtyvanii tvorcheskoi diskussii (rech' na plenume)," *Na literaturnom postu,* No. 23, August, 1931, p. 6.

57. Fadeev, "Zametki ob otstavanii," *Na literaturnom postu,* No. 2, January, 1931, p. 2.

58. G. Nikiforov, "Razreshite vyrugatsia," *Na literaturnom postu,* No. 29, October, 1931, pp. 43–47; "Za partiinost'," *Na literaturnom postu,* Nos. 35–36, December, 1931, pp. 94–95.

59. Speech of Seifullina, *Sovetskaia literatura na novom etape*, pp. 131–32.

60. A. Makedonov, "Pochemu 'Gidrotsentral', soiuznicheskoe proizvedenie?" *Literaturnaia gazeta*, January 22, 1932.

61. Speech of Lidin, *Sovetskaia literatura na novom etape*, p. 205.

62. Maiakovskii's suicide has been discussed from various points of view by practically all the commentators on Soviet literature. The current Soviet version is that he was "persecuted" and driven to this act by "enemies of the people" in RAPP who did not appreciate him. This of course fits into the current Soviet "devil theory" of their own history, and is not worthy of serious consideration, if only because it reduces to a childish level the stature of a fine and courageous poet. The problem cannot be taken up at length here, but I offer it as my opinion that the frustration which brought Maiakovskii to suicide was connected with the crippling of his individual ego in the disciplined and collectivized Soviet state of the late twenties. For Maiakovskii was above all an individualist.

For events in the Soviet literary world immediately following his suicide, see *Literaturnaia gazeta*, April 21 and April 28, 1930.

63. Averbakh, *Pamiati Maiakovskogo*.

64. Speech of Gronskii, *Sovetskaia literatura na novom etape*, p. 9.

65. *Ibid.*, speech of Prishvin, p. 66.

66. See above, note 25.

67. *Ibid.*, speech of Belyi, p. 69.

68. Zh. El'sberg, "Mirovospriiatie B. Pasternaka," *Na literaturnom postu*, No. 7, April, 1930, pp. 42, 50.

Chapter IX: Dissension in RAPP: the Litfront Controversy

1. For a RAPP statement on "backwardness," see L. Averbakh, "Zadachi proletarskoi literatury," *Na literaturnom postu*, Nos. 15–16, August, 1930, p. 3. This statement must be carefully evaluated in the context of events in which it was made. The month of August, 1930, witnessed the high point of left-wing criticism of Averbakh and the RAPP leaders for adopting theories and policies which had in fact held back proletarian literature from the tasks of the day. The "left" had heavy backing within the Party. Averbakh's admission of "backwardness" and his emphasis in this statement must be read in their context.

2. Boris Kushner, "Prichiny otstavaniia," *Krasnaia nov'*, No. 11, November, 1930, pp. 132–38; reprinted from *Pravda*, October 4, 1930.

3. *Ibid.*, pp. 137–38. Though *Pravda* opened its columns to

Kushner's criticism, its editors were later forced to admit that their action had been a "mistake." See "Za proletarskuiu literaturu," *Pravda*, April 19, 1931. Averbakh spoke up in no uncertain terms regarding *Pravda's* "mistake" in printing this article.

4. "Rechi RAPPovtsev na XVI s"ezde Partii," *Na literaturnom postu*, Nos. 13–14, July, 1930, p. 14.

5. Other elements hostile to the literary policy of RAPP had joined with the old On Guardists in the Litfront: for instance, several former followers of Professor Pereverzev and some former members of the Left Front of Art.

6. "Litfront," *Literaturnaia entsiklopediia*, VI (1932), 505–13.

7. See, for example, Averbakh's editorial, "Zadachi proletarskoi literatury," *Na literaturnom postu*, Nos. 15–16, August, 1930, p. 4, in which he points out that the policy of the *Literary Gazette* has not been equal to the task of bringing about a friendly union of fellow-traveler, peasant, and proletarian writer. See also "Otchët Literaturnoi gazety sekretariatu RAPPa, *Na literaturnom postu*, Nos. 13–14, June, 1930, pp. 119–21.

8. The first installment of the novel appeared in *Oktiabr'*, No. 1, January, 1930, pp. 4–53.

9. V. Ermilov, "Rozhdenie geroia," *Na literaturnom postu*, No. 12, June, 1930, pp. 14 ff.; also, "Gogolevskii Osip v kachestve literaturnogo kritika," *Literaturnaia gazeta*, April 7, 1930.

10. See above, chap. vii, p. 111.

11. For the Litfront criticism of *The Birth of a Hero*, see: T. Kostrov, "Rozhdenie geroia," *Literaturnaia gazeta*, March 24, 1930; Tarasov-Rodionov, "Mertvorozhdënnyi geroi," *Literaturnaia gazeta*, April 21, 1930; G. Gorbachëv, "O zhivom cheloveke i dialektike obshchestvennogo protsessa (Rech' na III Oblastnoi konferentsii LAPPa)," *Polemika*, pp. 166 ff.

12. Gorbachëv, *op. cit.*, p. 166.

13. *Ibid.*, p. 170. The last sentence is a rather obvious reference to the Sten controversy of 1929.

14. T. Kostrov, "O realizme, zhivom cheloveke, i stile proletarskoi literatury," *Literaturnaia gazeta*, March 31, 1930.

15. Ideas and quotations in this paragraph are from Kostrov, *op. cit.*

16. Gorbachëv, *op. cit.*, p. 169.

17. Bezymenskii, Gorbachëv, and Rodov, "O demagogii bez maski," *Na literaturnom postu*, No. 10, May, 1930, p. 41.

18. "Litfront," *Literaturnaia entsiklopediia.*

19. V. Ermilov, "Nashi tvorcheskie raznoglasiia," *Na literaturnom postu*, Nos. 13–14, July, 1930, pp. 23–31.

20. *Ibid.*, p. 31.

21. "Literaturnyi front," *Literaturnaia gazeta*, August 15, 1930.

22. *Ibid.*

23. The signers included the poets Bezymenskii and Rodov; Vishnevskii, a successful playwright and author of "First Cavalry Army" and "The Last Decisive"; T. Kostrov, once editor of the Youth League newspaper and a long-standing enemy of the On Literary Guardists; Zonin, formerly a member of VAPP, who left it in 1928, and the former pupils of Pereverzev, Bespalov and Gelfand.

24. "K diskussii v RAPPe," *Literaturnaia gazeta,* May 19, 1930.

25. Bezymenskii, "Golovokruzhenie ot neuspekhov; Partiia li RAPP?" *Literaturnaia gazeta,* May 12, 1930.

26. "Ko vsem chlenam RAPPa," *Literaturnaia gazeta,* July 25, 1930, p. 2. See Gorbachëv, *Polemika,* p. 157.

27. Averbakh, "Predrassudki," *Na literaturnom postu,* No. 7, April, 1930, p. 2.

28. *Ibid.,* p. 4.

29. Bezymenskii, "O tvorcheskoi ustanovke," *Literaturnaia gazeta,* April 14, 1930, p. 2.

30. *Ibid.*

31. "Rechi RAPPovtsev na XVI s"ezde Partii," *Na literaturnom postu,* Nos. 13–14, July, 1930, pp. 17–21.

32. "Za podlinnuiu konsolidatsiiu v sekretariat RAPP," *Literaturnaia gazeta,* July 25, 1930.

33. See, for instance, "Ko vsem chlenam RAPPa."

34. "Pervye uroki mobilizatsii," *Literaturnaia gazeta,* September 19, 1930.

35. *Ibid.*

36. See, for example, Fadeev, "Bolshevizatsiia proletarskogo literaturnogo dvizheniia," *Na literaturnom postu,* No. 11, June, 1930.

37. Averbakh, "Nado rabotat'," *Literaturnaia gazeta,* September 14, 1930.

38. *Ibid.*

39. "Prizyv udarnikov," *Na literaturnom postu,* No. 18, September, 1930, p. 112.

40. "O razvërtyvanii tvorcheskoi diskussii (pis'mo sekretariata RAPP)," *Literaturnaia gazeta,* October 14, 1930.

41. V. Il'enkov, "Prizyv udarnikov," *Na literaturnom postu,* No. 7, April, 1931, pp. 12–14.

42. *Ibid.*

43. *Ibid.*

44. "Rezoliutsiia plenuma pravleniia RAPP" (June 4, 1931), *Na literaturnom postu,* No. 22, August, 1931, p. 2.

45. *Ibid.*

46. *Ibid.*

47. "O pervykh itogakh prizyva udarnikov v literaturu (rezoli-

utsiia po dokladu Kirshona)," *Literaturnaia gazeta,* September 15, 1931.

48. *Ibid.*

49. See "V pomoshch udarniku (novaia programma litkruzhka)," *Na literaturnom postu,* No. 30, October, 1931, pp. 42–45.

50. See L. Subotskii, "O khode perestroiki," *Oktiabr',* December, 1932, pp. 182–83. See also Gleb Struve, *Soviet Russian Literature, 1917–50,* p. 249.

51. "Glavisskusstvo i poputchiki," *Literaturnaia gazeta,* March 17, 1930.

52. For a description of the devastating effect on engineers and technicians of these trials and of the public mood which they encouraged, see Alexander Baykov, *The Development of the Soviet Economic System; an Essay on the Experience of Planning in the USSR,* pp. 151–52, p. 281.

53. Joseph Stalin, *Leninism; Selected Writings,* p. 216.

54. For a generally accurate account of this affair, which, however, exaggerates the role of RAPP in it, see Max Eastman, *Artists in Uniform; a Study of Literature and Bureaucratism,* pp. 104–25; for the accusation and the reaction to it of the Writers' Union see B. Volin, "Nedopustimoe iavlenie," *Literaturnaia gazeta,* August 26, 1929, p. 1; and "Postanovlenie pravleniia VSP o Pilniake," *Literaturnaia gazeta,* September 9, 1929, p. 1.

55. An excellent Soviet novel dealing with the "proletarianization" of life in the late twenties and its adverse effect on the morale of intellectuals of the old school is Pantaleimon Romanov's *Three Pairs of Silk Stockings; a Novel of the Life of the Educated Class under the Soviet.*

56. "O razvërtyvanii tvorcheskoi diskussii (pis'mo sekretariata RAPP)," *Literaturnaia gazeta,* October 4, 1930.

57. *Ibid.*

58. *Ibid.*

59. *Ibid.*, October 9, 1930.

60. *Ibid.*, October, 14, 1930.

61. *Ibid.*

62. *Ibid.*

63. *Ibid.*

Chapter X: Further Pursuit of Proletarian Error, 1931

1. See V. Ermilov, "Za plekhanovskuiu ortodoksiiu," *Na literaturnom postu,* No. 19, October, 1929, pp. 1–7; and L. Averbakh, "Doloi Plekhanova!" *Na literaturnom postu,* Nos. 20–21, October–November, 1928, pp. 15–30.

2. For a discussion of the philosophical problems involved, see

John Somerville, *Soviet Philosophy; a Study of Theory and Practice,* pp. 213–29. For a Soviet account by one of the principals, see M. Mitin, *Boevye voprosy materialisticheskoi dialektiki* (Moscow, 1936). See also frequent articles by Deborin, Sten, Iudin, and Mitin in the journal *Pod znamenem marksizma* for the years 1930 and 1931. The Central Committee Resolution which directed that Mitin and Iudin be added to the editorial board of the magazine in question is very revealing as to the meaning of the dispute: "Postanovleniye TSK VKP(b) 26 Jan., 1931," *Pod znamenem marksizma,* Nos. 10–12, October–December, 1930, p. 1.

3. "Rezoliutsiia plenuma pravleniia RAPP" (February, 1931), *Na literaturnom postu,* No. 9, March, 1931, pp. 1–8.

4. M. Mitin, "Ocherednye zadachi na filosofskom fronte v sviazi s itogami filosofskoi diskussii," *Pod znamenem marksizma,* No. 3, March, 1931, p. 19.

5. *Ibid.*

6. *Ibid.*

7. *Ibid.*

8. *Ibid.*

9. *Ibid.,* p. 20. For the influence of Plekhanov on Voronskii and the proletarians of RAPP, see chap. ii and chap. v.

Plekhanov accepted the Hegelian thesis that the object of art is "the same as that of philosophy, namely, *reality*" (which for Hegel was the Absolute Idea), and Hegel's distinction between the activity of art and that of philosophy: "The philosopher perceives truth in concepts, while the artist beholds it in images." At the same time he admitted the "instinctive" as a factor in the appreciation of art. This laid him open to the charge of "idealism" and "intuitivism." Plekhanov was in general hostile to the intrusion of "logical" thinking in the form of conscious propaganda in artistic works. The work of *narodnik* Uspenskii, he felt, would have been improved if the latter had been more "objective." In his criticism of Gorky's novel *The Mother* he raised the question of the contrast between the language of logic and the language of image, and the unsuitability of the former in an artistic work. He regarded *The Mother* as propaganda rather than art. Soviet criticism of his aesthetic views at this time and later emphasizes that because of this "objectivism" he had lost sight of the function of literature and art as instruments in the class struggle. (See "Plekhanov," *Literaturnaia entsiklopediia,* VIII [1934], 703, 704, 715.)

10. Mitin, *op. cit.* Italics mine.

11. V. Polonskii, *Ocherki literaturnogo dvizheniia revoliutsionnoi epokhi,* p. 77.

12. A rather sizable tome containing nearly everything Lenin

ever said on questions of culture and art is available: M. A. Lifshitz, ed., *Lenin o kul'ture i iskusstve.* Shortly after the discussion described in this chapter a new periodical was established the purpose of which was to deal with questions of the Marxist interpretation of art. In it an absolutely exhaustive bibliography of everything Lenin ever said, wrote, or thought about literature and related fields was published: "Lenin o literature i iskusstve (bibliograficheskii ukazatel')," *Marksistsko-Leninskoe iskusstvoznanie,* No. 2, 1932, pp. 143–49.

13. Lifshitz, *op. cit.*, pp. 118–38. All the articles on Tolstoy are reprinted here.

14. Lifshitz, *op. cit.*, pp. 111–13. The article was first published in *Novaia zhizn'*, No. 12, November, 1905.

15. Lifshitz, *op. cit.*, p. 111.

16. "Bolshevistskaia partiia i sovetskaia literatura (kratkii obzor dokumentov)," *Novyi mir,* No. 5, May, 1947, p. 117.

17. The end result of the development of this cult of Lenin and the "Party Spirit" in literature is perhaps best shown in this statement from a recent account of the leadership of the Party in belles-lettres: "The Bolshevik leadership of Soviet literature is the deepest foundation of its creative growth. . . . At all stages, in all periods of its development, Soviet literature has heard the wise, encouraging, and often admonishing voice of the Party—the voice of Lenin and Stalin." "Bol'shevistskaia partiia," p. 148. One wonders whether literary life could possibly sink any lower than this. The events of 1931 and 1932, which we are now investigating, were a relatively early stage in its descent.

18. See above, chap. i, p. 9.

19. Lifshitz, *op. cit.*, p. 309.

20. *Pravda,* December 1, 1920. Quoted in "Khronika," No. 8, 1937, pp. 105–6.

21. *Ibid.*

22. Lifshitz, *op. cit.*, p. 298.

23. "Rezoliutsiia obshchego sobraniia iacheiki VKP(b) instituta L. i Ia. po dokladu Iudina ob itogakh filosofskoi diskussii" (May 14, 1931), *Na literaturnom postu,* No. 22, August, 1931, p. 37. Italics mine.

24. See "Kul'turnaia revoliutsiia i sovremennaia literatura (Resoliutsiia I vsesoyuznogo s"ezda proletpisatelei po dokladu L. Averbakha)," *Na literaturnom postu,* Nos. 13–14, July, 1928, pp. 1–11.

25. "Za proletarskuiu literaturu" (peredovaia), *Pravda,* April 19, 1931.

26. *Ibid.*

27. P. Iudin, "Zadachi perestroiki literaturno-khudozhestven-

nikh organizatsii v svete resheniia TSK VKP(b)," *Vestnik Kommunisticheskoi akademii*, Nos. 9–10, September–October, 1932, p. 51.

28. "Ustanovki tvorcheskikh gruppirovok," *Na literaturnom postu*, No. 23, August, 1931, pp. 7–32.

29. See above, chap. ix, pp. 167–71.

30. "Ustanovki," pp. 10–13.

31. *Ibid.*

32. *Ibid.*, pp. 14–20.

33. I. Makar'ev, "O kakom sorevnovanii idët rech'?" *Na literaturnom postu*, No. 25, September, 1931, p. 10.

34. *Ibid.*

35. "Ustanovki," pp. 20–22.

36. *Ibid.*, p. 22.

37. "Zakal," *Na literaturnom postu*, No. 30, October, 1931, pp. 46–47.

38. This slogan, while it does convey the RAPP emphasis on study and imitation of the classics, was never a central slogan of the RAPP leadership and was withdrawn as useless shortly after its first appearance. However, the idea that Soviet literature was still far from producing anything to equal the classics of bourgeois literature, and that its chief aim should be to produce a literature "greater than" that represented by, for instance, Shakespeare and Tolstoy, was frequently emphasized by Averbakh and other leaders of RAPP. See L. Averbakh, "Na temy literaturnogo segodnia," *Na literaturnom postu*, Nos. 23–24, December, 1930, p. 2.

39. Quoted in "Za druzhnuiu sovmestnuiu rabotu s Komsomolom (rezoliutsiia fraktsii VKP[b] sekretariata RAPP)," *Na literaturnom postu*, Nos. 31–32, November, 1931, p. 8.

40. *Ibid.*, p. 3.

41. This idea, which first occurred in Averbakh's address to the First Congress of Proletarian Writers, was elevated to the status of a RAPP slogan in the resolution of the secretariat of RAPP: "Rech' t. Stalina i zadachi RAPP" (August 12, 1931), *Na literaturnom postu*, No. 24, August, 1931, pp. 1–4. For a discussion of the slogan, see above, chap. v, p. 82.

42. Averbakh, "Iz RAPPovskogo dnevnika," *Literaturnaia gazeta*, October 12, 1931.

43. *Ibid.*

44. *Ibid.*

45. The writer Anna Karavaeva, for instance, said at the Organization Committee meeting in October, 1932:

One of the grossest of RAPP's errors was its position at the time of the dispute with the Youth League. The demands of the youth upon literature were correct. The generation of young Bolsheviks, who were taking part together with the old Bolshevik guard in the solution of the problems of socialist construction . . . had a right to demand a fuller expression in literature of their life, which is so rich in new experiences.

Speech of Karavaeva, *Sovetskaia literatura na novom etape,* p. 151.

46. Mitin, "Ocherednye zadachi," pp. 19–20.
47. Averbakh, "O perestroike RAPP," *Na literaturnom postu,* Nos. 35–36, December, 1931, p. 9.
48. *Ibid.*
49. *Ibid.*, p. 9.
50. *Ibid.*
51. *Ibid.*, p. 6.
52. Mitin, Iudin, Ral'tsevich, and Takser, "Proletarskuiu literaturu . . . na vysshuiu stupen'," *Pravda,* November 19, 1931.
53. *Ibid.*, quoted. Averbakh's remark appeared in *Literaturnaia gazeta,* October 27, 1931.
54. Iudin, the philosopher who has now turned literary critic, has had an interesting and apparently quite successful career in many fields in the Soviet Union. He brought about an "overturn" in the field of Marxist philosophy, he ran to earth the "errors" of RAPP in literary theory, he was active in the new Union of Writers as a representative of the Party; in 1937, as we shall see, he wrote speeches and articles describing the "Trotskyite" nature of Averbakh, Kirshon, and other leaders of RAPP. He has also been quoted as an authority on Soviet jurisprudence. In a word, he has functioned as a hatchet man for the Party in many of the intellectual fields, and is not to be taken seriously as a philosopher, literary critic, or jurist. His latest field of activity was Yugoslavia, where he was one of the Soviet functionaries forced out by Tito in 1948. See Jan Yindrich, *Tito v. Stalin; the Battle of the Marshals,* p. 88.
55. G. Vasilkovskii, "Sozdadim proizvedniia, dostoinye nashei epokhi," *Pravda,* November 3, 1931.
56. *Ibid.*
57. L. Mekhlis, "Za perestroiku raboty RAPP," *Literaturnaia gazeta,* November 21, 1931 (reprinted from *Pravda*).
58. *Ibid.*
59. *Ibid.*
60. *Ibid.*
61. *Ibid.*
62. *Ibid.*
63. *Ibid.*
64. "Zayavlenie sekretariata RAPP," *Literaturnaia gazeta,* November 21, 1931.
65. *Pravda,* December 21, 1931.
66. "V plenum pravleniia RAPP," *Pravda,* December 9, 1931.
67. V. Stavskii, "Litsom k tvorchestvu," *Pravda,* December 23, 1931.

68. *Pravda,* December 8, 1931, p. 3.

69. F. Panfërov, "Govorite golosom knig," *Na literaturnom postu,* No. 1, January, 1932, pp. 10–20, especially p. 17; and A. Bezymenskii, "Rech' na plenume," *Na literaturnom postu,* Nos. 35–36, December, 1931, pp. 20–24.

70. A. Troitskii, "Za Magnitostroi literatury (rech' na plenume)," *Na literaturnom postu,* Nos. 35–36, December, 1931, p. 16.

71. *Ibid.,* p. 17.

72. *Ibid.*

73. *Ibid.,* pp. 19–20.

74. Panfërov, "Govorite golosom knig," pp. 10–12.

75. The huge industrial *kombinat* in central Siberia.

76. Panfërov, *op. cit.,* p. 13.

77. *Ibid.,* pp. 13, 14.

78. *Ibid.,* p. 15.

79. *Ibid.*

80. *Ibid.,* p. 17.

81. *Ibid.*

82. Averbakh, "O perestroike," *Na literaturnom postu,* Nos. 35–36, December, 1931, pp. 6–13; No. 1, January, 1932, pp. 1–9; and No. 2, January, 1932, pp. 1–12.

83. Averbakh, "O perestroike," No. 1, January, 1932, pp. 4–5.

84. Averbakh, "Zlobodnevnoe posleslovie," *Literaturnaia gazeta,* November 17, 1931.

85. This accusation was applied particularly to the literary ideas of the Youth League.

86. Averbakh, "O perestroike," *Na literaturnom postu,* Nos. 35–36, 1931, p. 9. This statement of Averbakh is simply not true, but that is of no importance here.

87. Averbakh, "O perestroike," No. 2, January, 1932, p. 4.

88. *Ibid.,* pp. 8–9.

89. *Ibid.,* p. 7.

90. Troitskii, "Za Magnitostroi literatury," p. 19.

91. V. Kirshon, "Za bol'shoe iskusstvo Bol'shevizma," *Pravda,* December 13, 1931.

92. *Ibid.* (continuation), *Pravda,* December 20, 1931.

93. "Ob ocherednykh zadachakh RAPP (rezoliutsiia po dokladu Averbakha)," *Na literaturnom postu,* No. 34, December, 1931, pp. 1–5.

Chapter XI: The Party Liquidates Its Instrument

1. "O perestroike literaturno-khudozhestvennykh organizatsii," *Pravda,* April 24, 1932.

2. "Bolshevistskaia Partiia i Sovetskaia literatura (kratkii obzor dokumentov)," *Novyi mir*, No. 5, May, 1947, p. 136.

3. These are the names of well-known fellow-travelers who had contributed to the Five-Year Plan output.

4. I am aware of no important document produced by the RAPP leadership in which such a phrase occurs. The *Pravda* article gives no reference.

5. "Na uroven' novykh zadach," *Pravda*, May 9, 1932.

6. The offending issue was *Na literaturnom postu*, No. 11, April, 1932. The statement of the editors acknowledging the mistake they had made in not printing the Politburo resolution appeared in *Na literaturnom postu*, Nos. 13–14, May, 1932, p. 40, the last number of the magazine.

7. "Peredovaia," *Literaturnaia gazeta*, May 11, 1932.

8. *Literaturnaia gazeta*, May 23, 1932.

9. Both Makar'ev, who had been secretary of VOAPP, and Kirshon explain this failure to react properly as due to their not having understood the meaning of the resolution, and, in part, to the fact that the RAPP leaders felt an injustice had been done them. Makar'ev said: "The mighty idea of the resolution was not immediately clear to us, and there is no doubt that we acted as a brake on the realization of the resolution." See *Sovetskaia literatura na novom etape*, speeches of Makar'ev (p. 161) and of Kirshon (p. 195).

10. See above, p. 201.

11. "Za Leninskuiu literaturnuiu kritiku (o zhurnale *Na literaturnom postu*)," *Pravda*, April 15, 1932.

12. G. Vasilkovskii, "Ne na postu," *Literaturnaia gazeta*, May 23, 1932.

13. "Otvet kritikam," *Na literaturnom postu*, No. 12, April, 1932, p. 8.

14. The *Pravda* editorial of May 9, 1932, "Na uroven' novykh zadach," quotes out of context a statement by Averbakh which he made in the course of a polemic against Trotsky. In the course of this polemic Averbakh had rejected the term "fellow-traveler" as no longer applicable to the Soviet literary world. Averbakh had said, "Does the term 'fellow-traveler' fit those who today do *not* go along with the revolution? Isn't such a person an enemy?" ("Iz RAPPovskogo dnevnika," *Literaturnaia gazeta*, October 11, 1931, p. 2.) The *Pravda* editorial takes this quotation out of the context of a polemic against Trotsky, and substitutes for Averbakh's last sentence the statement, "All writers who do not conform to this formula are placed in the camp of counterrevolution." This is a relatively minor example of "misquoting out of context," but it is important to realize that in mentioning this "intolerable method," the

RAPP leaders had in mind not only Iudin and the Red Professors, but the editorial board of *Pravda.*

15. "Otvet kritikam," p. 9.

16. *Ibid.*

17. See above, n. 12.

18. That this was expected of all the former leaders of RAPP is clear from the self-accusatory speeches of Fadeev, Chumandrin, Makar'ev, Libedinskii, and Ermilov at that meeting, and also from the fact that Averbakh was directly criticized by the chairman of the meeting, Gronskii, for failing to admit his errors thoroughly and consistently. Other speakers also voiced their disappointment with Averbakh for his "egotism" and "lack of self-criticism." See *Sovetskaia literatura na novom etape,* speeches of Usievich (p. 147), of Averbakh (p. 120), where Gronskii interrupts Averbakh to say that what the meeting expected of him was "admission of his errors," and of Libedinskii, (p. 167).

19. L. Subotskii, "O khode perestroiki," *Oktiabr',* No. 12, December, 1932, p. 170.

20. *Ibid.,* p. 172.

21. P. Iudin, "Zadachi perestroiki literaturno-khudozhstvennikh organizatsii," *Vestnik Kommunisticheskoi akademii,* Nos. 9–10, September–October, 1932, p. 53.

22. *Ibid.,* p. 58.

23. A more or less complete stenographic record of this meeting is available in *Sovetskaia literatura na novom etape,* from which we have been quoting.

24. *Sovetskaia literatura na novom etape,* speeches of Lidin (p. 205), Tarasov-Rodionov (p. 176), Subotskii (p. 46), Efros (p. 104), Romanov (p. 135), and others. For favorable comments on RAPP activity made at this meeting see speeches of Prishvin (p. 66), Belyi (p. 69), and Olesha (p. 239). Further evidence of the narrow orthodoxy of certain RAPP workers is found in Fadeev's article published shortly after the dissolution. Even in the compiling of bibliographies and the like, the "labeling" proclivity of the RAPP experts was evidenced. A bulletin of the Bibliographical Institute, for instance, proclaimed Malyshkin's novel *Sevastopol'* a slander on the revolution. See Fadeev, "Staroe i novoe," *Literaturnaia gazeta,* October 17, 1932.

25. Iudin, "Protiv izvrashcheniia Leninskogo ucheniia o kul'turnoi revoliutsii," *Pravda,* April 23, 1932.

26. The "living man" P. Iudin might easily have been the prototype of Libedinskii's character Eidnunen in *The Birth of a Hero.*

27. Iudin, "K voprosu o proletarskoi sotsialisticheskoi kulture," *Bol'shevik,* Nos. 11–12, June, 1932, pp. 66–88.

28. See Appendix A, point 5.

29. Iudin, "K voprosu," p. 76.

30. Iudin, "Zadachi perestroiki," p. 57.

31. I have made a list of Five-Year-Plan works considered worthy of mention by four historians of the period, Kaun, Simmons, Slonim, and Struve. The following authors are included in this list: Pil'niak, Ehrenburg, Leonov, Kataev, Shaginian, Kaverin, Tolstoy, Fedin, Kirsanov, Gladkov, and Sholokhov. Only the last two are proletarians, and only Sholokhov was a member of RAPP.

32. J. Stalin, "New Conditions, New Tasks in Economic Construction," in *Leninism; Selected Writings*, p. 216.

33. "Rech' t. Stalina i zadachi RAPP (rezoliutsiia sekretariata RAPP, 12/VIII, 1931)," *Na literaturnom postu*, No. 24, August, 1931, pp. 1–2.

34. "O poputnichestve i soiuznichestve (rezoliutsiia plenuma RAPP po dokladu Selivanovskogo)," *Na literaturnom postu*, No. 26, September, 1931, pp. 1–6.

35. For a statement of the RAPP attitude toward this slogan, which was later rejected, see B. Kor, "Soiuznik ili vrag," *Na literaturnom postu*, No. 2, January, 1931, p. 39.

36. V. Ermilov, "Vopros redaktsii 'Novyi mir,'" *Literaturnaia gazeta*, February 23, 1932. In this article Ermilov sharply criticizes Tolstoy's *Chornoe zoloto* (Black Gold) for its attempt to represent the *émigrés* as "good people after all"; and he attacks Kaverin's book because it showed collectivization as "no different from life under capitalist exploitation."

37. Many of the articles criticizing RAPP which appeared after its dissolution emphasize that the RAPP leaders were unable to grasp the *political* significance of the Central Committee decision to dissolve separate proletarian organizations in the arts. They did not "see" that their organization had been dissolved because the fellow-travelers had already made the transition to the support of the Soviet power, and that therefore attacks on writers as "class enemies," and the "sharpening of the class struggle in literature" were no longer admissible. Averbakh, for instance, in a speech made a few days before the dissolution at a Poetry Conference, had made the mistake of declaring that the class war in literature was growing sharper, and he sharpened it himself by attacking several poets "of the right." The leader of RAPP seems to have missed the point (deliberately?) that the class war in literature was being dulled, not sharpened. (Averbakh, "My stroim sotsialisticheskuiu literaturu," *Literaturnaia gazeta*, April 23, 1932.)

On the political significance of the dissolution the *Literary Gazette* said in an editorial (May 17, 1932):

In his speech at the conference of business managers in June, 1931, Comrade Stalin, speaking of the transition of the cadres of the old intelligentsia to the support of socialism, and of the need for insuring normal conditions of work for them, indicated the inadmissibility of treating every specialist as an unapprehended wrecker. . . .

The successes of socialism have called forth in literature too a transition of the great majority of the cadres of the so-called "fellow-travelers" to the side of socialism. . . . A number of their artistic productions in the field of prose, drama, and poetry prove that—with varying tempos and varying depth—*the best*, and in a literary sense the most valued, writers are now organically included as part of socialist construction and now face the task of building socialist culture together with the proletariat.

Other aspects of this development are to be seen in industrial management. The change in policy is evidenced in the training of technical "cadres" (G. Bienstock, S. M. Schwarz, A. Yugow, *Management in Russian Industry and Agriculture* [London, 1944], p. 108):

Although the principal social ideas of the cadre policy remained unchanged until the mid-thirties, real education of new cadres was greatly modified as early as 1932. . . . Orders were issued to lengthen the period of education, revise curricula, and introduce a general system of strict entrance examinations. This last measure limited, in effect, the influx of workers (and their children) into colleges and technical schools. The section of the decree devoted to "recruiting for the engineering colleges and technical schools" did not mention a "workers' nucleus." While regulations on this point were not formally revoked, they were pushed into the background and little by little forgotten.

Alexander Baykov, in *The Development of the Soviet Economic System* (pp. 226, 227), has this to say about changes in the personnel policy:

From 1931 onward reforms were carried out on wages and the extension of piece-work rates, and eliminating hastily adopted and ill-prepared methods of intensifying production (the continuous week, the depersonalized use of lathes, and the functional subdivision of one production process among a number of workers), and strengthening the administrative legal provision for enforcing labor discipline and improving the material and social position of the engineering and technical staffs and their legal authority over production. . . .

Stalin's order was "to put an end to labour turnover, to abolish equal pay, readjust the wages system and improve the workers' living conditions." . . .

As already indicated in the survey of industrial administration, the new policy prescribed "a change of attitude towards engineers and technicians of the old school, greater attention and solicitude for them and more boldness in enlisting their cooperation"; at the same time providing "the USSR working class with their own technical-industrial intelligentsia, *i.e.*, specialists of working-class and peasant descent educated in Soviet schools . . . capable of understanding the policy of our country's working class and ready to put it conscientiously into effect."

38. "Peredovaia," *Literaturnaia gazeta*, May 17, 1932.

39. *Literaturnaia gazeta*, June 29, 1932.

40. See, for instance, articles in *Literaturnaia gazeta* on B. Lavrenev, May 5, 1932; on Leonov, May 23, 1932; on Il'f and Petrov, May 29, 1932; on Pasternak, May 29, 1932; on Slonimsky, June 5, 1932; on Tikhonov, June 17, 1932; on Ognëv, June 23, 1932; on Khlebnikov, June 29, 1932; on Nikulin, July 17, 1932; and many others.

41. A. Fadeev, "Staroe i novoe," *Literaturnaia gazeta*, October 17, 1932.

42. "Ustanovki tvorcheskikh gruppirovok," *Na literaturnom postu*, No. 23, August, 1931, pp. 29–30.

43. The emphasis on the talent and the literary ability of the fellow-travelers is very prominent in the documents of this period. See above, n. 37.

44. Alexey Tolstoy, for instance, whose works published during this period were anathema to the leaders of RAPP, became one of the richest, most successful writers in the Soviet Union of the thirties and forties.

45. Averbakh, *Nashi literaturnye raznoglasiia*, p. 90.

46. "Socialist realism" as the proper style for Soviet literature was already well-established by October, 1932. See *Sovetskaia literatura na novom etape, passim.*

47. Subotskii's speech at the Organization Committee meeting in October, 1932, is exceptionally rich in evidences of the Party's concern for the material welfare of writers. He announced that a huge Palace of Writers was being planned for Moscow, and large apartment buildings for writers would be built in order to solve their housing problems. There was to be a special rest home for writers on the Black Sea. A Literary Fund for the assistance of writers at work was promised. See Subotskii, "O khode perestroiki," *Oktiabr'*, No. 12, December, 1932, p. 187.

48. *Literaturnaia gazeta*, May 20, 1932.

An analysis of the reasons for the dissolution of RAPP which at some points is very similar to that given here is to be found in an article written in 1932 in Berlin by Vera Aleksandrova, a close student of Soviet literary development, and at present a contributor to the literary page of the New York Russian newspaper, *Novoe russkoe slovo*. Her article "Konets RAPPa" appeared in *Sotsialisticheskii vestnik*, No. 9, May 21, 1932. She says, among other things, the following:

The original core of proletarian writers had begun to be crowded somewhere into the background, and in the foreground there now appeared new writers "from those groups who are sympathetic to us" of the intelligentsia, and who, loudly and noisily, began to lay down their "path to the proletariat." These were the "allies" of the dictatorship . . . who shouted about "industrial tempos," about the enthusiasm of the masses, and who outdid each other in thinking up slogans. The administrative political leadership of RAPP . . . could hardly keep up with its agile fledglings.

Vera Aleksandrova points out that the "original core" of proletarian writers continued to develop along the lines of psychological realism, and that, because they were first of all artists, they often selected from "Soviet reality" glaring examples of disillusionment or degeneration. The official critics were stunned by the appearance of such works as *The Birth of a Hero* during the reconstruction period, and RAPP's position grew progressively weaker during the year 1931.

This analysis is in agreement with the evidence we have seen on the downfall and dissolution of RAPP.

Epilogue: the Fifth Anniversary

1. This was the viewpoint on RAPP given in a series of articles by A. Fadeev and featured by the Literary Gazette. See A. Fadeev, "Staroe i novoe," *Literaturnaia gazeta*, October 23, 1932. It is approximately the version given in the article "RAPP," in *Literaturnaia entsiklopediia*, already referred to.

2. See "Peredovaia," *Literaturnaia gazeta*, August 27, 1936.

3. *Ibid.*

4. In 1932 Fadeev took exception to the extreme violence of Stavskii's statements regarding the RAPP administration. Fadeev said that the remarks of Stavskii reminded him "of the days of Benvenuto Cellini, when artistic enemies were eliminated physically." See speech of Fadeev, *Sovetskaia literatura na novom etape*, p. 126. No explanation of Stavskii's motives in 1936 and 1937 is attempted here; probably he was only carrying out a "Party task." But Fadeev's 1932 remark offers interesting food for speculation. The fact is that most of the literary men "eliminated physically" in 1936–37 were former "artistic enemies" of Stavskii, as well as of Iudin.

5. *Literaturnaia gazeta*, August 27, 1936.

6. "Glavnaia zadacha" (peredovaia), *Literaturnaia gazeta*, February 26, 1937.

7. Fadeev, "My nepobedimy," *Literaturnaia gazeta*, February 1, 1937.

8. *Ibid.*

9. A. Kretov, "Politicheskaia slepota," *Literaturnaia gazeta,* March 5, 1937.

10. V. Stavskii, "Rabota po-novomu," *Literaturnaia gazeta,* March 5, 1937.

11. "Obshchemoskovskoe sobranie pisatelei," *Literaturnaia gazeta,* April 10, 1937.

12. *Ibid.* It may be that the *Literary Gazette* reporter is inventing the "nervousness" and "incoherence" of the victims' replies and deliberately exaggerating the hostility toward them at the meeting in order to make their guilt seem more certain. But it is not incredible that persons in the atmosphere of the treason trials and executions should have reacted with some agitation and fear to the charges.

13. *Ibid.* According to the verbal account given me by a man who was present at this meeting, Mirsky, because of his many contacts with foreigners, was publicly accused of hostility to the Soviet Union and possible spying and treason. According to this account, he did indeed but weakly defend himself, for he was extremely agitated at the time.

14. See *Report of Court Proceedings in the Case of the Anti-Soviet "Bloc of Rights and Trotskyites,"* p. 253.

15. "Piat' let," *Literaturnaia gazeta,* April 20, 1937.

16. *Ibid.*

17. "Uroki i vyvody," *Literaturnaia gazeta,* April 26, 1937.

18. *Ibid.*

19. P. Iudin, "Posledyshi Trotskogo—ob Averbakhovshchine," *Oktiabr',* No. 6, June, 1937, pp. 3–5.

20. *Ibid.*

21. *Ibid.*

22. "Vykorchevat' bez ostatka" (peredovaia), *Literaturnaia gazeta,* May 15, 1937.

23. *Ibid.*

24. "K otvetu" (peredovaia), *Literaturnaia gazeta,* May 1, 1937.

25. Iudin, "Piatiletiie resheniia TSK VKP(b)," *Literaturnaia gazeta,* April 26, 1937.

26. Bruno Iasenskii was a Polish Communist critic and author associated with Averbakh, not so much in the affairs of RAPP, but as editor of the international proletarian journal *Literatura mirovoi revoliutsii.*

27. Iudin, "Piatiletiie resheniia." Fadeev was indeed one of the first to break with Averbakh after the dissolution of RAPP in 1932, and praise was awarded him at that time for being the first of the former RAPP leaders to break the solid front which they had formed to defend their own interests. See *Sovetskaia literatura na novom etape,* speech of Ermilov (p. 181).

Apparently Iudin is referring here to Mirsky's very unfavorable review of Fadeev's work *The Last of the Udegs*. This review, which appeared in the *Literary Gazette*, June 24, 1934, taxed Fadeev with being too ready to adjust his writing to the new situation obtaining after 1932, and of exaggerating the role of the intelligentsia in the revolution. Mirsky was severely criticized for this attack on Fadeev, who has always had powerful friends, and the *Literary Gazette* in an editorial admitted that its publication had been a mistake. Mirsky the Russian prince had attacked Fadeev from a "proletarian" viewpoint which was not acceptable to the authorities after the dissolution of RAPP in 1932.

28. Averbakh had been in serious disfavor before the time of the events here described. Shortly after the Congress of Writers in 1934 he had been removed from Moscow and sent to the Urals. See Tsekhovner, "Averbakhovtsy v Leningrade," *Literaturnaia gazeta*, May 15, 1937. See also Marc Slonim and George Reavey, *Soviet Literature; an Anthology*, p. 46.

29. V. Vishnevskii, "Nuzhen otvet," *Literaturnaia gazeta*, April 26, 1937.

30. "Moskovskoe sobranie dramaturgov," *Literaturnaia gazeta*, May 1, 1937.

31. *Ibid.*

32. *Ibid.* On Solskii-Panskii, who is now a resident of New York City, see chap. iv, n. 27.

33. "Moskovskoe sobranie dramaturgov," *Literaturnaia gazeta*.

34. "Na sobranii partgruppy Leningradskogo soiuza sovetskikh pisatelei," *Literaturnaia gazeta*, May 10, 1937.

35. *Ibid.*

36. "Zasedanie pravleniia Leningradskogo soiuza sovetskikh pisatelei," *Literaturnaia gazeta*, May 20, 1937.

37. *Ibid.*

38. The *Literary Gazette* for May 20, 1937, carries a news item about a meeting of the Party group of the Leningrad Union of Writers at which it was decided that "Libedinskii could no longer be considered a member of the Party." It is not certain that action was taken to expel him. He remained active in literature.

39. "Zasedanie pravleniia," *Literaturnaia gazeta*.

40. Quoted in "Bolshevistskaia Partiia i Sovetskaia literatura (kratkii obzor dokumentov)," *Novyi Mir*, No. 5, May, 1947, p. 143.

41. A. Tolstoy, "Trends in Soviet Literature," *Science and Society*, VII, No. 3 (1943), 239.

42. L. I. Timofeev, *Sovremennaia literatura; uchebnoe posobie dlia 10-go klassa srednei shkoly*, p. 235.

43. "Bolshevistskaia Partiia," p. 134.

Bibliography

Averbakh, Leopol'd. Kul'turnaia revoliutsiia i voprosy sovremennoi literatury. Moscow, Gosudarstvennoe izdatel'stvo, 1928.

——— Na putiakh kul'turnoi revoliutsii. 3d ed., Moscow, Moskovskii rabochii, 1929.

——— Nashi literaturnye raznoglasiia. Leningrad, Priboi, 1927.

——— Pamiati Maiakovskogo. Moscow, Gosizdat, 1930.

Averbakh, Leopol'd, and Vladimir Kirshon. S kem i pochemu my boremsia. Leningrad, Zemlia i Fabrika, 1930.

Baykov, Alexander. The Development of the Soviet Economic System; an Essay on the Experience of Planning in the USSR. New York, Macmillan, 1947.

Bednyi, Demian. "Bez poshchady." *Pravda,* December 5, 1930.

——— "Slezai s pechi." *Pravda,* September 7, 1930.

Belinskii, V. G. Selected Philosophical Works. Moscow, Foreign Languages Publishing House, 1948.

Bezymenskii, A. Izbrannye stikhi. Moscow, Sovetskii pisatel', 1947.

——— "Sotsializm." *Pravda,* January 17, 1931.

——— Tragediinaia noch'. Moscow, Gosizdat, 1935.

——— Vystrel. Moscow, Gosizdat, 1930.

Bogdanov, A. A. Iskusstvo i rabochii klass. Moscow, Proletarskaia kul'tura, 1918.

——— O proletarskoi kul'ture. Moscow, Kniga, 1924.

Brodskii, N. L., B. L'vov-Rogachevskii, and N. P. Sidorov, eds. Literaturnye manifesty ot simvolizma k Oktiabriu. Moscow, Federatsiia, 1929.

Brodskii-Krasnov, M., and V. Druzin. Kratkii ocherk istorii russkoi literatury XIX i XX vekov. Saratov, Obedinënnoe gosudarstvennoe izdatel'stvo RFSFR, 1931.

Deutscher, Isaac. Stalin, a Political Biography. London, Oxford University Press, 1948.

Eastman, Max. Artists in Uniform; a Study of Literature and Bureaucratism. New York, Knopf, 1934.
Fadeev, A. Poslednii iz Udege. Moscow, Gosizdat, 1936.
——— Razgrom; roman. Moscow, Gosizdat, 1932.
——— The Nineteen. Trans. R. D. Charques. London, Lawrence, 1929.
Gerasimova, V. "Sëstry." *Oktiabr'*, No. 7, July, 1929, pp. 41–62.
Gorbachëv, Georgii. Polemika (sbornik statei). Leningrad, Gosizdat, 1931.
——— Sovremennaia russkaia literatura. Moscow, Gosizdat, 1931.
Goriely, Benjamin. Les Poètes dans la revolution russe. Paris, Gallimard, 1934.
Gorky, Maxim (Maksim Gorkii). Nesobrannye literaturno-kriticheskie stat'i. Ed. S. M. Breitburger. Moscow, Gosizdat, 1941.
——— O literature, stat'i i rechi 1923–36. Ed. N. F. Bulchikov. 3d ed., Moscow, Sovetskii pisatel', 1937.
Gurshtein, M. Marksistkoe literaturovedenie. Moscow, Gosizdat, 1931.
History of the Communist Party of the Soviet Union (Bolsheviks); Short Course. Edited by a Commission of the Central Committee of the CPSU(B). New York, International Publishers, 1939.
Il'enkov, V. Vedushchaia os'. Moscow, Gosizdat, 1934.
Karavaeva, Anna. Krutaia stupen'; rasskazy kontrol'nika. Moscow, Gosizdat, 1931.
Kaun, Alexander. Soviet Poets and Poetry. Los Angeles, University of California Press, 1943.
Kaverin, Veniamin. Prolog. Moscow, Gosizdat, 1931.
Kirsanov, S. Piatiletka. Moscow, Gosizdat, 1931.
Kirshon, Vladimir. Bread. Trans. Sonia Volochova; ed. Eugene Lyons, *Six Soviet Plays*. Boston, Houghton Mifflin, 1934.
Klingender, F. J. Marxism and Modern Art; an Approach to Social Realism. New York, International Publishers, 1945.
Kogan, P. S. Literatura etikh let (1917–1923). 2d ed., Ivanovo-Voznesensk, Osnova, 1924.
——— Literatura velikogo desiatiletiia. Moscow, Moskovskii rabochii, 1927.
——— Proletarskaia literatura. Ivanovo-Voznesensk, Osnova, 1926.
Kolosov, M. "Individual'noe vospitanie." *Oktiabr'*, No. 3, March, 1929, pp. 4–12.
Kopylova, L. "Sad ottsa Arseniia." *Oktiabr'*, No. 2, February, 1929, pp. 59–64.
Lenin, V. I. Collected Works. Vol. XIII: Materialism and Empirio-Criticism; Critical Notes Concerning a Reactionary Phi-

losophy. Trans. David Kvitko. New York, International Publishers, 1927.

Levin, B. "Zhili dva tovarishcha." *Oktiabr'*, No. 1, January, 1931, pp. 64–96, and No. 2, February, 1931, pp. 83–119.

Lezhnëv, A. Sovremenniki, literaturno-kriticheskie ocherki. Moscow, Krug, 1927.

Libedinskii, Iurii. General'nye zadachi proletarskoi literatury. Leningrad, LAPP, 1931.

——— Rozhdenie geroia. 2d ed., Leningrad, LAPP, 1930.

——— A Week. With an introduction by Arthur Ransome. New York, Huebsch, 1923.

Lifshitz, M. A., ed. Lenin o kul'ture i iskusstve. Moscow, Gosizdat, 1938.

Literaturnaia entsiklopediia. Moscow, Gosizdat, 1929–39.

London, Kurt. The Seven Soviet Arts. Trans. Eric S. Bensinger. London, Faber and Faber, 1937.

L'vov-Rogachevskii, B. Ocherki proletarskoi literatury. Moscow, Moskovskoe aktsionernoe izdatel'stvo, 1927.

Maiskii, I., ed. Proletariat i literatura (sbornik statei). Leningrad, Gosizdat, 1925.

Makarov, I. "Smert'." *Oktiabr'*, No. 1, January, 1929, pp. 86–96.

Marshall, Herbert. Mayakovsky and His Poetry. London, Pilot Press, 1945.

Marx, Karl, and Friedrich Engels. The German Ideology. Parts I and III, edited with an introduction by R. Pascal. New York, International Publishers, 1939.

Milyukov, P. N. Outlines of Russian Culture. Part II: "Literature." Trans. Valentine Ughet and Eleanor Davis; ed. Michael Karpovich. Philadelphia, University of Pennsylvania Press, 1942.

Mirsky, D. S. A History of Russian Literature. Ed. Francis J. Whitfield. New York, Knopf, 1949.

Mitrofanov, A. "Iiun'-iiul'." *Oktiabr'*, No. 7, July, 1930, pp. 96–160.

Olesha, Iv. Envy. Trans. P. Ross. London, Westhouse, 1947.

Olkhovyi, B. Na zlobu dnia. Moscow, Zemlia i fabrika, 1930.

Ovalov, L. "Lovtsy somnenii." *Oktiabr'*, No. 6, June, 1930, pp. 89–152; No. 7, July, 1930, pp. 8–59.

Panfërov, F. Brusski. Moscow, Moskovskii rabochii, 1928. Translated by Z. Mitrov and J. Tabrisky as *Brusski: a Story of Peasant Life in Soviet Russia.* New York, International Publishers, 1930.

Patrick, George Z. Popular Poetry in Soviet Russia. Berkeley, University of California Press, 1929.

Paul, Eden and Cedar. The Proletcult (Proletarian Culture). New York, Thomas Seltzer, 1921.

Pereverzev, V. F., ed. Literaturovedenie (sbornik statei). Moscow, 1928.

Pervyi vsesoiuznyi s"ezd sovetskikh pisatelei. Stenograficheskii otchët. Moscow, Gosizdat, 1934.

Pil'niak, Boris. Volga vpadaet v Kaspiskoe more. Riga, Novyi golos, 1931.

——— The Volga Falls to the Caspian Sea. Trans. Charles Malamuth. London, Davies, 1932.

Plekhanov, G. V. Sochineniia, Vol. XIV. Moscow, Gosizdat, 1924.

Poggioli, Renato. Politica letteraria sovietica: Bilancio d'un ventennio. Instituto Nazionale di cultura Fascista, 1937.

Pogodin, N. Tempo. Trans. Irving Talmadge; ed. Eugene Lyons, *Six Soviet Plays*. Boston, Houghton Mifflin, 1934.

Polonskii, Viacheslav. Ocherki literaturnogo dvizheniia revoliutsionnoi epokhi. 2d. ed. Moscow, Gosizdat, 1929.

Popov, N. N. Outline History of the Communist Party of the Soviet Union. New York, International Publishers, 1934.

Pozner, Vladimir. Panorama de la littérature russe contemporaine. Paris, Kra, 1929.

Problems of Soviet Literature; Reports and Speeches at the First Soviet Writers' Congress. New York, International Publishers, 1935.

Report of Court Proceedings in the Case of the Anti-Soviet "Bloc of Rights and Trotskyites." Moscow, People's Commissariat of Justice of the USSR, 1938.

Resheniia partii o pechati. Moscow, Politizdat pri TSIK VKP(b), 1941.

Romanov, Pantaleimon. Three Pairs of Silk Stockings; a Novel of the Life of the Educated Class under the Soviet. Trans. Leonide Zarine, ed. Stephen Graham.

Rozanov, I. N. Putevoditel' po sovremennoi Russkoi literature. Moscow, Rabotnik prosveshcheniia, 1929.

Schiller, F. P., and M. A. Lifshitz. Marks i Engel's ob iskusstve i literature. Moscow, Sovetskaia literatura, 1933.

Selivanovskii, A. V literaturnykh boiakh (sbornik statei). Moscow, 1930.

Shaginian, M. Gidrotsentral. Leningrad, Izdatelstvo pisatelei, 1931.

Sholokhov, Mikhail. Podniataia tselina. Moscow, Gosizdat, 1946.

——— Seeds of Tomorrow. Trans. Stephen Garry. New York, Knopf, 1942.

——— Tikhii Don. Leningrad, Gosizdat, 1945. Translated by Stephen Garry as *The Silent Don*. New York, Knopf, 1942.

Simmons, Ernest J. An Outline of Modern Russian Literature (1880–1940). Ithaca, Cornell University Press, 1943.

Slonim, Marc. Portrety sovetskikh pisatelei. Paris, Parabola, 1933.

Slonim, Marc, and George Reavey. Soviet Literature; an Anthology. New York, Covici, Friede, 1934.

Somerville, John. Soviet Philosophy; a Study of Theory and Practice. New York, Philosophical Library, 1946.

Sovetskaia literatura na novom etape. Stenogramma I-go plenuma orgkomiteta Soiuza sovetskikh pisatelei. Moscow, Sovetskaia literatura, 1933.

Stalin, Joseph. Dialectical and Historical Materialism. New York, International Publishers, 1940.

——— Leninism; Selected Writings. New York, International Publishers, 1942.

——— Sochineniia, Vols. XII and XIII. Moscow, Gosizdat Politicheskoi literatury, 1949–51.

Struve, Gleb. Twenty-five Years of Soviet Russian Literature (1918–1943). New and enlarged edition of Soviet Russian Literature. London, Routledge, 1944.

——— Soviet Russian Literature, 1917–50. Norman, University of Oklahoma Press, 1951.

Timofeev, L. I. Sovremennaia literatura; uchebnoe posobie dlia 10-go klassa srednei shkoly. Moscow, Uchpedgiz, 1946.

Trotsky, L. D. Literatura i revoliutsiia. 2d ed., Moscow, Gosizdat, 1924.

——— *Literature and Revolution.* Trans. Rose Strunsky. London, Allen and Urwin, 1925.

——— My Life; an Attempt at Autobiography. New York, Scribner, 1930.

Tsentral'nyi komitet RKP(b), Otdel pechati. K voprosu o politike RKP(b) v khudozhestvennoi literature. Moscow, Izdanie Krasnaia nov', 1924.

Usievich, E. F. Za chistotu Leninizma v literaturnoi teorii. Moscow, Gosudarstvennoe izdatelstvo, 1932.

Voronskii, A. K. Iskusstvo i zhizn'. Moscow, Krug, 1924.

——— Literaturnye tipi. Moscow, Krug, 1925.

——— Literaturnye zapisi. Moscow, Krug, 1926.

——— ed. Nashi Dni. Moscow, Krug, 1922.

Wolfe, Bertram. Three Who Made a Revolution; a Biographical History. New York, Dial Press, 1948.

Yindrich, Jan. Tito v. Stalin; the Battle of the Marshals. London, Ernest Benn, 1950.

Zamiatin, E. We. Trans. Gregory Zilboorg. New York, Dutton, 1925.

The following periodicals have been examined for the dates indicated. Full reference to specific articles quoted from them will be found in the notes. They are all published in Moscow, except where indicated otherwise.

American Slavic and East European Review, New York, 1948–52.
Bol'shevik, 1924–48.
International Literature, 1933–45.
Izvestiia, 1926–32.
Knizhnaia letopis', 1924–33.
Komsomol'skaia pravda, 1930–31.
Krasnaia nov', 1921–33.
Language, Baltimore, 1951.
Le Monde Slave, Paris, 1928–38.
Literatura i iskusstvo, 1930–31.
Literaturnaia gazeta, 1929–38.
Literaturnyi kritik, 1933–37.
Literatura i marksizm, 1929–30.
Literatura mirovoi revoliutsii, 1931–32.
Marksistko-Leninskoe iskusstvoznanie, 1932.
Na literaturnom postu, 1927–32.
Na postu, 1923.
Novyi LEF, 1927–28.
Novyi mir, 1928–47.
Oktiabr' 1924–37.
Pechat' i revoliutsiia, 1921–30.
Pod znamenem marksizma, 1930–32.
Pravda, 1926–37.
Revue des études Slaves, Paris, 1930–33.
Science and Society, New York, 1936–43.
Slavonic and East European Review, London, 1928–39.
Sotsialisticheskii vestnik, Berlin, 1931–32.
Versty, Paris, 1926.
Vestnik Kommunisticheskoi Akademii, 1932.
Zvezda, Leningrad, 1924–33.

Index